THE COACHING PROCESS

In this fresh and engaging introduction to sports coaching, Lynn Kidman and Stephanie J. Hanrahan guide students through the coaching process. Focusing on the practical aspects of sports coaching, the book helps students to develop their basic technical skills as well as strategies for working with individual and team athletes, and to plan and implement effective coaching sessions.

The book develops an 'athlete-centred approach' to sports coaching, by which athletes take ownership of their learning, in turn strengthening their abilities to retain key skills and to make effective decisions during competition. Useful pedagogical features in each chapter, such as real life case studies, activities, self-reflection questions, and summaries of current research and best practice, encourage reflective practice and help student coaches to develop and extend their coaching techniques and philosophies.

The Coaching Process is invaluable reading for any student starting a sports coaching course at college or university, and for any coach working with athletes or children in sport who wants to improve their practical skills.

Lynn Kidman recently moved from the University of Worcester in England to take up a lecturing position in Sports Coaching at Auckland University of Technology in New Zealand.

Stephanie J. Hanrahan is an associate professor in sport and exercise psychology for the Schools of Human Movement Studies and Psychology at the University of Queensland, Australia.

D0420488

THE COACHING PROCESS

A PRACTICAL GUIDE TO BECOMING AN EFFECTIVE SPORTS COACH

THIRD EDITION

**LYNN KIDMAN
AND STEPHANIE J. HANRAHAN**

PHOTOS BY CHÉRIE HARRIS

Routledge
Taylor & Francis Group

LONDON AND NEW YORK

First published 1997 by Dunmore Press
Second edition 2004 by Dunmore Press

This edition published 2011
by Routledge
2 Park Square, Milton Park, Abingdon, Oxon OX14 4RN

Simultaneously published in the USA and Canada
by Routledge
711 Third Avenue, New York, NY 10017

*Routledge is an imprint of the Taylor & Francis Group, an
informa business*

© 2011 Lynn Kidman and Stephanie J. Hanrahan
Photos © Chérie Harris

The right of the authors to be identified as authors of this work
has been asserted by them in accordance with sections 77 and
78 of the Copyright, Designs and Patents Act 1988.

Typeset in Melior by
GreenGate Publishing Services, Tonbridge, Kent
Printed and bound in Great Britain by
CPI Antony Rowe, Chippenham, Wiltshire

British Library Cataloguing in Publication Data
A catalogue record for this book is available from the British Library

Library of Congress Cataloging in Publication Data
The coaching process : a practical guide to becoming an effective
sports coach / by Lynn Kidman and Stephanie Hanrahan. -- 3rd
ed.
p. cm.
1. Coaching (Athletics) I. Kidman, Lynn, 1955- II. Hanrahan,
Stephanie J., 1961-
GV711.C6225 2011
796.07--dc22
2010024672

ISBN: 978-0-415-57053-4 (hbk)
ISBN: 978-0-415-57054-1 (pbk)
ISBN: 978-0-203-85742-7 (ebk)

DEDICATION

Lynn: To my family, Bobby, Matthew, Amanda, Simon, Toni, and Izzy.

Stephanie: To the coaches who create positive and supportive environments to help their athletes grow and excel.

CONTENTS

FIGURES

ABOUT THE AUTHORS

Lynn Kidman recently moved from the University of Worcester in England to take up a lecturing position in sports coaching at Auckland University of Technology in New Zealand. Lynn has coached athletes for many years in various sports, but now enjoys developing coaches of all levels. She has recently co-edited a book with Bennett J. Lombardo entitled *Athlete-centred Coaching: Developing Decision Makers*.

Stephanie J. Hanrahan is an associate professor in sport and exercise psychology for the Schools of Human Movement Studies and Psychology at the University of Queensland in Australia. In addition to teaching swimming and ice skating, she has coached volleyball in three countries – novice and state level players, children and adults, males and females. As a psychologist she has worked with athletes and coaches from a wide variety of sports – from ballet to football, and from bocce to skydiving. After 17 years of representative volleyball at the open level, Stephanie currently spends her recreational time Latin dancing.

PREFACE

Over the past two decades, Lynn and Stephanie have been dedicated to the development of coaches who enable their athletes to learn. The third edition of *The Coaching Process: A Practical Guide to Becoming an Effective Sports Coach* provides coaches with information about how to create a successful sporting environment, where success is measured by athletes' satisfaction and performance improvement. The third edition covers the same topics as the first two editions, but has been revised to reflect the latest developments in skill learning and the process of coaching. This new edition also has an increased focus on coaching-related research, with selected studies highlighted in most chapters. In this book we emphasise opportunities for coaches to identify and practise coaching strategies using an athlete-centred approach.

This edition continues the concentration on what to improve, how to improve, and the recognition of what has improved. We focus on a technical level of reflection, where the coaching process is about reaching session objectives and gaining knowledge to apply to the sporting environment. The techniques include setting objectives, understanding and applying management principles to a coaching session, understanding and applying basic coaching strategies, and understanding the positive approach.

In *The Coaching Process*, we challenge you, through a self-directed approach, to enhance your coaching. The self-directed approach is an educational tool that enables coaches to apply coaching strategies in their own settings, and then encourages them to reflect on how the strategies were applied. *The Coaching Process* is designed for coaches to be able to learn at their own pace.

The Coaching Process acknowledges the complexities and intricacies of coaching by addressing some of the pedagogical and psychological aspects. Every chapter provides technical and thoughtful processes to help coaches be aware of how they are coaching. Examples of various coaching strategies and solutions about how to implement them are included.

In each of the chapters in the third edition we continue with the theme of providing activities and/or self-reflective tasks that will enhance thought processes and practices about coaching. Self-reflection provides a non-threatening means of analysing coaching without the outside pressures of job security or political implications that often can be encountered. Self-reflection is a tool that determines how well coaches are working with their athletes. Being a successful coach is not measured by a win–loss record, but by how athletes learn and how successful their sporting experiences are.

The Coaching Process is a useful text for tertiary study in coaching as well as a valuable reference for practising coaches. This book is well suited for coaches who are interested in enhancing their and their athletes' performances.

FEATURES OF THE CHAPTERS

For this edition, the authors have maintained the format of self-help for coaches to apply the information to their coaching with a group of athletes.

Introductions

In each chapter we introduce the topics to be covered. The introduction includes information about why the topics were chosen, insight into experiences of coaches who have applied these strategies, and how the strategies can be linked to other information covered in the book.

Information about an aspect of the coaching process

In each chapter we provide a base of information under different headings about at least one coaching strategy. We introduce the theory and provide practical examples of the strategy. We designed the practical examples to provide experiences that may relate the theory to personal situations that readers are likely to encounter.

ACTIVITY

In the activity sections in each of the chapters we provide opportunities for development by applying information about coaching strategies to individual sport settings. The activities are written using a workbook approach with tables and short-answer questions provided. These activities encourage further thought about situations that may arise in coaching. **If you choose to write in the text, consider using pencil. You may prefer to photocopy the activities or use a separate notebook that will serve as a record as you change and monitor strategies and continue developing as a coach.**

SELF-REFLECTION

Research and comments from coaches have confirmed the value of the appropriate use of self-reflection to enhance coaching. We designed the self-reflection exercises to provide you with a way to practise selected coaching strategies and apply what you have learned to your own coaching situations. You will be able to practise the tasks without the pressures of someone looking over your shoulder. After attempting the coaching strategy at your own pace, you will be able to analyse and reflect on how you applied the strategy. The learning and development of these coaching strategies is entirely in your hands. You can experiment and try different methods to apply coaching strategies and therefore find the best method for your own and your athletes' needs.

Using video in self-reflection

As part of the self-reflective process, coaches are asked to video themselves coaching. Accessing a camera should be fairly easy; ask friends, family or sport organisations if there is a camera that can be used. There is usually a parent or friend who will volunteer to video your coaching. The video will provide you with valuable insights as to how you coach and challenge your athletes.

Reflective questions

To enhance the self-reflective process, we include reflective questions to provide structure and guidelines about specific coaching strategies. We know that great coaches often analyse themselves to seek better ways to coach. They often ask questions such as, 'Did that work?', 'How did the athletes respond to that message?', or 'Was that the right way, or should I have tried something different?' We hope that the reflective questions we have provided will facilitate self-analysis to determine what works and what doesn't work.

Points to ponder

'Points to Ponder' throughout the text can be related to your own coaching, someone else's coaching, or your athletes. Draw on your own experience to determine a solution where necessary. Sometimes these points are quotes from well known coaches or sports participants.

Points to remember

We have also provided important 'Points to Remember' about coaching. They may be points for consideration, or essential points to apply while coaching.

Recent research

In most chapters we have included boxes where we have summarised recent research articles related to the topics presented.

Summary

Chapters conclude with a list of points about particular coaching strategies and an overall summary of the chapter.

We hope that your athletes experience great success. Enjoy your journey through the coaching process.

ACKNOWLEDGEMENTS

We continue to acknowledge our students who study with us. They challenge our thinking, experiment with various strategies, discuss and debate many issues, and continue to reflect on best coaching practice. These people are our coaching future and we thank them for their reflections.

PART 1

INTRODUCTION

CHAPTER 1

SUCCESSFUL COACHING

This chapter covers

- The coaching process
- Self-reflective learning process
- The enjoyment of coaching athletes

Coaching is about striving to contribute to the success of each athlete. The *Australian Oxford Dictionary* defines success as 'a favourable outcome; attainment of what was desired or attempted'. In sport, an outcome is seen traditionally as winning or losing a particular competition. This view of outcomes is narrow and limited. Winning is important, it is one of the reasons for organised sport; however, as an outcome, it is uncontrollable. Though success is commonly defined as an outcome, we need to look more broadly at what it means. Ralph Waldo Emerson has written about success as more than just an outcome:

> To laugh often and much, to win the respect of intelligent people and the affection of children; To earn the appreciation of honest critics and endure the betrayal of false friends; To appreciate beauty, to find the best in others; To leave the world a bit better, whether by a healthy child, a garden patch or a redeemed social condition; To know even one life has breathed easier because you have lived. That is to have succeeded.
>
> (Ralph Waldo Emerson in Smith, 1997, p. 43)

As coaches we can have a dramatic influence on the development and lives of those we coach (Smoll & Smith, 2002). What is considered to be successful coaching is dependent on how we develop our own skills and behaviours to meet athletes' needs.

THE COACHING PROCESS

Becoming a great coach is an ongoing process (Cross & Lyle, 1999). Coaches do not just complete a coaching course, coach for a specified period of time and then, presto, become perfect coaches. Coaches' abilities are diverse and complex and each coach is at a different development level (Kidman & Lombardo, 2010a). Nevertheless, every coach can always improve. As we continue to coach, we constantly refine and enhance our coaching skills. It is important to judge the effectiveness of that process rather than any particular outcome. If coaches are not achieving success (however it is defined), they need to look at changing what they are doing, that is, changing the process. Even if coaches believe they are successful, they need to be aware of the process so they can continue to strive for athlete achievement.

4

For each of the behaviours in the following list, mark with an 'S' the points you believe are an indication of success (what you are trying to achieve) and with a 'C', aspects of effective coaching (part of the process). Some items may be marked with both 'S' and 'C'.

☐ Being flexible to meet the individual needs of athletes

☐ Willing to experiment with new ideas

☐ Valuing the coach–athlete relationship

☐ Understanding and appreciating human nature

☐ Being honest and strong in character

☐ Being committed to individual integrity, values, and personal growth

☐ Enabling athletes to feel comfortable and happy with training sessions and competitions

☐ Improving athletes' techniques

☐ Having fun

☐ Appreciating individual differences

☐ Understanding the value of time

☐ Cherishing the satisfaction of perseverance

☐ Comprehending the meaning of effort

☐ Discerning the dignity of humility

☐ Developing character

☐ Enhancing athletes' decision making

☐ Giving athletes ownership of their learning

☐ Being kind

☐ Appreciating the rewards of cooperation

☐ Valuing/developing friendships

☐ Learning new skills

- [ ] Meeting challenges
- [ ] Overcoming obstacles
- [ ] Experiencing new things
- [ ] Having a positive sense of self (feeling good)
- [ ] Feeling it is OK to make mistakes
- [ ] Winning
- [ ] Communicating effectively
- [ ] Getting recognition
- [ ] Maintaining involvement (being active throughout life)
- [ ] (Add your own) _____

Now go back and look at your responses. Are there common themes in what you have stated as an indication of success and what you have stated as an indication of coaching ability? These concepts will be revisited in the next chapter when your coaching philosophy is developed or refined.

SELF-REFLECTIVE LEARNING PROCESS

It is likely that you are reading this book because you are interested in improving your coaching. What you probably have realised already is that developing as a coach is an ongoing process. As mentioned in the preface, you are asked in this book to reflect on your current coaching practices. Before determining what changes need to be made, it is important to be aware of how you coach now. More than one technique can be used for self-reflection (Cassidy et al., 2009).

One of these techniques is the use of video. Throughout the book coaches are asked to video themselves coaching. Many coaches use this technique to enhance the coaching process. At first, many coaches find it to be a threatening task. Confronting yourself on video is daunting, but once past that initial stage, looking at coaching strategies becomes easier. After you have become accustomed to your personal mannerisms, you can begin to reflect on your coaching. Video is a useful tool for self-reflective learning in teacher education and has also proven to be

6

effective in changing and monitoring coaching strategies (Kidman & Carlson, 1998).

Reflective questions are often part of the learning process, providing structured guidelines and information about coaching behaviours. Such questions are used to direct coaches to focus on particular aspects of coaching. Reflective questions can be designed by you or other experts.

Another useful aid in the self-reflective process is a second opinion (Whitmore, 2002). By obtaining feedback from another respected colleague, coach or teacher, and even from the athletes, the self-reflective processes in coaching will be enhanced.

Hints for participating in self-reflection using video

1   Remember that people generally go through a self-confrontation phase when viewing themselves on a video (e.g., 'I didn't know that I was so fat', or 'I didn't know that my nose was so big'). Coaches are no different, but the good news is that the confrontation passes and attention can then be given to coaching strategies.
2   Ensure the camera is focused on you, the coach. Observing your own body signals is important.
3   Use this book as a guide to the 'how to' of coaching. Use the reflective questions provided or design questions based on information you gather.
4   Remember that learning a coaching skill is like learning a physical skill. It takes practice. When focusing on improving a particular coaching skill, other coaching skills may falter, which is to be expected. Coaching strategies will begin to gel the more they are practised.
5   When searching for someone to provide coaching feedback, pick someone you respect and trust, a critical friend.

Self-evaluation technique

Another technique to improve your coaching effectiveness is to complete self-evaluation forms after coaching (both after training sessions and after competitions). Figure 1.1 provides a simple example of a form that could be completed after your next coaching session. Later in the book, coaches will be asked to create their own, more detailed self-evaluation forms.

7

Date: _____	Venue: _____

Strategy/Characteristic	Rating (circle as applicable)
	(1 agree – 5 strongly disagree)
I listened to my athletes	1 2 3 4 5
I was well prepared for the session	1 2 3 4 5
I was positive	1 2 3 4 5
I gave effective feedback	1 2 3 4 5
I was enthusiastic	1 2 3 4 5
I kept my cool	1 2 3 4 5
Athletes were treated equally	1 2 3 4 5
Athletes had good learning experiences	1 2 3 4 5
I varied my tone of voice	1 2 3 4 5
Athletes enjoyed the session	1 2 3 4 5
Athletes were enabled to make decisions	1 2 3 4 5

One thing I did really well this session was

_____

One thing I want to remember for next time is

_____

Figure 1.1 An example of a self-evaluation form

THE ENJOYMENT OF COACHING ATHLETES

Coaching demands time, energy, preparation, enthusiasm and patience (to name just a few of the requirements). People coach for different reasons (Leidl, 2009), both extrinsic and intrinsic. Extrinsic reasons are the external rewards that are available. These rewards are not limited to money or material gains such as free sporting equipment or discounted access to venues. Indeed, only a small percentage of coaches get paid for their efforts. Awards, trophies, and other less tangible forms of recognition from others also can be extrinsic reasons for coaching. Coaches who are coaching mostly for extrinsic rewards are generally coach-centred. A person who is coach-centred tends to be prescriptive, espouses knowledge on to athletes, and can actually inhibit athletes' learning (Kidman & Lombardo, 2010a).

8

Intrinsic reasons for coaching are based around the personal sense of satisfaction that can be achieved. Intrinsic motivation involves doing things that make people feel competent or self-determining, that can have an influence on the way things happen (Duda et al., 1995). For example, a coach may experience satisfaction from team performances and the realisation that what the team worked on together allowed them to achieve their personal goals. People who coach for intrinsic reasons and are athlete-centred tend to promote a sense of belonging as well as give athletes a role in decision making and ensure a shared approach to learning (Kidman & Lombardo, 2010a). Coaches who are intrinsically motivated to coach, coach for the love and fun of the sport and personal satisfaction. Obviously, enjoyment is a major component of intrinsic motivation.

POINT TO PONDER

Why do you coach? This may seem like a simple question, but please take time to answer now.

Figure 1.2 The personal sense of satisfaction achieved through coaching usually outweighs the glory of awards and medals

The media tend to equate enjoyment in sport with winning (Coakley, 2009). Winning is great! Everyone loves to win, but the day to day aspects of participation in sport and of coaching should be enjoyable. For coaches, satisfaction should be experienced whenever any form of success is achieved or when coaches believe they have contributed to athletes' learning. A wide variety of experiences in coaching, not just winning the grand final, can be enjoyable and satisfying. The following are just a few examples of stories coaches have told that express satisfaction and enjoyment.

- A rugby coach and his team undertook a wilderness experience at Mt Kosciuszko in Australia. His story was, 'We had to climb the mountain, which could only be done with the help of your mates. We reached the peak, but we did it by working together. We contrasted this with how we had achieved success ... when we had stuttered along as individuals, not really gelling as a team until it was almost too late. Whilst standing on top of the mountain I said to the players, "You are standing on the highest point in Australia", which was significant – we had conquered Australia. [A player] was standing next to me and said, "No, that peak over there is higher!" (There was another one about 100 metres away which was slightly higher.) Still, with a bit of imagination and symbolism, the point was made!'

- A tennis coach, Chris, experimented by designing a series of lessons with the aim of enabling the student to make decisions and become self-aware of her skill and tactics. After three lessons, it rained for almost a month causing lessons to be cancelled for four weeks. Prior to the next lesson, a number of coaches told Chris that he'd have to start over with such a large break between the third and fourth lessons. Chris expected that the student would remember some of what she had learned because of the decisions for which she took ownership. He was amazed when the player performed as if there had been no break in the lessons. The sense of satisfaction experienced caused him to change all of his coaching plans to follow the same guidelines as his initial experiment.

- Jan, a BMX coach, had an athlete whose bike was damaged so badly that it was not rideable. At the last minute, a substitute bike was found. This bike was not the correct size for the athlete, did not have the proper gear ratios and was virtually little better than not having a bike at all.

10

Although highly skilled and experienced, Jan's athlete found himself well behind during the competition, but continued to do the best he could at every jump and turn. In the end he didn't win, in fact he had one of his worst outcomes ever. Jan, however, was ecstatic with the athlete's performance. He never once complained or made excuses.

■ A child with an intellectual disability came to the rink with her school for ice skating lessons. This child would not walk at school or anywhere else outside the home without firmly gripping on to an adult. As the skating lessons progressed (once a week for four weeks), her classmates were learning to turn, skate backwards and stop (without grabbing on to the wall). One or two children even learned simple spins and jumps. The coach's greatest and warmest memory of coaching that year was when the child with the intellectual disability made it across the rink by herself. Even though she walked more than skated, it was an amazing achievement.

<hr>

POINT TO PONDER

What story might you remember about your satisfying and enjoyable experiences while coaching?

<hr>

Enjoyment does not have to rely on special, isolated incidents. Often enjoyment is the result of seeing athletes having fun, learning new skills, improving their self-confidence, or helping each other. Sometimes when caught up in the daily frustrations of last-minute changes to schedules, having to cut or eliminate athletes because of limited space, or dealing with behaviour problems, we can forget about the enjoyable experiences. Every now and then we should remind ourselves why we are coaching in the first place.

ACTIVITY

List three things you most enjoy about coaching. These may be specific moments you have experienced, or everyday experiences.

1

2

3

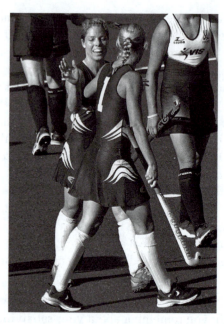

Figure 1.3 There can be enjoyment in seeing athletes support each other

SUMMARY

1   To enhance your coaching, focus on process rather than outcome. Striving to be a great coach is an ongoing process.

2   Athlete-centred coaching is about catering to athletes' needs; coach-centred coaching is about coaches catering to their own needs.

3   Self-reflection is important for improving coaching strategies. Techniques facilitating self-reflection include the use of videos, reflective questions and self-awareness forms, and feedback from others, including your athletes.

4   Coaching can be a rewarding experience, offering both intrinsic (personal satisfaction) and extrinsic (tangible) rewards.

5   The improvement in athletes, the little humorous remarks, the friendships, and the memories are just some experiences that make coaching a worthwhile venture.

6   The enjoyment of coaching is an individual experience and is closely related to coaching motivation.

CHAPTER 2

DEVELOPING A COACHING PHILOSOPHY

> I have come to a frightening realization. *I* am the decisive element on the track or on the field. It is *my* personal approach that creates the climate for learning and personal performance. It is *my* daily mood that makes the weather bright or dreary. As a coach, *I* possess tremendous power to make my athletes' lives miserable or joyous. *I* can be a tool of torture, or an instrument of inspiration. I can humiliate ... or humor, hurt ... or heal. In all situations, it is *my* response that decides whether the experience of sport is positive or negative and whether my athletes gain or lose self-esteem.
>
> (Adapted from Dr Haim Ginott, n.d.)

The notion that coaches have as much power as this quotation suggests can be quite foreign to coaches and athletes, but true. Power is a word that conjures up many negative images, but by creating and communicating a coaching philosophy, power can be exercised in a sincere, meaningful way (Jones & Standage, 2006). Coaches have the power to help athletes reach their goals by providing positive experiences and ensuring physical and emotional safety (Cassidy & Potrac, 2006). They have the power to increase and maintain integrity in sport through their actions and words. Coaches' actions determine the influence of their power because they have the potential to be a definer, creator, provider, deliverer, and facilitator of a positive sporting experience (Nakamura, 1996). This power is reflected through coaches' personal beliefs, values, principles, and priorities which are the basis for their behaviour. Coaches can influence whether athletes' experiences are full of frustration or satisfaction and whether they experience success or failure (Jones et al., 2004). As Cassidy et al. (2009) suggested, the power constructs of the coach–athlete relationship are important to consider when developing a coaching philosophy (see box for Recent Research on elite rowers' perceptions of their coaches).

RECENT RESEARCH

ATHLETES' EXPECTATIONS OF THEIR COACHES

Elite athletes come to any situation with a wealth of experience and understanding of whether coach behaviours are 'good' or 'bad'. Their perceptions and expectations can influence how they evaluate and react to coaching pedagogies.

Using ethnographic research methods (indepth interviews, informal conversations, participant observation, field notes, and the first author's reflexive journal), Purdy and Jones (in press) examined the pedagogies of a coach of an elite group of rowers, specifically focusing on how the rowers interpreted their coach's instructions and feedback over the length of a season. The results reported that the coach demonstrated a didactic, traditional, authoritative manner (mostly aural in delivery of instructions and feedback). The athletes initially were dissatisfied with the coach's instructions and frequency and quality of feedback, feeling that they weren't receiving the help they needed to improve their performances.

As the season progressed, the athletes became critical of the coach, who began to lose credibility. Building on the athletes' dissatisfaction, the research delved into what happened after the coach lost credibility with the athletes. Once the rowers scorned the coach, the athletes began to make fun of the coach behind his back. Due to the athletes' perceived social position (i.e., one of subversion), when they were with the coach, they met the role boundaries of power expected in such an athlete–coach relationship, that is athlete silence (just doing as they were told).

14

At this stage, there was evidence of a shift in power to the athletes as they tried to manage this unsatisfactory situation. Through loss of trust and respect for the coach, and due to the dissatisfaction of the quality and frequency of instruction, they began to search elsewhere (e.g., video footage, sport scientists) for the knowledge and instruction necessary for them to continue to train at an elite level. They became self-coaches, and used other mechanisms to help them perform. This result demonstrated that people learn differently rather than relying on a coach's aural transmissions of knowledge.

Conclusions from this study were that the pedagogical strategies of coaches are effective only when the expectations of the athletes are honoured. Athletes were able to examine the nature of the pedagogical strategies and, when the coaching pedagogies didn't meet their needs, they found alternatives to enable them to keep learning and performing so that their expectations were better met. The research reinforces coaching as a complex process with many influences from social forces (including role boundaries). It is essential that coaches gain respect from the athletes in the first instance. To understand them, coaches must also consider the complex situations surrounding athletes and their social environment. The essence of coaching is that coaches need to use their abilities to act in the best interests of the athletes.

Source: Purdy, L. & Jones, R. (in press). Choppy waters: Elite rowers' perceptions of coaching. *Physical Education and Sport Pedagogy*.

The aim of this chapter is to help coaches develop foundational beliefs about coaching and provide insightful reflection about the role and the importance of developing a coaching philosophy. Coaching philosophies are individually determined and are based on individual values and beliefs, as well as personal objectives. The education of athletes is in coaches' hands. For every coach who has educated athletes to have pride, there is another coach who has instilled shame. The coach's role in the education, growth and development of athletes is essential to ensuring that athletes are provided with opportunities to excel (Cassidy et al., 2009). We do not claim that this chapter has all the answers, but it may provide some insight, enabling coaches to reflect on their coaching.

A COACHING PHILOSOPHY

We begin this chapter by discussing how coaches can formulate a philosophy based on beliefs and values (Cassidy et al., 2009). It is a coach's responsibility to communicate a positive philosophy to athletes that will help them achieve their goals. Every sport setting needs guidelines that can be developed and followed. Coaches have input into defining the nature of these guidelines and following them in the way they coach athletes. By clarifying these guidelines, coaches can make choices and set priorities. For example, if your goal is to develop athletes without considering the outcome of the competitions, this philosophy would dictate the coaching methods you would use. Developing a philosophy will enable you to set up the foundations for the entire season and follow through with consistency. It is important that the philosophy developed can be actioned. Words must be meaningful, but also true to your beliefs.

One of the first things to consider is the athletes. Sport belongs to the athletes, therefore coaches should have an athlete-centred approach. A coach's purpose is to develop athletes and increase the quality of the sporting environment. The quality of experience that the athletes get out of a season will depend on a coach's value systems, principles, and beliefs. If, for example, you decide that winning is the purpose of the season, what will be the implications for the team? What will happen to the less skilled players? What will you have to give up when focusing on winning? Are you able to support a philosophy with actions or are you a 'Do as I say, not as I do' coach?

16

Success vs winning

Success is not forever – and failure isn't fatal.

(Don Shula, American football coach)

Success is a peace of mind, which is a direct result of self-satisfaction in knowing you did your best to become the best that you are capable of becoming.

(John Wooden, basketball coach)

To many, success is measured by how many games or competitions are won. Many coaches' jobs depend on how many matches have been won or lost. Success, however, is not just winning. Striving to win is more important than actually winning. An athlete can win without performing well and lose even though the performance has been outstanding.

Winning is important and is a major factor in sport participation. Winning and losing are fairly tangible outcomes. But success is more important; it is a measure of how well the athletes are performing. Success can be measured by how many athletes come back the following year. 'It is about understanding, meeting and supporting the athletes' emotional and social needs and teaching athletes about responsibility, self-discipline, social interaction, and self-reliance through athletics' (Nakamura, 1996, p. 5).

There are many success stories about famous coaches, but how many coaches have ensured the success of all athletes? It is common for children's coaches to sacrifice learning by focusing on winning. Coaches who are interested only in winning will ensure that athletes are robots, performing exact plays and moves (Renshaw, 2010). These athletes often move on to the next season with little to offer because they do not understand the skills and movements. Until athletes are enabled to think and become self-aware, they will not learn. Penney (2006) discussed how coaches need to focus on what learners (athletes in this case) bring to the context. The context (environment, task, and individual) needs to be considered for learning to occur (Renshaw, 2010).

How many athletes do coaches scare away because they are too adamant about winning? The pressure to win can take over the enjoyment of performing. Athletes rarely win if they are not enjoying their sport or their lives. The 'win at all costs' attitude is quite prevalent in mainstream Western society, but there is a heavy cost. One of the most frequent reasons for dropping out of sport is related to the coach and an emphasis on winning (Smoll & Smith, 2002).

Sadly, we rarely hear of a coach being described as successful because he or she provided a great environment and encouraged those participating to do their best. The media rarely portray a successful coach as an educator (Jones, 2006). Nevertheless, one of the biggest jobs in coaching is educating athletes – preparing them physically, psychologically, cognitively, socially, and spiritually for their sporting challenges. Knowing the athletes and drawing out their full athletic capabilities is success. Coaching is a people job and coaches must know how their athletes tick and what to provide to bring out the best in each athlete (Kidman & Lombardo, 2010a). Coaches should have an understanding of and commitment to the individuals with whom they work.

Fundamental to the authors' beliefs in this book is the necessity to provide athletes with caring, trust, positive communication and commitment that enables them to learn. Athletes need to be able to make their own decisions in their sport. They are the ones who compete, so enabling them to learn includes ensuring they can make informed decisions (Kidman, 2001). This philosophy encourages athletes to be the best that they can be. Sport is only part of athletes' lives, not their entire lives. They have different reasons for participating in sport (Smoll & Smith, 2002). Success should be determined by whether athletes continue to participate in their chosen sport. Sport offers an environment in which athletes can gain a sense of competence, achievement, and recognition. The important coaches are not only the ones who take athletes to the Olympics or coach elite professional teams, but those who offer a profound, enjoyable, and positive experience for athletes. What is a worrying trend is the evidence that the positive experience can be hindered by a coach. A research project completed in Australia suggested that the top three reasons athletes are often discouraged from participating in sport have to do with the coaches (Clough et al., 1993). Coaches influence the quality of the experience, and our athletes deserve good coaches – those who are dedicated to their betterment and to the development of proud, motivated, successful, and happy people (Lombardo, 1987). An example of a coach who promotes this positive experience is Wayne Smith (international rugby coach). He suggests that his philosophy and practices are:

> ... to create an environment so that players feel comfortable in making decisions. In this way, they can cope with responsibilities and they can take ownership of their learning. Players should own the team culture. They should set their own expectations, establish

the team protocols … create the vision and the values. We (as coaches) guide them and facilitate them, but it is their total 'buy in' (collectively) that we are after. It's their programme, their campaign. So, my philosophy is to create empowered players and to have … a holistic type approach so that the players are not just sport jocks, not just training for rugby, but have outside interests. I believe coaching is all about trying to develop better people, not just better players and it's important to enjoy the whole experience.

(Kidman, 2001, p. 18)

WRITING YOUR COACHING PHILOSOPHY

I try to operate on the same theory at all times, whether I win or not. I never put pressure on a player to win. I tell all my players that if they keep their heads up and can be satisfied with themselves, more often than not they will outscore their opponent.

(John Wooden, basketball coach)

This section will give you the opportunity to structure and write a personal philosophy. Many coaches have never done this. They just go and do the job and do not think about why they are there. As mentioned earlier, a coaching philosophy is a personal statement that is based on values and beliefs that direct your coaching. It is a valuable exercise to try writing down these values and beliefs. Some may feel threatened by doing this, others will be enlightened, but it is important to understand the value systems that guide your coaching and govern your actions. Writing a guided philosophy clarifies personal values and goals and provides a tangible reference point. You can then regularly check to see that you are abiding by the philosophy. With experience, your philosophy may change, so it should be updated periodically.

Your coaching philosophy will be shaped by your experiences (Cassidy et al., 2009). Think back to when you were competing, or had a teacher who had an enormous effect on you. Determine how those experiences influence your coaching actions. Your views and opinions may also be influenced by knowledge gathered over the years. You may have noticed other coaches and said, 'I will never be like that because she destroys the athletes. She scared many of the athletes away.' You will also have to look into the future. In which direction do you want the athletes to go?

Coaches are constantly in a predicament as to whether to do what they believe or to do what other people say. For example, because winning appears to be important to society and in the media, is it more important to accept the values of the media or hold on to your own?

> The most effective way to forge a winning team is to call on the players' need to connect with something larger than themselves.
>
> (Phil Jackson, NBA basketball coach)

ACTIVITY

To develop your coaching philosophy, answer the following questions:

1 What do you value about sport?
2 What do athletes value about sport?
3 Why are these athletes participating?
4 What can I do to ensure these athletes reach their goals and expectations?
5 What are the qualities of people who have influenced you?
6 What type of coach do you wish to be? It may be the coach you wish you had had!

Based on your answers to the above questions, write down the key identified beliefs, values, and assumptions of athletes' development, your coaching goals and your views on success. Use your answers to activities in Chapter 1 to help formulate your ideas.

Once the points have been developed, write your complete philosophy. An example of one by Brutus Hamilton (an athletics coach) is:

> To create within the athletes an interest and enthusiasm for the events ... then direct that interest and enthusiasm along the lines of sound fundamentals, taught imaginatively, intelligently, purposefully, and even inspirationally. It sounds rather simple, but it isn't.

Establishing mutual direction

Once your philosophy is formulated, it is important to communicate it to the team. The philosophy can be communicated in many ways, and it is up to the coach to determine how they will handle this process. The

20

key is that the athletes, parents, and administrators should know what coaches believe and understand their values about coaching and sport.

The athletes themselves should play a major role in determining the direction of the team (Kidman & Lombardo, 2010a). Sometimes the direction they choose may be different to the coach's. This situation is where the 'art' of coaching is important and the complex nature of coaching is evidenced (Lyle, 2002). Coaches need to determine if they should change to meet athletes' needs or if they need to market a philosophy that is important to the success of the team. Whatever the decision, the direction of the team should be agreed upon by the coach, athletes, and support staff so that the team functions optimally. To establish a mutual direction, questions should be asked of the athletes such as:

- What would we like people to say about our team at the end of the season?
- Why are we competing in this sport for the season?
- What are our goals/purpose of the season?
- What do we need to do to achieve these goals?
- What do we each enjoy most about this sport?
- What do we need to do to ensure that this experience is satisfying?
- If the expectations are not satisfied, what do we need to do?

These questions are only examples to ignite thinking of the athletes and enable them to 'buy in' to expectations, values, and visions of the team. Essentially coaches are the facilitators of the process and can probe further to ensure total team agreement. Once the team 'buys in' to the direction of the team, athletes tend to take responsibility for their own learning and commitment (Galipeau & Trudel, 2006).

Also important is the team's rotation policy. When athletes feel that they are contributing, they are confident and perform well. Coaches who have trust in their athletes will ensure that their athletes are considered for their strengths and encouraged to contribute at all times. At some stage, you will need all athletes to perform. Often, coaches save their 'reserves' for substitutions into pressured situations, for example when there are injuries in crucial matches. Nevertheless, if these reserves have not practised or had a chance to compete in pressure situations, they often struggle and disappoint when called upon to perform.

The other rotation consideration is the position of each athlete. When younger, children grow and change, and therefore before puberty athletes should try every position (except when unsafe; Smoll and Smith, 2002). Also, if coaches want truly innovative thinkers, it is useful to rotate players to unfamiliar positions in order that they can understand those roles. If athletes understand all roles on the team, they will have a good understanding of the total game.

No matter what approach (e.g., autocratic, athlete-centred, laissez-faire) is used, coaches should explain their methods. If coaches are going to be prescriptive and directive, the athletes need to understand the coaches and why they are using that approach. If coaches are questioning, problem-solving coaches, the athletes need to be aware that they will have to think. If the athletes do not know or understand the coaches and their philosophies, they will have certain expectations that may not match the coaches' intentions and there will be limited trust and understanding. In any team or business situation, open communication is a key to the success of the team (Nakamura, 1996).

SELF-REFLECTION

After you have written down your coaching philosophy, share it with another coach and discuss the implications. Reflect on the following questions:

- How will I communicate my philosophy to my athletes, their parents, and administrators?
- How will I ensure I follow my coaching philosophy?
- What will I do to ensure that the team (or group of individuals) has a mutual direction, that they 'buy in' to the way the team is coached and organised?
- What are the key values and principles that I will follow? Do I always follow them?

Once you have developed and written down your philosophy, keep it at hand so that you can revise and update it as circumstances change. As you reflect and challenge your own and others' belief systems, consider the current trends and continue to search for knowledge and wisdom. This book will not have all the answers for you, but hopefully it will provide ideas for reflection. Question everything you read, and relate it to your own value and belief systems.

FAIR PLAY

Ethics is the study of values or moral philosophies and how individuals ought to behave in certain situations (McNamee, 2010). In sport, ethical behaviour is called sportsmanship or fair play. Coaches acting ethically and in accordance with the principles of fair play will behave as they should, even in situations where they might want to do otherwise. Coaches have a responsibility to their athletes to develop self-control that demonstrates their beliefs of fair play. They should be aware of their own belief systems, values, needs, and limitations and the effect of these on others. One facet of a coach's job is to be a mentor for their athletes. An objective therefore should be to foster in their athletes the strength of character to act with integrity, honesty, fairness, and respect for others. Integrity is a powerful coaching asset and its absence can drastically affect the tenor of sport for athletes, parents, spectators, officials, supporters, and others involved. Integrity is thus not only in one's own interest, but is an essential principle to follow for a fulfilling and satisfying life and to gain and maintain self-esteem. Integrity also influences those with whom one works or relates.

Coaches may be tempted to cheat or take short cuts to impress someone, for monetary gain or to avoid failure (Cushion & Jones, 2006), but the odds are that their behaviours will eventually catch up with them. Cheating may often take the form of trying to fool an individual such as the coach of an opposing team, the opponents, or even an official. It is dishonest, and may result in an outcome that denies others a just reward for their efforts. Condoning or ignoring cheating or unfair play is also cheating. Athletes should play or perform their best, but it is the coach's responsibility to keep athletes playing fair.

The concept of fair play thus includes not only how athletes behave, but also how coaches behave. Fair play means coaches and athletes are abiding by the rules, treating opponents with respect, and showing modesty and composure in victory and defeat by not taking unfair advantage of opponents (Coaching Association of Canada, n.d.). The concept of fair play is all-encompassing because it can be related to other aspects of life and demonstrates the educative value that sport can have (Kidman & Lombardo, 2010a). Without fair play, any victory becomes hollow and worthless. Imagine winning an important competition when one of the opponents was severely injured during the game because of a cheap tackle.

Figure 2.1 Teach your athletes to respect their opponents

A fair play philosophy in coaching is built on the belief that participation in sport should be a moral pursuit. The fair play philosophy encourages all to participate in a fair, moral fashion and have respect for others, themselves, and material possessions. The principles of fair play include:

1 Respecting the rules of the competition
2 Respecting officials and accepting their decisions
3 Respecting the opponent
4 Providing all participants with equal opportunities
5 Maintaining dignity by setting examples worthy of imitation.

24

These principles apply to all situations and to all who are involved in sport – coaches, officials, athletes, parents, spectators, and supporters.

Rules

The rules and regulations of various sporting endeavours were devised to allow fair competition. The rules of each sport generally have been thoroughly researched and have continued to be updated as new issues arise (Hanlon, 2009). Fair play is based on these rules and whether or not they are followed. Rules give sport its form and values. Rules are created to enhance the spirit of the game. They are developed by people who care about the sport and have a vested interest in the safety, interests, and enjoyment of athletes. Some rules have even been created to enhance the interest for spectators and even now for television viewing (Reeves, 1989). For example, there is a tie-break rule in tennis for television scheduling purposes, and time-outs are taken in basketball for television commercials. Whatever the origin of the rules, coaches have a responsibility to teach and follow them in their sport, and to educate young people as to the value of respecting them.

When rugby started in Britain, there was no referee to call the game. The rules were designed by those who played several years after Webb Ellis arguably ran with the ball. At that time fair play included a gentlemanly call when a rule was broken (RugbyFootballHistory.com, n.d.). Imagine that concept in today's society. In some sports there are now parent problems on the sidelines, even though there is an official (Kidman et al., 1999). Rules are created to ensure fair play. Once the coach acknowledges, implicitly or otherwise, that 'rules are made to be broken', the athletes acquire that understanding and the concept of cheating is perpetuated.

Officials

The referees, umpires, or judges are perceived to be the most controversial people involved in sport, but are necessary to keep the competitions fair. Officials do their best, no matter what the spectators and coaches believe. An extreme example of abuse of an official was demonstrated in a professional rugby game in South Africa (August 2002) where a spectator came on the field and tackled the referee. He was upset at some of the calls that were going against South Africa. The rugby players defended the referee by trying to get the spectator away from him. The referee, nevertheless, had to be carried off the field because of a dislocated shoulder. What was the point to this exhibition? What effect did this display have on the players? What effect did this display have on the referee? How did the public view this situation? What did the children watching this game learn from the incident?

Coaches must come to terms with the purpose of officials in competitions. Both coaches and officials should ensure a fair game by making athletes abide by the rules. Just as coaches have a job to do, officials have a job to do. Just as coaches dislike being criticised and sometimes take the criticism personally, officials feel the same way. Remember that the purpose of officials is also to promote sportsmanship.

ACTIVITY

Think of three ways of showing officials appreciation and understanding for their officiating at a competition. An example is thanking them afterwards.

1

2

3

Figure 2.2 Fair play?

26

Opponents

Without opponents, there would be no competition. Respecting opponents and their abilities is essential to the principles of fair play. Fair play is helping the opponents up when they are injured, or congratulating them at the end of the competition for a job well done. International netball and volleyball seem to have it right. They shake hands before the game (and often exchange gifts) and then again after the game. Understanding the abilities and potential of athletes and challenging them to do better demonstrates respect for the opponent, because by trying their hardest, athletes are giving the opponents an opportunity to demonstrate what they can do. If by trying their best the athletes completely outdo the other team, then coaches might consider providing the opponents with a more even competition. For example, the athletes' positions could be rotated or they could work on specific goals, such as tactical or skill practice, that do not focus on winning. There are many clubs that are overloaded with extremely talented athletes. Some clubs believe in such an overload, so that they can win all the time. A golden rule to follow is to treat the opponents as you and your athletes want to be treated.

When coaches are trying to develop or become better coaches, we often see that coaches, especially at the professional level, are reluctant to share ideas with other coaches (Mallett & Rynne, 2009). By sharing learning activities, and general strategies, even at the professional level (see Kidman, 2001), the competition becomes challenging and fun. Also, sharing ideas on how to ensure athletes are enjoying their sport can enhance motivation levels (e.g., fun activities with lots of variety or coaching methods that focus on athletes' needs).

Equity issues

The Australian Coaching Council, the Coaches Association of Canada, and the United States Olympic Committee (USOC) are three organisations that have written codes of ethics for coaches. These codes provide a common set of values so coaches can build their philosophies and provide equitable opportunities for the athletes they coach. Many coaches in the USA are professional, but the general principles of the code of ethics should apply to all sports and levels of competition. It is the individual coach's responsibility to advocate a common set of values, to aspire to the highest possible standards of conduct, as well as to educate his or her athletes to abide by the same high standards.

Coaches should seek to contribute to the welfare of their athletes, which includes considering athletes' individual rights. These rights and athletes' needs are the essence of an athlete-centred approach. When conflicts occur, coaches should be able to resolve them responsibly and maturely. If individual rights are ignored, sport will increasingly lose its value as a humanising experience (Lombardo, 1987). All athletes should experience the joy and delight of participation (Kretchmar, 2005). Coaches have a legal, ethical and moral duty to ensure all athletes are fairly treated. The equity issues to consider include disability, race, gender, ability levels, sexual orientation, cultural considerations, and socioeconomic status. Equity ensures everyone's needs are met by respecting the fundamental rights, dignity, and worth of all participants (Burrows, 2004). Coaches should strive to eliminate biases based on these factors and not knowingly participate in or condone unfair discriminatory practices. Participants include athletes, families, coaches, officials, volunteers, administrators, and spectators. Equality ensures everyone has equal opportunities, despite individual differences. Athletes have a right to an equal opportunity to develop their talents in their chosen sport. They have a right to receive fair treatment from the coach and their fellow athletes. They need to be encouraged to develop as independent persons who respect themselves and others.

We often have the misconstrued idea that a particular type of person is 'normal'. We tend to think we are normal and we compare our 'normality' to other people (Buck, 1992). Nevertheless, there is no single idea of what is normal. What is normal in one subculture could be distinctly odd in another. Everyone is different in looks, experiences, skill, and genetic makeup. In sport some individuals have a more difficult time than others, but everyone has something to offer. Rarely will one of our athletes be an Olympic competitor; therefore Olympic competitors are, by definition, abnormal! Coaches should learn about the athletes who join their teams or squads and should provide every possible opportunity for all of them, valuing the team's diversity. Lyn Gunson, an international netball coach, discussed how this diversity makes up a community:

> there are sometimes five different cultures in the team. Netball seems to be a game where there are socioeconomic differences, intellect differences, age differences and life experience differences. I actually believe more in the concept of community. You've got a community

28

of people on your hands for a period of time … Also you need to leave a door open … for competitive pressure outside [and] for those people who will grow and develop within the group … who come from other aspects, like another country. It would be highly unlikely that you could pick a team at the beginning of a four-year cycle and have the best group and it remain the same for all that time. The culture rises out of the group you've got. However, I strongly do believe in having some basic principles which establish a connecting forum from which to go [forward] and pull them together.

(Lyn Gunson, cited in Kidman & Lombardo, 2010a, p. 83)

Coaches may experience conflict at times, but should accept the obligation to provide an equitable environment for all athletes. You may have to gain an understanding of your own biases and why you hold them, and also be aware that messages conveyed, both verbally and non-verbally, are critical to the equitable environment for which you are responsible.

SELF-REFLECTION

All of us have certain biases that may affect our intention to communicate equally with all people. In the list below, write '1' if the word or phrase has little influence on your personal biases, through increasing numbers to '5' for a word that has great influence.

☐ religion   ☐ culture   ☐ homosexuality

☐ gender   ☐ body shape   ☐ age

☐ hair style   ☐ occupation   ☐ socioeconomic status

☐ behaviour   ☐ parenting   ☐ 'elite' athlete

☐ physical appearance   ☐ type of sport   ☐ rival

☐ differing opinion   ☐ smoker   ☐ drug user

☐ accessories worn   ☐ attitude   ☐ drinking problem

☐ type of clothing   ☐ mannerisms   ☐ political activism

☐ ethnicity   ☐ criminal record   ☐ temper

☐ body piercing   ☐ tattoos   ☐ previous mistakes

☐ laziness   ☐ acceptance of mediocrity

By observing the range of your responses, you are acknowledging that particular biases exist and will then be able to work on reducing them.

Language

Meaning what we say and saying what we mean enhances our values and attendance to equal opportunity. Many equity problems in our society stem from people saying things that contain implicit biases towards a particular person or group (Staurowski, 1998). For example, some coaches still use the phrase, 'You're throwing like a girl.' Gender challenges are particularly problematic. The connotations of the masculine identity still pervade sport (e.g., 'How gay', or 'You're a wimp').

Gender-neutral language should be a goal. Ensuring politically correct terms are always used is difficult, but coaches should value the need for the use of correct terminology. An example is man-to-man defence. Should we say, instead, person to person? Does 'son' still signify the male gender? How far do we take the issue (e.g., sportspersonship)? The important consideration here is to ask your athletes which terms they want to use. This acceptance, combined with terms that are currently politically correct and include gender, race, disability, and cultural considerations, should promote equality. Coaches' best contribution to equality will always be through their own words or actions.

Coaches as role models

Children model themselves on significant adults in their lives. Children learn what they observe and will copy behaviours accordingly (Smoll & Smith, 2002). Bandura's social learning theory (1977) suggests that people learn by observing others' behaviours. When these behaviours are reinforced, people tend to continue to exhibit them. For example, if athletes see a coach yelling at a referee, they will see that behaviour as appropriate and will think that they can yell at the referee as well. If coaches tell athletes not to yell at referees, but then continue to do so themselves, then the yelling is reinforced by the coaches. Therefore, coaches' actions towards fair play reinforce the notion of what is appropriate.

30

Children can recite every principle of fair play, but saying and doing are two different things. They may have had coaches who value a fair play philosophy and abide by it through their actions and communication. Those coaches are terrific role models and the children value fair play and act like good sportspeople. Nevertheless, there have been coaches who say one thing and do another. Children not only talk about coaches behind their backs, but during competitions they talk back to the referee and the opponents. In some sports, children have been seen spitting in their hands before shaking the opponents' hands and the coach on the sideline has laughed, reinforcing behaviour that will likely continue throughout the season.

TIPS TO PROMOTE EQUITY

- Include all sorts of athletes on posters and newsletters.
- Mention all different athletes when discussing sports.
- Do not laugh at or tell racist or ethnic jokes that make fun of a different individual.
- Expect all athletes to behave differently.
- Do not allow athletes to tease about equity issues.
- Avoid loaded terms such as gay, sissy, clumsy, or wimpy.
- Make sure that low-skilled athletes are not picked last, and assign them tasks they can do successfully.
- Elicit and monitor feedback on equity issues.

What are other strategies that would promote equity on your team?

Coaches' expectations

The expectations coaches have for their athletes are often realised by their athletes. Coaches frequently go into sporting situations where they have varied expectations of individuals on their teams. These expectations can be derived from what other coaches have pointed out, their own opinions based on brief interactions, or other influences on the coaches' lives (Nakamura, 1996). There is a direct connection between coach expectations and athlete behaviour. The sequence of coach expectations is a) coach forms expectations; b) coach's expectations influence athletes' behaviour; c) athletes' behaviour influences athletes' performances; and d) athletes' performances confirm coach's expectations (Nakamura, 1996). An example of this expectation–performance relationship is Kyle, an 11-year-old football player who started with a new coach. The old coach had a discussion with the new coach about his team from the year before. When he discussed Kyle, the old coach related that Kyle was hopeless, uncoordinated, and not very athletic. The new coach took this opinion on board and expected little from Kyle, so continued to treat him as incompetent. Kyle was going through a growth spurt when he was on the previous team and was uncoordinated, but this year he was starting to grow into his body. Kyle was continually berated and continued to underperform (just as the coach expected) and eventually dropped out of football all together. Kyle lived up to the new coach's expectations.

There are many effects of these expectations including the frequency and quality of coach–athlete interactions (Nakamura, 1996). Coaches who spend more time with those whom they perceive as high-ability athletes, or show more warmth and positivity with those athletes, can negatively influence the performances of perceived lower-ability athletes. The perceptions of the coaches can label athletes as low ability or high ability, whether they demonstrate those characteristics or not. For example, if coaches lower their expectations of what skills some athletes will learn, thus establishing a lower standard of performance, they may allow the perceived low-ability athletes less time in learning activities, and be less persistent in teaching difficult skills. The type and frequency of feedback can be aligned to coaches' expectations. For example, coaches may provide more frequent and positive feedback to perceived high-ability athletes after successful performances. The high-ability athletes get more instructional and informational feedback, as well as more praise and affirmations. The perceived low-ability athletes exhibit poorer performance due to less effective reinforcement and often, as a result, have less playing time. They then exhibit lower levels of self-confidence and perceived competence over the course of a season. Low-ability athletes attribute their failures to lack of ability, thus substantiating the notion that they aren't any good and have little

32

chance to succeed in the future. Although it is difficult for coaches not to form expectations, it is important that they reflect on their behaviours towards each athlete to ensure the expectations do not influence athletes' performances or confidence levels.

ACTIVITY

You will need to do this activity with another person – a coach, partner, friend, or colleague. Read each of the following case studies out loud and discuss the consequences of each. What would you do differently? What actions would you suggest?

CASE STUDY 1

You are coaching an Under-12 speed skating group. At the start of the season, one of the parents suggests to you that Donald (who is nine years old) is hopeless. She says that he cannot stand up straight, loses his balance all the time, and basically hangs on to the side a lot. The parent relates the story about how the previous coach knew he was hopeless and therefore never gave him much attention. The previous coach also played lots of elimination-type games, whereby Donald was always the first one out.

CASE STUDY 2

Isabelle (age 10) is an athlete with a hearing impairment, and is self-conscious that she is different. When she plays sport, she has to take out her hearing aids and therefore cannot hear the coach or the other children. Isabelle is quite adept at lip reading, but needs to be able to see the person who is speaking. When the coach calls all the athletes in, Isabelle is often left standing out in the middle of the field before she realises that she is supposed to be somewhere else. Unless Isabelle is close to the coach, she cannot lip-read any instructions. The coach does not give Isabelle much feedback, because it is so difficult to get her to understand. None of the other athletes has been told that Isabelle has a hearing impairment, but some of them are making fun of her and her inability to respond quickly.

Robert is playing basketball with one of the local high school teams. The coach has called training for Saturdays, but Saturdays are Sabbath days for Robert and his family. Because of Robert's religious beliefs and commitments, he cannot make Saturday training sessions. The coach has suggested that Robert should not play with his team this year.

Louisa is an outstanding volleyball player. She has the ability to make the national volleyball team. During her club team's training sessions, the coach spends 50 per cent of her time with Louisa. Often the other players are left to fend for themselves. Many of the players are upset about the limited attention they receive and are beginning to resent Louisa. A couple of the players have approached the coach and complained that they are not getting a fair chance.

At a Saturday game, your field hockey team is playing a rival team. During the game, the parents of the other team continue to verbally abuse your team, put down players from their own team, and shout abuse at the referees.

General guidelines of fair play

As a coach you should consider adopting the following guidelines to ensure a high standard of fair play for teams and/or athletes:

- Emphasise that the process of performance is an important aim in and of itself.
- Ensure your actions are an example of how athletes and spectators should behave; be a good role model.
- Encourage participants to respect the spirit of the game, not just the outcome. The quality of, and participation in, the sport experience is more important than who wins or loses.
- Actively encourage athletes, parents, and spectators to respect officials and other competitors. Point out that competitors cooperate by competing and that there would be no competition without opponents.

34

- Recognise that all participants are special and important in their own ways and should be treated with respect and dignity.
- Recognise that sport is only one aspect of life.
- Listen to what athletes say and adjust your expectations and programmes according to their needs and desires.
- If you are unsure how to handle a situation, talk to another coach confidentially and ensure no names are mentioned.

SUMMARY

1 A coaching philosophy is based on our foundational beliefs, values, principles, concepts, and priorities. A coaching philosophy should govern our actions.

2 Personal philosophies are related to ethics, how people ought to behave in certain situations. Ethical behaviours form the basis of fair play.

3 Striving to win is more important than actually winning. Winning allows coaches and athletes to compare themselves against others, whereas success is a measure of how well participating athletes are performing and comparing themselves against themselves.

4 The authors' coaching philosophy is to provide athletes with caring, trust, positive communication and commitment that enables them to be the best that they can be physically, psychologically, cognitively, socially, and spiritually.

5 Coaches need to determine the method of communicating their philosophies.

6 Coaches need to establish mutual team goals, values, and strategies so that athletes take responsibility and ownership for their team culture.

7 All coaches should take the time to write down their coaching philosophies as the basis for their day-to-day coaching and their longer term goals.

8 Having integrity – demonstrating self-control, honesty, fairness, and respect for others – is a powerful coaching asset.

9 The principles of fair play include respecting the rules of the competition, respecting officials and accepting their decisions, respecting the opponent, providing all participants with equal opportunities, and setting examples worthy of imitation.

10 Athletes often live up to coaches' expectations, so coaches need to be open-minded about their athletes.

PART 2

ATHLETE DEVELOPMENT

CHAPTER 3

YOUR ATHLETES

This chapter covers

- Characteristics of athletes
- Athletes' reasons for participating
- Developing a team from a collection of individuals

Being a successful coach is a challenging undertaking. An approach that works well with one athlete may not work at all with another. Coaches often need to spend a lot of time and effort thinking of and trying different alternatives to teach athletes certain skills and tactical awareness. Flexibility, innovation, and patience are the tools of a good coach. The feeling of satisfaction rewards the effort expended when a way is finally found to reach a particular individual. Nevertheless, coaches may feel frustration when the same method does not work with everyone and they have to renew the search for another approach.

Yes, coaching is challenging because all athletes are different. These differences, however, keep coaching interesting and ensure we never get bored. The important thing to remember is that all athletes are individuals. How they acquire skills and knowledge is influenced by their personal differences.

CHARACTERISTICS OF ATHLETES

Physical characteristics

Probably the most obvious difference between individuals is their physical appearance. Athletes come in all shapes and sizes. Although body build may contribute to how readily individuals learn particular skills, it is not always necessary to have a particular body build to perform well (or have fun) in a particular sport. For example, being tall can be an asset when playing basketball, but it is not a requirement. A 5 ft 7 in (170 cm) player has won the Slam Dunk Contest in the National Basketball Association (NBA) in the United States and a 5 ft 3 in (160 cm) player ('Muggsy' Bogues) scored 6,858 points and made 1,369 steals as a professional NBA player (Electro-Mech, 2009). A particular body build may be beneficial, but it is not a requirement (although there are probably few jockeys over 6 ft (183 cm)). Coaches should not discourage people, particularly children, from participating in any activity just because they do not match an 'ideal' shape. Even though their body builds may make it difficult for them to make it to the elite level (as only a few will), they may get a lot of enjoyment out of participating at a lower level, or even beat the odds and make it to the top.

In youth sport, it is imperative to keep in mind that individuals' growth and maturity characteristics affect performances (Malina et al., 2004). Early maturers, who have physique advantages in youth sport compared to their later maturing peers, may not be the ones with the most desirable physical characteristics once they become teenagers or adults (something to remember if trying to identify young talent).

Within any group of athletes a range of fitness levels will be represented. Various aspects of fitness will influence how individuals are able to practise physical skills. If Chris, for example, has limited muscular strength, he will have to put more effort into any activity requiring strength than does someone who is stronger. If he has a weakness in part of his body, coordination may be affected. Similarly, if Lisa has poor endurance, she may learn a task, but not be able to practise adequately. Seemingly lazy training habits may be due to problems with muscular endurance or aerobic fitness rather than a slack attitude or short attention span. Coaches need to be sure that athletes have the endurance to repeat skills and learning activities in their sport. Just because some athletes cope well with the workload does not mean that everyone will be able to do the same.

40

Figure 3.1 Approaches that work well for one athlete may not work well for another

Individuals will also differ in their flexibility. Not everyone will have the same range of movement in their joints. Poor range of movement in a joint that is important to the development of a particular skill may limit achievement. Flexibility is not only important for sports such as gymnastics or skating, where it is an obvious requirement, but also for any activity that requires a broad range of movement of a particular joint. For example, shoulder flexibility is needed for correct and efficient technique for backstroke in swimming and for spiking in volleyball. Although Stuart may appear to be fit and coordinated, poor shoulder flexibility could limit his achievement as a backstroker or a spiker. Rather than continually repeating drills designed to change his technique, developing a stretching programme to increase his shoulder flexibility would be more beneficial (and probably less frustrating for Stuart).

Of the athletes you currently coach, write the initials of the athlete you believe to be best and least suited for your sport according to each of the physical characteristics listed. You may have different athletes in mind for each characteristic. Then, in the column provided, indicate what might best help the athlete with the potential disadvantage.

Characteristic	Best	Worst	How to support or help
Body build			
Strength			
Muscular endurance			
Aerobic fitness			
Flexibility			

The senses

Most of us learn about the five basic senses in primary or elementary school. We see, hear, smell, taste, and touch what is around us. Although athletes' abilities to smell and taste have little, if any, bearing on how they learn skills, the other senses play a role in learning most skills. Athletes usually use multiple senses when learning physical skills. People with no obvious sensory impairments may, nevertheless, learn more or less effectively depending on the sensory modality that is stressed during instruction. Some individuals prefer visual demonstrations, some a precise verbal description of what is required, and yet others learn best through physically feeling their own bodies performing the skill (Baribeau, 2006). Because of these individual differences, coaches will be effective with more athletes if they are able to incorporate multiple sensory modalities into their instruction of physical skills. Coaches who have had opportunities to coach athletes who are sensory impaired often have strengthened their abilities to use the senses not affected by the impairment, particularly when the impairment was in a sense on which the coach had relied for instruction in the past. This section will cover the senses of hearing, vision, touch, balance, and kinaesthetic awareness.

42

Hearing

Hearing is important when learning motor skills. If athletes have a hearing impairment or for some other reason cannot hear clearly, it is difficult for them to listen to and understand directions. Even athletes with good hearing may have problems when there is a lot of other noise in the environment or when the people speaking have their backs turned. Hearing is also important for team sports where calls or suggestions from teammates are commonplace. Hearing can also provide clues for how to react to what others are doing. For example, in softball or baseball, the sound made when the bat hits the ball can indicate how the ball was hit, providing clues about distance and speed.

In many sports being able to hear whistles, starting guns, or officials is important for athletes to know what they should be doing and when. When coaches or officials are not aware of hearing impairments, they may mistake an individual's inability to hear for a poor attitude or lack of respect.

Vision

Vision contributes to learning and performance in many ways. Probably the most obvious effect of vision in learning physical skills is where athletes are asked to watch demonstrations or models. We often rely on the saying that 'a picture is worth a thousand words'. Demonstrations are effective, but for an athlete with a visual impairment an equally clear verbal description is needed.

Another influence of vision on learning – one that is so common it is usually taken for granted by those with good vision – is visual feedback about our performance. Whether we are hitting a tennis ball, throwing a javelin, or sailing a boat, we learn a lot about the effectiveness of our technique by the visual feedback we are constantly receiving. In coaching situations it is imperative that another source of feedback is found for the athletes who are blind or visually impaired.

Run through the same 15–20 minute section of one of the videos of your coaching twice. The first time, turn the sound off and just watch. The second time, turn away from the screen and just listen.

- Which sense, hearing or vision, provided you with the most information?
- Are there any sections of the recording that lost meaning when you only watched or only listened?
- If you were coaching an athlete with a hearing impairment, what could you do visually that would make your communication clearer?
- If you were coaching an athlete with a visual impairment, what could you do to communicate more effectively with that athlete?
- What effect would it have on all your athletes if you were equally clear verbally and visually?

Touch or pressure

The sense of touch is also important when learning some skills. In many ball sports there is an implicit acknowledgement that some individuals have better hands, or a better feel for the ball, than others. How you catch a soft sponge ball versus a hard ball is influenced by your sense of touch. How well developed someone's sense of pressure is can also affect how easily some skills are learned. For example, when swimming, the hands should feel maximum pressure when pushing the water. If you move your hand straight through the water you will be pushing against water that is already moving and will therefore have less pressure on your hand. If, however, you move your hand through an S-shape when pulling it through the water, you will be pushing against still water and therefore feel more pressure on your hand (and move further forward). Understanding the technique intellectually is one thing, but being able to feel the difference in the pressure on the hand means the individual once again gets continual feedback while swimming. If Gloria cannot feel the difference in pressure, learning correct technique will take longer because of limited feedback. In this situation, patience is needed, because it would be detrimental to Gloria for you to mistake her slow learning as a sign that she simply does not understand what she is meant to do.

44

Balance

A sense not included in the basic five senses is the sense of equilibrium or body balance. Balance is the basis for voluntary movement and control (Shumway-Cook & Woolacott, 2007). Without balance individuals cannot control their movements. An example is a newborn giraffe's first attempt at walking. In less than an hour after being born it can stand, but learning how to walk is another matter. Initially when standing it has all four legs fairly wide apart. When it tries to take a step, it falls in the direction of whichever leg it picked up. The baby giraffe has no control for voluntary movement until it develops a sense of balance. Once that sense of balance is developed, however, the giraffe quickly moves from its hesitant first steps to a carefree frolic.

Sometimes when athletes are having difficulty learning a new skill, it is not because they do not understand what it is they are supposed to do, it is because when trying the skill they are off balance and cannot control their movements. All voluntary movement requires balance if that movement is to be controlled.

POINT TO PONDER

Consider how balance is necessary for your sport. How might you help your athletes develop their senses of balance?

Kinaesthetic awareness

Kinaesthetic awareness is being aware of changes in your body position, direction, or acceleration. It is related to the sense of touch, but it is more about how your body feels when you are moving than how it feels to touch external objects. Athletes with outstanding physical skills have well-developed kinaesthetic awareness. If athletes are not aware of where their bodies are in space or what positions their limbs are moving through, it is difficult for them to modify technique. How can they change something if they do not know what it is they are currently doing?

Many coaches have probably experienced the situation where they are telling an athlete to move an arm or a leg into a particular position only to have the athlete say that the arm or leg is already there, because of poor kinaesthetic awareness. The person is not trying to be difficult, but honestly believes that the limb is in the correct position. Showing athletes videos of themselves can help develop their self-awareness (see Chapter 6). It is also useful to regularly focus on how the movement feels. Coaches can ask athletes to move through different positions and focus on how the positions feel rather than what they look like.

Personality

In addition to physical or sensory characteristics, athletes also differ in terms of personality. Coaches may respond differently to certain personality types, and the personalities of individual athletes may influence how they learn skills and cope with competitive situations. There are many personality qualities that could be discussed in this section, but we will limit the discussion to values and attitudes, attentional style, the need to achieve and anxiety.

Values and attitudes

Individuals have their own sets of values and attitudes. Although appreciation of individual differences is necessary, it is also important to know that particular values or attitudes may affect learning effectiveness. If Anita does not value hard work, determination, and persistence, it could be difficult for her to fit in with a programme where these values are paramount. If Eric does not respect his coach, he will not learn effectively from that coach, because anything the coach says will be considered unimportant or incorrect. Athletes' attitudes towards their coaches (as well as the coaches' attitudes towards their athletes) will influence how well athletes learn. Attitudes and values related to excellence, fair play, teamwork, winning, and fun also influence the performance of athletes – and coaches (Cassidy et al., 2009).

Attentional style

People you know may walk past without even noticing you because they are so caught up in their own thoughts. On the other hand, some individuals cannot seem to focus on any one thing because they are continually distracted. These differences relate to their attentional

46

styles. Attentional style refers to how we generally attend to the world around us. There are two main dimensions of attention – internal/external and broad/narrow (Williams et al., 2010). We may have a tendency toward either an internal focus (our own thoughts, feelings, or actions) or an external focus (the environment or what other people are doing). Similarly we may tend to have a broad focus of attention (aware of everything that is happening) or a narrow focus of attention (restricting our attention to a particular thought or object).

If Nathan is putting a golf ball, a narrow focus of attention can be useful. If Nathan is playing rugby, however, a narrow focus of attention might result in his turning the ball over to the other team or being flattened by an unnoticed member of the opposition. Most sports require our attention to shift at various times. Individuals who are predisposed to a certain attentional focus may find it difficult to adopt other foci. Coaches may need to create learning activities to help athletes develop an appropriate focus. For example, in volleyball, the setter should be aware of what the blockers are doing on the other side of the net in addition to focusing on the ball and knowing the patterns to be run by the spikers. Coaches can help setters broaden their focus of attention and get them used to looking at the other side of the net by holding up coloured paper for them and having them call out the colour before setting the ball. Once they are used to looking at the other side of the net, progressions of the activity could require decisions about setting to be determined by what is happening on the other side of the net. TGfU (see Chapter 6) is a model that develops this ability of broad attention because it enables athletes to learn how to 'read the game'.

ACTIVITY

Determine when in your sport it would be appropriate to have each focus of attention.

Broad and internal: _____

Broad and external: _____

Narrow and internal: _____

Narrow and external: _____

Now pick one of the above and explain how you could help an athlete develop that focus of attention.

Need to achieve

Achievement motivation theory suggests that there are two primary motives – the motive to approach success and the motive to avoid failure (Reeve, 2009). People with a strong motive to avoid failure tend to avoid voluntary participation in sport. They would rather not participate at all than take the chance of failing. We all have a mixture of both motives. If our desire to approach success outweighs our desire to avoid failure, we tend to choose activities where there is approximately a 50:50 chance of success. We want to have some chance at success, but we also want the success to mean something when we achieve it. On the other hand, if our motive to avoid failure is stronger than our motive to approach success, we will tend either to not participate, or to choose options where success is practically guaranteed or, paradoxically, virtually impossible. With a strong motive to avoid failure, we will pick either the easiest or the most difficult option.

Sometimes when athletes continually clown around and try the impossible, they are hiding a strong motive to avoid failure. If they fail at something at which no one would be expected to succeed, they have not really failed. These individuals need to learn that never making a mistake means never improving. Mistakes need to be looked at in a positive light (Halden-Brown, 2003). If Bob is learning to ice skate and is afraid of falling, he may never let go of the boards. If he never falls, he is not trying anything he cannot already do. If he tries something new and falls, he needs to consider what he could do differently to stay on his feet the next time. Learning requires taking chances through trial and error.

Anxiety

Anxiety is the tendency to perceive a situation as threatening, stressful, or challenging. People interpret the same situation differently. Thelma may enter a major competition and feel anxious because she perceives the situation to be threatening. She worries that she might blow it or let down her coach. Terry might enter the same competition and, even with the same level of skill, feel that the situation is a challenge. She may feel that she now has a chance to show what she can do.

The tendency to view situations as threatening or challenging relates to individuals' trait anxiety levels, or how they generally perceive situations. State anxiety, on the other hand, relates to how anxious

48

individuals are in a specific situation at a specific point in time. Anything that increases athletes' uncertainty or the importance of the outcome will increase state anxiety levels. When coaches say, 'we've trained all year for this moment', they usually make their athletes anxious rather than excited. The more certain athletes can be about their own abilities, their positions on the team, and whether they are liked by their teammates and coaches, the less likely they are to be anxious.

Different backgrounds

All athletes come to a team with different backgrounds and experiences that will influence how they react to their coaches and how they learn. For example, if Maureen and Sharon are both learning to swim, but one of them had a frightening experience in water when younger, they will approach the water differently. Also, previous coaches will influence athletes' attitudes towards their present or future coaches. Individuals who have had coaches who yelled whenever anyone made a mistake may be hesitant to try something new. If they had coaches who encouraged feedback, they may offer suggestions even when they have not been asked for them.

Cultural differences can lead to misunderstandings and conflict (Hanrahan, 2010). For example, people from individualistic cultures (i.e., societies that encourage the needs and wishes of individuals over group concerns) may be accustomed to people owning their own equipment, striving for personal improvement, taking responsibility for their own fitness training, and making decisions about strategy. Individuals from collectivistic cultures (i.e., societies that value the needs and wishes of groups over individuals, often emphasising conformity) may be accustomed to equipment being accessible to anyone, focusing on team rather than individual performances, waiting for others to lead fitness training, and relying on the coach or experienced players to decide on strategies. In the global society in which we work, we need to ensure that we do not assume that everyone has similar beliefs or ways of doing things. Waiting to be told to do fitness training or not independently making decisions about strategy may be indicative of respect for those of higher status, not signs of laziness.

A discussion about how backgrounds and experiences influence athletes could take up the remainder of this book. Family and cultural expectations and values, the sporting successes and failures of siblings and parents, and societal expectations in terms of gender-appropriate activities are just a few examples of factors that may influence each athlete. The main thing is to remember that each athlete is an individual. Instead of expecting athletes to be clones and to conform to a single method of learning, coaches should be flexible and accommodate and appreciate their differences.

ATHLETES' REASONS FOR PARTICIPATING

Athletes participate in sport for many reasons and coaches should consider the motives of their athletes. Not only do athletes begin a particular sport for various reasons, they also have different incentives to continue participating. For athletes to continue, coaches need to determine what it is that attracts each athlete to participate. Coaches have a responsibility to ensure athletes' needs are met according to the reasons they participate and continue in the sport (Kidman & Lombardo, 2010a). Athletes have an incentive to continue when their experiences are enjoyable or satisfying. If not, they will eventually find more satisfying sports or activities or drop out altogether.

Athletes' motives to participate include affiliation, mastery, desire for sensation, self-direction, and social comparison (McCullagh et al., 1993). Most athletes have more than one of these motives.

Affiliation

An athlete's affiliation incentive is based on a desire to have positive, friendly relationships with others. Athletes with an affiliation incentive are socially reassured by making new friends or maintaining friendships. Coaches can aim to provide an environment that is conducive to social affiliation by making interaction with others a part of each training session. Examples are developing partner or group learning activities, encouraging partner stretching, or having participants provide constructive feedback to each other. Coaches may also have brief team talks after each training session. These talks should be informal and encourage athletes to be open and honest. It is useful to encourage athletes to help one another and to do things together. Some teams have found success in developing mini-groups that have the responsibility for various needs of the team. For example, groups can be formed to analyse skills or tactics, scrutinise other teams, or design warm-ups or other learning activities. Athletes should be reminded that everyone is a valued member of the team. The provision of opportunities for social get-togethers outside the sport can also contribute to feelings of affiliation.

Mastery

Another incentive to participate is a desire for mastery. In the achievement motivation literature this focus on mastering skills is called a task orientation (Hanrahan & Cerin, 2009). Athletes with this incentive or orientation wish to improve skills, master new skills, and pursue excellence. If athletes tend to have a mastery incentive to participate, coaches should endeavour to point out individual improvements, keep written records of progress in diaries and logs, and arrange regular meetings to discuss progress and re-evaluate athletes' goals. Athletes with an incentive for mastery are characterised by doing something well for its own sake. For example, Jonah has been practising a smash shot in badminton. He is so keen to master this smash shot that he spends a lot of time just improving that shot. When he gets to a competition, he decides to try it on an opponent whom he has been unable to beat for a long time. Success for Jonah in this situation would be making a great smash shot, regardless of whether or not he wins the match.

Desire for sensation

A desire for sensation is another incentive to participate. This sensation may be derived from the sights, sounds, excitement, and physical feelings surrounding a sport (Kidman & Lombardo, 2010a). This incentive focuses on the thrill, tension, pressure, and pure action that sports can provide. For athletes who have a desire for sensation, coaches should try to arrange workouts in areas with pleasant sights, sounds, smells, and physical feelings. For example, athletes could warm up to music. Coaches should provide enough activity for everyone – not too much, not too little. Within the training session, games and activities should be provided that are fun and use different resources. Workouts should be varied by changing routines, creating new drills, and allowing participants to work on exciting new moves.

Desire for self-direction

Some athletes may participate in sport because of a desire for self-direction. These athletes have a wish to feel a sense of control or to feel in charge. This motive can be addressed by giving athletes responsibilities, for example positions of leadership. Coaches may consider having self-directed athletes lead warm-ups or choose activities to develop certain skills. Coaches can enhance self-direction by giving athletes chances during practices or competitions to make their own decisions about what strategy to use (what pitch to throw, what play to run). In some situations athletes can also be given the responsibility for determining training times, uniform styles, and social activities. As discussed throughout the book, self-direction can also be catered to by structuring practice sessions so that athletes discover the answers to questions about technique and strategy through problem-solving activities. Instead of coaches always telling the athletes what to do, the coaches provide the environment in which the athletes learn through experimentation and structured questioning (Kidman & Lombardo, 2010a).

Social comparison

Some athletes participate in sport because of the opportunity to compare themselves to others socially. In the achievement motivation literature this focus on being better than others is called an ego orientation (Hanrahan & Cerin, 2009). Athletes with this incentive or orientation seek status and prestige through winning competitions or beating others. They are most happy when they can demonstrate that they are better than others. A major consideration with athletes who are primarily motivated in this manner is that if their skill levels are relatively low, they tend to drop out of sport. To cater for athletes motivated by social comparison, coaches can include competitive games within training sessions, such as relays or games that have a winner and a loser. The purpose of these games is to give points or some other reward to ensure there is an outcome to the various learning activities in which the athletes are participating. When using this tactic try to avoid elimination activities where athletes sit out when they have lost. Those who are eliminated first are often the ones who have lower skill levels. If eliminated, they practise less and perpetuate their lower levels of skill. Also, try to match ability levels as evenly as possible. Athletes should not give up because they perceive themselves to be outclassed. Similarly, beating an opponent is not particularly satisfying when the opponent is notably less skilled.

Athletes are usually motivated by more than one of the incentives listed above. It is quite possible for coaches to ensure that each athlete has the opportunity to master skills in her or his chosen sport, be given feedback on personal performance, and experience some form of self-direction, yet at the same time have the opportunity for social interactions. When coaches understand these motives they can cater for a variety of needs and develop athletes who are motivated to continue to be involved in the sport.

ACTIVITY

Write the initials of each of your athletes in Figure 3.2. Work out the incentive(s) for each athlete's participation motivation. In the last column, identify activities or ways that you can ensure the athlete meets his or her motives.

Athlete initials	A	M	S	SD	SC	Methods to ensure athletes have an incentive to participate

Figure 3.2 Athletes' incentives to participate
(A = affiliation; M = mastery; S = sensation;
SD = self-direction; SC = social comparison)

DEVELOPING A TEAM FROM A COLLECTION OF INDIVIDUALS

So far this chapter has focused on how individual athletes are different from each other. Although we need to recognise individual differences, we usually have the added challenge of finding a way to encourage these individuals to form a team. Bringing a group of athletes together does not automatically create a harmonious team. Even though athletes may wear the same uniform, rarely do they spontaneously form a cohesive team.

A cohesive team is one where the members like each other and stick together in pursuit of the group's goals or objectives (Carron et al., 2005). Cohesion is a process. Cohesion does not just happen and then remain as a permanent feature of the team. How athletes feel about each other and how effectively they work together change over time. Throughout a team's existence, there is a continual build up and decline of cohesiveness.

There are two types of cohesion: social and task. Social cohesion refers to how much the team members like each other and enjoy each other's company. Even individual sports, where there is limited interaction between athletes during competition or training, can benefit from social cohesion. Task cohesion refers to how well the members work together towards achieving goals. Most interactive team sports such as hockey, football, or basketball require high levels of task cohesion if the team is to perform effectively. Task cohesion, however, is not limited to interactive team sports. Athletes in individual sports, such as golf or skateboarding, can benefit from task cohesion when individuals support each other.

Benefits of cohesion

Individuals are likely to remain with a team when it is cohesive (Carron et al., 2002). Cohesiveness enhances stability. Although there are examples of elite teams with poor cohesion performing well, cohesiveness generally enhances performance, particularly for interactive sport teams. From an individual point of view, athletes gain satisfaction from being in a cohesive team. Most people prefer teams where there is harmony and unity rather than antagonism and disquiet. In addition, satisfaction is gained from success. When cohesion enhances performance, it also, indirectly, creates satisfaction.

54

Getting to know each other

When a group of people first come together, they can feel awkward or inhibited because they do not know each other and do not know what to expect. This lack of familiarity can cause hesitant performances in sport. A multitude of ice-breaking activities exist that allow people to get to know each other (see Hanrahan & Carlson, 2000). Several activities focus on learning names. The more effective ones allow individuals to learn more about each other than just their names.

One activity (applicable to both male and female athletes of all ages and ability levels) involves bringing a collection of soft toys and objects to the group. Be sure to have more items than there are people in the group. Display the toys and objects so that everyone can see them, then ask each individual to choose the item that best represents them. It is useful to provide examples such as, 'One of you may think you are like a knife – always getting into everything, fairly sharp, and rather direct and to the point. Another may be more like a possum – appearing to be very shy, particularly in new surroundings, tending to fall asleep during the day but being the life of the party after dark.' Do not include in the display the items that you use as examples. After each individual has selected an object, organise the athletes into pairs where they are to explain to their partners why the item they selected is representative of them. Next, the athletes form a circle and place their objects in the middle of that circle. Then each athlete selects the object that represents their partner and explains to the entire group who the item represents and why it is an appropriate choice. The activity becomes a fun and creative method of getting to know each other. Sometimes the objects selected in this activity contribute to nicknames that can stick for the season or even longer. An extension of this activity is to ask the athletes to select a second object that represents what they want to achieve or what changes they would like to see in themselves during the forthcoming season. This extension can be a good introduction to goal setting (see Chapter 5).

Your confidence in the value of the exercise will influence how much energy individuals invest in the activity. A note of caution: when working with children make it clear at the outset that toys and objects must be returned at the end of the exercise. Otherwise you may find a few of your cuddly friends have been kidnapped!

A relatively simple activity that we have found to be effective for representative teams made up of athletes who previously competed against each other is having them list 10 things they have in common. The list cannot include anything that would be true for all the other athletes in their league or conference (e.g., we all play sport X, we all have two eyes). All team members need to genuinely agree with all items on the list.

ACTIVITY

There are other ice-breaking activities that you may have used or experienced. Talk to at least one other coach and swap ice-breaking activities. Try to gather three new activities to use with your squad or team.

1

2

3

Trust

One component of cohesion is trust. In a cohesive team, the individual members trust each other. In addition, the development of trust can enhance cohesion (Statler, 2010). When individuals trust each other, they are likely to be open with their feelings, ideas, and information. This openness will enhance communication. Although specific trust exercises and games can be incorporated into training sessions, the day-to-day behaviour of group members has a powerful influence on establishing trust. Individual athletes and coaches can facilitate the development of trust by displaying particular behaviours.

For each of the behaviours in the following list, note whether you believe it enhances trust and/or cohesion (mark them 'T' and/or 'C'). Your athletes can also do this activity.

- [ ] Smiling
- [ ] Spending time small-talking about pleasant things
- [ ] Making eye contact when talking
- [ ] Having a good laugh with others
- [ ] Listening to others
- [ ] Telling others when you agree with them
- [ ] Shaking hands
- [ ] Confirming that you understand what others have said
- [ ] Including others in your activities
- [ ] Clarifying to make sure you understand others
- [ ] Encouraging others by recognising them for something they have done
- [ ] Finding interests you have in common with others
- [ ] Finding experiences you have in common with others
- [ ] Offering to help others
- [ ] Telling jokes
- [ ] Taking small risks
- [ ] Feeling free to disagree with others and giving them the freedom to disagree with you
- [ ] Asking others for feedback
- [ ] Cooperating with others
- [ ] Not always disagreeing with others
- [ ] If you do disagree, criticising others' ideas, not them
- [ ] Providing others with information that checks out

- [ ] Going the extra mile
- [ ] Reassuring others when things aren't going well
- [ ] Sympathising with others
- [ ] Offering constructive criticism
- [ ] Empathising; taking the time to feel how others feel
- [ ] Getting to know others
- [ ] Accepting others for who they are
- [ ] Appreciating individual differences
- [ ] Helping settle conflicts
- [ ] Telling others they are valuable to the team
- [ ] Being honest with others
- [ ] Sharing with others
- [ ] Being sincere
- [ ] Keeping your word
- [ ] Spending time with others
- [ ] Being genuine
- [ ] Saying hello
- [ ] Asking others how it's going
- [ ] Forgiving mistakes
- [ ] (Other) _____

Now go back through the behaviours that you noted as enhancing trust and/or cohesion. Select three behaviours that you think are important. Ask your athletes to select three behaviours that they think are important to the team. Together pick behaviours that you think will have a positive effect on the team. Make an agreement with your athletes to display these three behaviours during the next few training sessions or competitions. Periodically review the list.

1

2

3

58

Developing cohesion by creating distinctiveness

Encouraging team identity by making team members distinctive from other teams enhances unity (Dimmock & Gucciardi, 2008). The most common source of distinctiveness is the team uniform. Other possibilities include everyone styling their hair the same way, applying the same colour of zinc cream, wearing the same bathing cap, having a team emblem or pin, or even something subtle such as having team shoe laces. Allowing the athletes to determine their own distinct identity may be better than imposing an identity on them, but be prepared to provide some structure or guidelines. Cost may be an issue, as may parental approval for junior teams (more than once we have heard the suggestion of team tattoos).

Developing cohesion by establishing team goals

Chapter 5 will go into detail about the process of setting goals. In terms of increasing cohesion, it can be useful for coaches to encourage the group to set team goals and then take pride in their accomplishment (see box for Recent Research on team goal setting and cohesion). Team goals can give the individuals on the team a common sense of direction and purpose. Once two or three team goals have been established, posting the goals at the training venue can serve as a reminder of what the team is trying to achieve. Effort levels at training can sometimes be increased by athletes understanding that drills have been designed to help them achieve agreed goals (see box for Case Study involving team goals).

Developing cohesion by cultivating ownership

Athletes need to feel that the team is their team and not the exclusive property of the coach, the school, or the club. Ownership is accomplished by enabling and encouraging members to become involved in decisions that affect the team and themselves personally, such as direction, training times, learning activities, or tactics. As alluded to above, a sense of ownership can also be fostered by encouraging the athletes to choose how they will be distinct from other teams.

TEAM GOAL SETTING ENHANCES (OR AT LEAST MAINTAINS) COHESIVENESS

Because of the relationship between cohesion and performance in sport, many coaches are interested in enhancing cohesion through a process known as team building. A limitation of team-building research has been the absence of a control group. Previous research has typically used a team-building intervention with a single team either briefly or over a season, and then reported any changes in cohesion. Without a control group, there is no way of knowing if any changes in cohesion were due to the intervention or just the result of the athletes spending more time together (or some other factor). The purpose of this study was to determine whether the team-building intervention of team goal setting would increase perceptions of cohesion compared with a control condition that received no team-building intervention.

Eight high school female basketball teams participated in the study, four in the team goal-setting condition and four in a control condition. The teams in the two conditions did not differ in terms of team tenure, playing experience, or win/loss record during the season in which the study took place. The teams in the goal-setting condition selected team goals, established targets for the goals, were reminded by coaches of the goals, and reviewed and re-evaluated the goals. All teams completed the Group Environment Questionnaire, which measures perceived team cohesion, at the beginning of the season and at the end of the regular season.

There was no difference between the two groups in perceived cohesion at the beginning of the season. At the end of the season the athletes in the team goal-setting condition had significantly higher perceptions of team cohesion than did athletes in the control condition. Even though the focus of the goal-setting intervention was on specific basketball skills (i.e., the task), the differences between the intervention and control teams were in both task and social cohesion. Athletes in the goal-setting condition did not significantly increase their perceived cohesiveness over the season.

The athletes in the control condition, however, significantly decreased in perceived cohesiveness over the season (even though they reported that their coaches implemented one-off team-building activities such as team dinners, outings to the movies, or team meetings). Players in the intervention reported that team goal setting helped them play better together as a team, enabled them to be focused on common goals, allowed them to work together to reach their goals, forced them to work harder, and helped them set realistic and manageable goals.

Source: Senecal, J., Loughead, T.M. & Bloom, G.A. (2008). A season-long team-building intervention: Examining the effect of team goal setting on cohesion. *Journal of Sport and Exercise Psychology*, 30, 186–199.

Figure 3.3 Creating distinctiveness to develop team cohesion

Developing team culture

Guy Evans, as a developing basketball coach, attempted to implement a team culture that involved a mutual discussion where the team created the goals, values, and strategies to develop the team's culture. Guy was adamant that it was important to take the time to create this team culture formally.

To create this culture, he organised several training sessions away from the basketball court. During these sessions the team and coaches co-constructed team goals, values, strategies for living up to those values, and rules and responsibilities. Players then signed a resulting co-constructed document to indicate their agreement to follow it for the season. The process of co-construction began by splitting the team into small discussion groups in which they considered a series of questions. First, to establish team goals, Guy asked what they aimed to achieve from the season (see also Chapter 5 for how to set goals). After the small groups of players had provided numerous suggestions, Guy asked players to vote on the six areas they thought were most important for this season. These six areas then became the team's goals for the season:

- Gain promotion from Midlands Conference 2A.
- Get to the final of our university competition.
- Incorporate and develop a team atmosphere through training and games.
- End the season with a sense of team and self-achievement.
- Have fun.
- Have individual training sessions a minimum of three times per week.

Although many coaches co-construct or set goals for the team, often these goals are put into place with minimal consideration as to how they will be achieved and what values are required for the team to fulfil these goals. To create and prioritise team values and strategies for living up to these values, the team went through the same process as for the team goals and came up with the following:

Team values

- Inclusion – value everyone's role
- Work hard and give maximum effort

- Show respect
- Have trust in and loyalty to the team
- Have a winning mentality
- Show dedication/commitment.

Strategies

- Be on time
- Use positive reinforcement
- One person talks at a time
- Always ask for help if needed
- Mentally and physically prepare for each training session and game
- Listen and learn.

The final part of the co-construction process involved identifying rules and responsibilities that the team should live by to govern their behaviour. These rules and responsibilities were to action the values and strategies and aim towards the team goals. The rules and responsibilities created by the team were as follows:

- Any player late for practice gets 16 sidelines for every minute late. Cut-off point is five minutes.
- Any player who misses practice with no prior reason misses the following game.
- Table officials – a free-throw shoot-out will be held at training to decide the table officials for the ladies' basketball home fixtures. The last two players in the competition will have this responsibility.
- Referees are elected for each game.
- Players pay £2 per game – home and away.
- Everyone will chip in with after-game responsibilities before getting changed.

Guy suggested that the team was successful in implementing the culture and that the players 'bought into' and practised the goals, values, and strategies developed. In his reflection Guy highlighted that one of his shortfalls was the lack of frequent reinforcement and reminders of the goals, values, and strategies to keep everyone accountable to the culture.

Adapted from Edwards (2010)

Select three decisions that you will encourage your athletes to make during the next training session that will affect the team as a whole. Determine the process that you will recommend your athletes use to make each decision. Will you leave it entirely in their hands, take a vote, or let different subgroups make different decisions?

Decision	Process
1	
2	
3	

Developing cohesion by determining role identities

All members of a team need to learn their respective roles and believe these roles to be important (Carron et al., 2005). Each member of a team has a unique role. If individuals do not feel they have something to contribute, they will not feel they are a part of the team, which in turn will detract from team cohesion. Additionally, each member of the team should be acquainted with the responsibilities of other members and appreciate their importance. In team sports, this appreciation of teammates can be accomplished either by rotating positions during training or by performing team drills with one position removed. Playing other positions can help athletes understand the demands on their teammates, and playing without a position highlights the importance of that position.

Developing cohesion by avoiding turnover and cliques

Ongoing changes in team membership make it difficult for members to establish good rapport. Excessive turnover causes individuals to be unfamiliar with each other and uncertain about the team's durability and permanence. Therefore, to the extent that it is compatible with team requirements, excessive turnover should be avoided. When new members do join an existing team, steps should be taken to integrate the newcomers both socially and in terms of task-related roles. Sometimes it can be effective to use a buddy system where continuing athletes are each responsible for welcoming a specific new athlete, helping that athlete to become familiar with the team. Within existing teams, care should be taken to avoid the development of cliques. A clique is an exclusive subgroup of individuals that actively excludes others from joining. Cliques work in opposition to team goals. Studies in basketball and football have demonstrated that athletes who like each other tend to pass the ball more often to each other than to less-liked teammates, even when the latter athletes may be in preferable positions (Woodman & Grant, 1977). Changing partners during learning activities, including the integration of newcomers as part of team-meeting agendas, and emphasising activities that require group cooperation will all help develop team cohesion.

SUMMARY

1 Athletes are individuals. How they acquire skills and tactics is influenced by their personal differences.
2 Athletes differ in terms of the physical characteristics of body build, strength, muscular endurance, aerobic fitness, and flexibility.
3 Athletes' senses of hearing, vision, touch or pressure, balance, and kinaesthetic awareness influence their acquisition of skills.
4 Personality attributes such as values and attitudes, attentional style, the need to achieve, and anxiety influence how individuals behave.
5 Cultural backgrounds and the various experiences that individuals have had both in and out of sport will influence each athlete personally.
6 Athletes usually participate in sport for one or more of the following reasons: the need for affiliation, the desire for mastery, the desire for sensation, the desire for self-direction, and the desire to get status and prestige by being better than others.
7 There are two types of team cohesion. Social cohesion refers to how much the team members like each other and enjoy each other's company. Task cohesion refers to how well the members work together towards achieving the goals of the team.
8 Cohesiveness can increase performance and satisfaction as well as increase the likelihood that athletes will remain in the team.
9 Trust is a component of cohesion.
10 Cohesion can be developed by creating distinctiveness, establishing team goals, cultivating ownership, determining role identities, and avoiding member turnover and cliques.

CHAPTER 4

MANAGING ATHLETES

This chapter covers

- Planning a successful training session
- Managing the environment
- Managing time during training

In the first chapter we introduced characteristics and qualities of a successful coach. Planning to maximise learning is one of those essential qualities (Cross & Lyle, 1999). Providing an environment that is conducive to learning requires some creative, yet logical, steps. To help coaches develop athletes and ensure a smooth flow to training sessions, this chapter will discuss three coaching strategies that create a positive, caring environment: session planning, positive management, and managing time during training. The goal of this chapter is to provide coaches with methods to optimise opportunities for athletes to learn about their chosen sport and about life.

In coach development programmes coaches often ask, 'How do I organise these athletes?', 'How do I control these children?' This chapter provides some guidelines and perhaps some answers to these sorts of questions. We do not suggest that the answers are the only ones; we only want to provide some opportunities for you to learn by thinking about the methods that work best for you when coaching. To continue developing and searching for the best methods of coaching, coaches should regularly ask themselves questions such as 'Why did this work?', 'Did I achieve my objectives for the training session today?' or 'How can I improve the managing of my athletes in training sessions?'

PLANNING A SUCCESSFUL TRAINING SESSION

A productive training programme begins with good planning. Many coaches hate to plan, yet planning for the season and each training session is one of the most important aspects of coaching. Without planning, coaches can spend too much time organising and deciding what to do during the training session (Crisfield et al., 2003). Coaches tend to meet with their athletes for a limited amount of time each week. This valuable time needs to be used for preparing athletes to learn and improve skills and tactics for competitions (Morgan, 2008). If you spend a lot of time organising during a training session, the athletes have less time to participate in the activities, and therefore less quality practice time.

One important coaching strategy is to provide a variety of learning experiences throughout the season that give athletes a solid foundation from which to improve skills and tactics (Smoll & Smith, 2002). Coaches need to be aware of unbalanced programmes in which athletes learn only one aspect of the sport. Athletes need to be given opportunities to understand everything about the sport, play every position, or for youngsters, try a variety of sports. Most athletes do not stay with the same coach in all their years of participation, so a balanced programme enables athletes to move forward and continue to develop and improve. The focus on athlete development is essential to aid in athletes' growth (Burrows, 2004).

It can be tempting to avoid planning, yet it is an essential aspect of great coaching. Can you think back to a time when you had a teacher or coach who was not prepared? Was there a clear purpose to each training session? How did you feel about not being able to touch the ball more than once during a training session or only getting one attempt on the vault? Did you understand what you were supposed to do? Did you spend a lot of time moving between activities or standing in line waiting your turn? These are the sorts of planning considerations that will be addressed in this chapter.

Designing a successful training plan

You have probably been involved with the process of planning a season or an individual training session. For the purpose of enhancing individual training session planning and to prepare for future sessions, we ask you later in the chapter to design a training session within your own current season, using the format provided or one that you create. But first, we will discuss the process of planning a training session.

67

A first step in the process of planning is to determine your learning objectives for the training session (McMorris & Hale, 2006). By establishing objectives, a coach can select, design, and evaluate the learning activities for that session. A learning objective is a statement describing a task and the situations under which it will be performed (Siedentop & Tannehill, 2000). These objectives show purpose and help provide focus for that session. Coaches can determine this purpose and focus from previous competitions, athletes' requests, or other training needs.

There are three domains of learning that should be considered when designing learning objectives: performance, cognitive, and affective (Siedentop & Tannehill, 2000). Performance objectives are the movement skills athletes will perform during the training session. Cognitive objectives are the tactics, strategies, decision making, rules, or other knowledge-type learning that athletes are to gain during the training session. Affective objectives are the mental skills, attitudes, and values expected in the training sessions. Coaches generally have been concerned mostly with performance objectives, but all three domains should be encompassed and planned in each training session. When developing objectives, remember that they should be achievable. Objectives should be written so that they can be reviewed and evaluated. You should attempt to incorporate all three learning domains in every training session to enhance the holistic learning of the athlete. Figure 4.1 provides a sample format of objectives for a basketball training session.

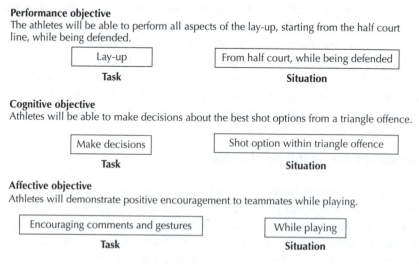

Performance objective
The athletes will be able to perform all aspects of the lay-up, starting from the half court line, while being defended.

Lay-up		From half court, while being defended
Task		**Situation**

Cognitive objective
Athletes will be able to make decisions about the best shot options from a triangle offence.

Make decisions		Shot option within triangle offence
Task		**Situation**

Affective objective
Athletes will demonstrate positive encouragement to teammates while playing.

Encouraging comments and gestures		While playing
Task		**Situation**

Figure 4.1 An example of training objectives

In Figure 4.2 use the blank form provided to write down objectives for the next training session that you will coach. Then identify the task and situation to meet each objective. Remember that you may have more than one objective in each domain of learning.

Performance objective

_____

_____

Task	Situation

Cognitive objective

_____

_____

Task	Situation

Affective objective

_____

_____

Task	Situation

Figure 4.2 Blank form to create your own training objectives

Now that you have established the objectives for a training session, ask yourself, 'What will athletes need to do to achieve each learning objective?' The answer will contain a list of skills, knowledge and understandings. By determining this information the content of the training session will be identified and then learning activities can be designed. To develop the content of the objectives listed in our examples below, we first considered the main skills, knowledge, and understandings.

Performance objective

The athletes will be able to perform all aspects of the lay-up **[skills and knowledge]***, starting from the half court line, while being defended* **[understandings]**. The main content needed to ensure the objective is met is a purposeful, game-like situation where players perform lay-ups against defensive players.

Cognitive objective

Athletes will be able to make decisions **[knowledge]** *about the best shot options* **[skills]** *from a triangle offence* **[understandings]**. The main content needed to ensure the objective is met is a purposeful, game-like situation that includes decision making within a triangle offence.

Affective objective

Athletes will demonstrate positive encouragement to teammates **[skills and knowledge]** *while playing* **[understandings]**. The main content needed to ensure this objective is met is reinforcing athletes about their value of respect (which may be developed as part of their team culture).

ACTIVITY

Using the above as an example, list the main skills, knowledge, and/or understandings for the objectives you wrote in Figure 4.2.

Performance objective tasks:

Cognitive objective tasks:

Affective objective tasks:

POINT TO PONDER

Learners learn, coaches only help the process … sometimes.
(Rod Thorpe, Teaching Games for Understanding
(TGfU) developer)

70

Designing learning activities

Thus far, you have developed the objectives for your session and identified the content. You now need to design the learning activities that will meet the requirements of the selected content. You will need to look at the learning needs of your athletes, then identify the way you will coach them. (See box for Recent Research on different approaches to learning.) Often as coaches, we focus on what we will do to coach athletes rather than how we can help athletes learn. We go into training sessions worried about what we are going to do to coach, rather than evaluating and designing activities to suit the needs of the team and the individual athletes in a realistic context (Renshaw, 2010). When finalising the plans about how to teach the learning activities of the training session, it is important to think about the process involved in learning the task.

Monitor the sizes of the steps that are taken from one activity to the next, because if the steps are too large, athletes can experience failure and lose the motivation or enthusiasm necessary to perform the task successfully. If the steps are too small, the athletes can become bored. Try to establish steps that are large enough to continually challenge the athletes and small enough so that they can experience frequent success. Consider the environment that will best suit the athletes' motivation to learn.

RECENT RESEARCH

STUDENTS WITH DIFFERING APPROACHES TO LEARNING PERCEIVE TEACHING/LEARNING ENVIRONMENTS DIFFERENTLY

Campbell et al. (2001) described students' approaches to learning as either surface or deep processing of information. A person with a deep approach to learning intends to gain personal understanding and attaches meaning to the learning task. A person with a surface approach to learning intends to avoid failure by using strategies that facilitate memorisation of facts without attending to the meaning of the learning task.

71

In this research project the authors first determined the learning approaches of 490 secondary school students using the Learning Process Questionnaire (LPQ). Once the learning approaches were identified, two students from each approach from 24 different classes were interviewed using semi-structured interviews. The student interviews focused on the perceptions of how their teachers taught, what the teacher wanted students to learn, how the student learned, what they learned, and what the purpose of learning that subject was.

The results showed that students with deep approaches to learning tended to describe a variety of teaching strategies used, compared to those with a surface approach. The deep approach students tended to understand the reason for active learning and higher order thinking, whereas the surface approach students tended to focus on the transmission and reproduction of information. The students with deep approaches to learning took a more active role in their learning experiences than the surface approach students.

The findings suggest that teachers (and coaches) need to teach the skills and show students how to actively participate in various learning experiences, because there are a range of learning ability levels and different rates of learning. When teachers focus strongly on actively involving students in the learning process (student-centred learning), and create a supportive environment, students with both approaches to learning benefit.

Source: Campbell, J., Smith, D., Boulton-Lewis, G., Brownlee, J., Burnett, P.C., Carrington, S. & Purdie, N. (2001). Students' perceptions of teaching and learning: The influence of students' approaches to learning and teachers' approaches to teaching. *Teachers and Teaching: Theory to Practice*, 7(2), 173–187.

Athlete learning

A key point to learning is for athletes to experience the skills and tactics in realistic, authentic settings (Renshaw, 2010). Learning is a dynamic, complex process and often done best in an environment that replicates the realistic sport setting. There are many factors to help athletes learn, including their motivation, the environment provided, learning from modelling others, to name a few. A useful resource about athlete learning is written by Wayne Smith and located at the website: http://www.sparc.org.nz/en-nz/communities-and-clubs/Coaching/Coach-Development--Education/Framework-programme-materials/Coach-Development-Modules---Learning-Resources-and-Materials/. Further discussion on some of these factors and the dynamic systems approach to skill learning will be provided in Chapter 6.

POINT TO REMEMBER

A coach's plan is only as good as the coach's execution and management of the plan. Be flexible and ready for the unpredictable.

Planning for different ability levels

One of the many challenges coaches have is to provide all athletes with maximum opportunities to improve and practise their tactics, techniques, and skills. At all levels of competition, variance in individual skill, technique, and fitness must be considered. Coaches may have a tendency to give more time to the higher skilled athletes because they get excited by the demonstration of talent, or they may tend to focus on the lower skilled athletes because these need the most help. By focusing on one skill level, coaches tend to ignore other athletes. Consider the demands and structure of your sport. For example, in a novice game of touch rugby, invariably the action is in the middle of the field and therefore any player on the wing probably has little contact with the ball. If a lower skilled player is put on the wing, the player's rate of success may be decreased because the player will hardly ever get to touch the ball.

Elimination games or drills tend to inhibit athletes' opportunities to participate and their rates of success. The lower skilled person is almost always the first to get eliminated, thus taking away the opportunities to practise. For example, in basketball, when a shooting elimination game is played, the player who gets knocked out first is usually the one who does not shoot as well as the others. Therefore, the low-skilled athletes' opportunities to practise in such a game are minimal.

Maximum opportunities to practise will increase the skill level, tactical awareness, and the success rate of athletes. You need to ensure that you seek ways to provide maximum opportunities to practise, so when designing your session plans, see if you can provide learning experiences for all levels of skill development.

For this activity, observe someone else's training sessions and look for new learning activities that enhance practice opportunities for athletes. List some learning activities that you can use in your trainings.

Equipment

As well as planning each training session's learning experiences, you must plan for field/gym space and equipment needs and have contingencies in case something interrupts your plan. If there is not enough equipment, athletes do not get enough practice. Keep the equipment well maintained. There is nothing worse than having flat balls or broken racquets. A variety of equipment should be available. For example, in cricket, try using harder balls for the more skilled and softer balls for the less skilled, or in batting, the less skilled could practise using a stand (a stationary ball) and the more skilled could practise from a bowl. Equipment can be modified to suit the skill being practised. It is not necessary, for example, to have a particular ball to practise ball handling skills; any ball will do. But if it is necessary for athletes to bounce a ball, then it is the coach's responsibility to ensure the balls are filled with air; or if athletes are rehearsing the kinaesthetic feel of the ball, then practising with the appropriate ball for the sport is necessary.

POINT TO PONDER

Every child should have a ball with which to practise. If every child has a ball, there will be fewer disruptive children and children will have more chances to improve their skills and techniques because they will all have every opportunity to practise. Observe some of your own training sessions. If an athlete does not have a piece of equipment to play with or practise on, what is the athlete doing? Is the athlete paying attention? Is the athlete interested in what is going on? Is the athlete helping other athletes who do have the needed equipment? How long does the athlete stand in line waiting for a turn?

What are the equipment needs in your sport? Exchange ideas with other coaches in your sport on how to enhance athlete practice using equipment. Make a list of these ideas.

Preparing to coach the session

Your training session plan now needs to be prepared. When designing the plan, ask yourself how the material will be presented or, even better, how the athletes might learn this content in the realistic setting of the sport. Some sections that should be included in the plan are: objectives, things to remember, equipment needed, injuries, training schedule, learning activities, and diagrams.

Once your plan is designed you will need to prepare the training session. Some useful questions to consider when preparing for the training session are:

- How will you introduce the learning activity? Will you explain it? Demonstrate it? Use questioning?
- How will you know that the athletes understand what they are going to do?
- What materials or instructional aids will you need to teach the tasks and enable athletes to practise effectively?
- How safe are the tasks and activities that you have planned? Do you need to check equipment?
- Are the progressions of the skill at the athletes' level?
- Do your activities cover all domains of learning?
- Will both your higher- and lesser-ability athletes get something out of the session?

As you can see from the list of questions, coaching is complex. The questions listed here are important ones, but don't worry if you are a bit confused about how to demonstrate, explain, question, analyse, or provide effective feedback. In Chapters 5, 6, and 7 we will go into the practical applications of these coaching strategies.

Your learning objectives for a training session plan are prepared. Using the other information in this chapter as a basis, prepare a training session plan. Use a form with which you are familiar, design one of your own or borrow a sample from a colleague. Have the plan ready before going on to the Self-reflection exercise. See Figure 4.3 for an example of a session plan.

After you have designed your training session plan, implement the plan and video your training session. Personally review the training session before answering the reflective questions on planning. Remember that you generally go through a self-confrontation phase when viewing yourself on video for the first time.

Evaluate the application of your training plan by answering the following questions when viewing the video:

- Did you reach your learning objectives? Why or why not?
- Reflect on your session by answering these questions:
  (a) What did you like best about the session?
  (b) What did you like least about the session?
  (c) How would you improve the session?
- Did all athletes have equal opportunities to practise?
- How well did you plan for different ability levels?
- How well did you plan for the use of equipment? Did all athletes have maximum time to practise?

SESSION PLANNER

Club/School: LOOK SHARP
[Secondary age]
Sport: Volleyball
Training Objectives. The players will be able to:
1 Demonstrate passing to the front using accurate passing technique (**performance**).
2 Read the situation so that the pass goes to the setter (**cognitive**) to initiate game play.
3 Show the value of the team (**respect**) when working on the tactics (**affective**).

Things to remember

Remind athletes of Parent Night
Sort out transportation for Saturday

Injuries

Brett, slight back strain

Equipment needed

16 volleyballs
Net, set up by team
4 hoops
12 markers

Warm up

1 Animal Tag, Alan to lead
2 Dynamic stretches
3 Partner volleyball skills

Learning activities

Game One: Predator

The focus of Predator is:
■ To develop understanding about, and skill in, ball placement.
■ To develop understanding of the need to read opponents' positions to decide the best place to aim for open space.

How to play, score, rules, space, and number of players

■ Two teams, one of three, one of six on full-sized volleyball court.
■ Play is started by the coach who throws the ball into the team of three.
■ Players score a point by putting the ball on the opponents' floor.
■ The game is restarted by the sideline thrower, who throws the ball to the team of three.

Game Two: Server Butterfly

The focus of Server Butterfly is:
■ To make a decision about which serve to use and where to serve.
■ To enable passers to pass, setters to set and servers to serve.

How to play, score

■ The court is divided vertically down the middle. One team of three on the right side of the court on each side of the net.
■ Server serves to the passer (who is on the other side of the net), who passes it to the setter who catches the ball. They then rotate positions (i.e., the server swaps sides of the net and becomes the passer, the passer becomes the setter and the setter joins the server line on the same side of the net).
■ Players get a point if they served to the passer and the passer passed to the setter within one step of their position (the coach is the final judge).

Game Three: King of the Court

The focus of King of the Court is:
■ To develop tactical understanding about, and skill in, ball placement.
■ To develop the skills of 'reading the game' and deciding on the next move.
■ To look for weaknesses in opponents' play.

How to play, score

■ Two teams of three on each side of a full-sized volleyball court.
■ The ball is started by the team, who are not the kings, serving.
■ If the kings' team wins the point, they stay on the court. If the challengers' team wins the point, they become the kings and take the reigning kings' place on court.

Possible questions to ask athletes:

What did you notice about the option you took in that situation?
Where did the receivers go to defend that situation?
How could you ensure that you get under the ball to get it to the setter?
In that situation, how did you demonstrate respect?

Cool down

Figure 4.3 An example of a session plan

MANAGING THE ENVIRONMENT

The sport environment is holistic. A holistic environment ensures all three domains of learning are met: performance, cognitive, and affective. There are two main aspects to managing an optimal learning environment for athletes. One is the methods that are used to maintain desired behaviours (Siedentop & Tannehill, 2000); the other is a learning environment that provides optimal time for quality practice (Renshaw, 2010). A successful learning environment is difficult to define, but it is the coach's responsibility to develop an encouraging environment so that the athletes have opportunities for optimal learning. Factors that influence the environment include how we manage behaviour, use equipment and organise successful and enjoyable training sessions that enhance learning. An important coaching goal is to ensure athletes enjoy their experiences and want to come back for more.

Positive management

As part of developing managing skills, coaches should learn how to ensure appropriate behaviours of athletes so that an optimal learning environment exists. They should develop an environment that allows them to teach and athletes to learn. The managerial element of such an environment establishes the limits and expectations of athletes' behaviour. We often hear about the difficult athlete who causes trouble, seeks attention, or is generally disruptive. When developing a positive behavioural environment for learning, remember that the athletes have a right to a coach who provides them with positive support, but also facilitates consequences for inappropriate behaviour. Because athlete behaviour is a concern for coaches, we provide suggestions about how to strive for a positive behavioural environment.

Positive management refers to proactive rather than reactive strategies used to develop and maintain a positive, on-task environment in which minimal time is devoted to managerial issues (Siedentop & Tannehill, 2000). The positive aspect focuses on the 'good' rather than the 'bad'. An example of positive management is 'Thank you, Jo, for getting into line so quickly', or 'Well done, Mark, the net is at a perfect height, thank you.' An example of negative management would be 'Be quiet, Frank!' or 'Amanda, get over here!'

For the successful management of athlete behaviours it is essential that coaches:

■ Reinforce appropriate behaviour
■ Ignore negative behaviour (as much as is safely possible)
■ Avoid reinforcing negative behaviour (Siedentop & Tannehill, 2000).

Look for athletes who are demonstrating desirable behaviours and praise them. How do you feel when people praise you? How do you feel when people criticise you? Which do you prefer? The positive approach has been researched and proven successful in coach education literature (Nakamura, 1996). People prefer praise and positive reinforcement to punishment. In this book positive management is a method of reinforcing appropriate behaviours. The basic idea is to catch people doing good things.

Figure 4.4 Coaches need to position themselves where they can see what all athletes are doing

If coaches do not attend to ensuring suitable athlete behaviours, then by default they are left to disciplining techniques that are unpleasant and create a negative environment (Weinberg & Gould, 2007). If a training session is run with negative comments or threats of punishment, athletes will participate and strive to *not* make mistakes, rather than strive to learn and perform correctly. When coaching sessions are characterised by negative interactions, athlete achievement is typically low (Smoll & Smith, 2002).

A factor that can be detrimental and frustrating to the smooth flow of the training session is dealing with athletes who are attention-seekers. If you acknowledge athletes' appropriate behaviours, you will be giving them positive attention. If you acknowledge their negative behaviours, you will still be giving them attention and reinforcing negative behaviour (Weinberg & Gould, 2007). The attention received is not determined by whether the behaviour was appropriate or inappropriate, but rather by simple acknowledgement of the athlete or behaviour.

The first step in positive management is to define appropriate behaviours. Appropriate behaviours are those behaviours that the team is willing to accept as part of the training sessions. What athlete behaviours do you accept? What behaviours do your athletes expect from themselves and the coach? If athletes contribute to the formation of the rules, they will take ownership and responsibility to ensure these are followed (Kidman & Lombardo, 2010a). When defining expected behaviours, be sure to communicate them in a positive way. Once you add the words 'don't' or 'will not', the emphasis is on the negative. For example, if you listed 'The athlete will not talk while someone else is talking', you would have listed a negative approach. If you list 'The athlete will listen while someone else is talking', you have set a positive tone.

For this activity, write down the expectations of the team's behaviours, stating them in a positive fashion. You are encouraged to complete this activity with your athletes.

Agreed expected behaviours for the team:

1

2

3

4

5

A second step in positive management is to emphasise clear expectations and rules to athletes and parents (see Chapter 9 for more information about parents). Mean what you say and say what you mean. Your and the team's agreed-upon behaviours must also be consistently enforced. Both rewards and punishments need to be planned. If your team has decided that athletes will not compete on Saturday if they have exhibited poor behaviour, then that decision has to apply equally to everyone, even the most skilled athlete. Be consistent in enforcing expected behaviours with all athletes. If penalties are used, they should be the same for all similar behaviours. See Chapter 5 for further discussion about punishment.

A third step in positive management is to observe and praise expected behaviours that you see occurring in your training sessions. Giving praise can be a significant challenge. But if successful, the positive environment created will be conducive to optimal learning and enjoyment (Nakamura, 1996). Some guidelines to help you provide effective praise are:

■ Provide encouraging comments and gestures to athletes who follow rules. For example, 'I like the way Jane is ready to train early.'
■ Set high, yet realistic expectations.
■ Give plenty of praise. People thrive on praise. Be sincere in your praising comments and gestures.
■ Use effective, positive non-verbal cues that are compatible with your positive verbal communications. For example, a smile when praising tells athletes that you were sincere about your praising comments, whereas throwing your hands on your hips and frowning would not provide encouragement even if your words were positive.

A fourth step in positive management is to create a plan for decreasing inappropriate behaviour. To stop an inappropriate behaviour immediately, use effective desists. A desist is a verbal cue that reprimands a behaviour (Siedentop & Tannehill, 2000). An example of a desist is 'Warren, stop bouncing the ball.' Desists are most effective when combined with a positive management system. For example, if Warren continues to be a problem, you must look for desired behaviours he exhibits and praise those. Desists should be clear, be accompanied with firm eye contact, well timed, and well targeted, but not rough, judging, or harsh. Try to ignore attention-seeking behaviour. By ignoring behaviour you will eliminate the interaction that provides the reinforcement for attention. If you choose to ignore behaviours as part of your positive management, ensure the environment is safe. If athletes are being unsafe, stop them immediately.

An environment based on positive management will enhance the opportunities for athletes to learn (Graham, 2008). Practise these positive management strategies. If you have never tried this approach before, it will take time to learn. Athletes will also need to become accustomed to the new you. It is difficult to learn how to be positive, but the benefit of the approach and the look on athletes' faces when they are successful and enjoy the training is well worth the effort. The ultimate goal in positive management is for athletes to have respect for each other and their environment and for you to provide a productive climate (Nakamura, 1996).

MANAGING TIME DURING TRAINING

Time on task is the time that athletes are actually engaged in the targeted task (Graham, 2008). It is the time that athletes are practising what they are supposed to be practising. Coaches need to provide high rates of time on task for optimal learning to occur. To maximise time on task, coaches need to plan their sessions to ensure minimal time is devoted to managerial tasks. Managerial tasks are non-instructional tasks that include things such as organising teams, gathering athletes for explanations, and demonstrations, sending athletes to start the activity, administrative duties (passing out gear, balls), and waiting time (the time athletes wait for their turn).

82

Non-managerial tasks are those tasks that are related to the activity or subject at hand (Graham, 2008). Feedback about a skill is an example of non-managerial time; however, if you are giving feedback about behaviour, the activity is classified as managerial. If you tell Martha that her backhand swing is really great, but she needs work on her follow-through, then this is considered non-managerial, but if an athlete is playing up, dealing with the misbehaviour is classified as managerial. An example of a demand on managerial time is if Lucy is elbowing her partner rather than watching a demonstration.

Research suggests that if athletes spend more time on optimal learning activities, they will have a higher success rate (Renshaw, 2010). Athletes need many opportunities to practise and therefore coaches should maximise the time on task. Factors that increase time on task include providing activities with high participation rates, decreasing instruction time, having appropriate equipment, and reducing the time it takes to move from one activity to another (transition) (Siedentop & Tannehill, 2000). Traditionally, junior sports tend to provide an average of one hour per week for youth athletes. Within that hour there should be as much opportunity to practise as possible.

ACTIVITY

In the following list, decide which activities help to maximise the time on task (M), or are potential barriers (B) to athletes spending time on task.

1 Fiona's parents are talking to you about her uniform. ☐

2 Alexander is dribbling around the cones and you tell him to switch hands. ☐

3 You are explaining an activity, then tell a story about a famous football player. ☐

4 You are demonstrating the chest pass. ☐

5 Scott is playing with the ball while you are explaining the activity and you ask him to stop doing that while you are talking. ☐

6 You are chatting with another coach as the athletes are waiting to start an activity. ☐

7 You are teaching the freestyle arm stroke using problem solving and Lisette answers a question you ask about the arm stroke. ☐

8 Athletes are asking you to clarify what they are supposed to be doing. ☐

9 Simon has suggested a different game plan. ☐

10 You and the athletes are moving cones to set up for the next activity. ☐

Now that you understand which activities are managerial and non-managerial, you will be able to record the number of minutes that you use for management during your training session. There will be a chance to do this in the Self-reflection section towards the end of the chapter.

(Answers: 1=B; 2=M; 3=B; 4=M; 5=B; 6=B; 7=M; 8=M; 9=M; 10=B)

Increasing the amount of time athletes have to practise

To reach a high level of skill, an athlete should have performed a skill or game situation thousands of times (Davids et al., 2008). As suggested earlier, it is important to organise learning activities/games so that the athletes have multiple opportunities to practise and perform the skills and focus on tactics. The following are strategies that will assist in providing time, within a training session, for athletes to practise.

Routines

One of the ways to increase time on task is to establish organisational routines for the training sessions (Graham, 2008). For example, do you provide a signal for the athletes to come in for an explanation or demonstration, or do you just call and wait for them to come in? How can you make gathering more efficient? Establish a signal for gathering and dispersing. If such a signal is established, athletes will understand your expectations. For example, when you blow the whistle, athletes are to come to where you are within five seconds.

Another important routine to create regards distributing equipment. Often coaches have limited budgets and therefore ask their athletes

84

to bring personal equipment. If athletes supply their own equipment, then it is easy to get each athlete to retrieve theirs quickly. If coaches supply the equipment, then routines to distribute and collect it should be established. For example, once the whistle blows, the ball must be put on the ball rack.

What do athletes do when they arrive at your training session? Time on task will increase when athletes have routines to follow when they first arrive at training. An example in gymnastics would be to have task cards with warm-up drills for each gymnast. Athletes could be provided with recording sheets to keep track of their progression in these skills. It is important to create activities that do not require a lot of physical exertion because the athletes will not be warmed up. Alternatively, they could warm up and stretch by themselves and be ready to train by a certain time.

ACTIVITY

Provided here is a list of tasks for which routines can be established. Write the routines you could or do use with your team:

Entry

Warm-up

Attention/quiet

Home base (meeting place)

Gain attention

Disperse

Collect equipment

Put equipment away

Boundaries and safety considerations

End of training

Leaving

Housekeeping (e.g., collecting uniforms, organising game times)

Such routines should be established in the first few training sessions of the season. When a learning activity is being run, practise the routine so that athletes know what to do and what you expect from them. For example, if you are in the first training session and the team is playing a dribble tag game, in the middle of the game use your gathering signal so the athletes can practise coming in quickly. Praise those athletes who do come in quickly to help communicate your expectations.

Prompts and hustles

Prompts and hustles are cue words to remind athletes what should be done. If these cues are used when establishing the routines, it will remind them to quickly complete the managerial task. An example would be 'Huddle', or 'Come in, quickly.' The cue words should encourage quick action. The comments should avoid sarcasm that creates a judging environment.

Positive reinforcement

As you may have noted by now, positive reinforcement is essential to establish expected behaviours and a positive environment for the athletes. When directing or prompting athletes, coaches should use positive comments to reinforce what was done appropriately, for example 'Way to go, Sarah, you are the first one ready to train' or 'Thanks for picking up the equipment, Jason.' The more you positively reinforce those who are doing wonderful things, the smoother the sessions will be.

Flow

To decrease managerial time, a fast-paced or smooth-flowing session is a priority (Graham, 2008). Try to avoid disruptions or explanations that go off on tangents. Some coaches have fantastic stories, but they should be told before or after training sessions or at team social activities, not during precious training time.

Management games

Because most sports are competitive in nature, athletes can be encouraged to compete to decrease managerial time. Management tasks can be made fun and somewhat competitive. An example of a management game (Siedentop & Tannehill, 2000) is:

Coach: Let's play a game to see how quickly you can be ready. When I call you to come in, if you come in within five seconds, you get a point. If you come in after five seconds, I get a point. If you have the most points at the end of the training session, you can choose a game to play. If I have the most points at the end of the training session, I choose what we do.

In summary, to increase the amount of time athletes have to practise:

■ Have routines that include signals for athletes to come in or start their learning activities. For example, use the word 'huddle' as a gathering signal for explanations, demonstrations, and feedback.
■ Use prompts and hustles to encourage quick action.
■ Use plenty of positive reinforcement.
■ Try to keep a flow going in your session. Try to avoid disruptions or long-winded explanations.
■ Make management tasks fun or competitive.

Organising athletes into groups

The organisation of athletes into groups creates several issues. Remember the child that for one reason or another always got left out? How can we ensure that all athletes are included? There is a multitude of ways to organise athletes into groups. We have to be careful, however, not to hurt athletes' feelings or decrease their self-esteem when organising these groups (Hanrahan & Carlson, 2000). Coaches should consider the most appropriate way to deal with athletes with behavioural problems or who are slow to pick up new skills.

One of the quickest ways to select groups or partners is to say 'Get a partner', or 'Get into groups of four.' This method generally works quite well with athletes, but can result in the same people always working together. It is useful to have alternative methods to get athletes into small groups. One difficult area is choosing teams, either for relays or games.

In these cases you can use a numbering-off system or have the teams listed on your plan. When athletes choose teams, there is invariably someone who usually gets chosen last.

ACTIVITY

There are other more creative ways of getting athletes into groups. For example: 'Those with white shoes go into this team', or 'Those with a last name that is between A and K, go into this team.' List three creative systems that you use or have seen other coaches use. Observe how other coaches organise their athletes. See Hanrahan and Carlson's (2000) book for some useful and creative games to get people into groups.

1

2

3

SELF-REFLECTION

For this exercise you will need to have videos of several of your training sessions. Answer the questions with reference to your current coaching and then again after specific work on developing your managing skills, for a comparison. Focus on looking for two things in your coaching: the use of positive management and the amount of time that athletes actually practise. The following are reflective questions to answer about your coaching.

Positive management

- How many positive comments for appropriate behaviours did you make? How many negative comments did you make about behaviour? Were you happy with the ratio of positive to negative comments?
- What were the reactions of the athletes who were praised?
- How many desists did you give? Were they necessary? Why or why not? Did they work?
- Were you consistent in reminding and reinforcing athletes about the expected team behaviours?

- What did you learn about your positive management this session?
- What did you learn about your athletes' behaviours?
- How do you think the training session could be improved?

Time on task

- What percentage of time did you spend on managerial tasks?
- Were you happy with the amount of time that the athletes were able to practise in this session? Why or why not?
- Get a spectator to observe one athlete during your session and record the number of times that athlete performed using the equipment. How much time did the athlete spend waiting for his or her turn? Were you happy with this result? Why or why not?
- What will help you decrease your management time?

SUMMARY

1 Planning is important for providing quality learning experiences for athletes and ensuring a smooth flow to your training sessions.
2 The first step to planning is to establish learning objectives for the training session. These objectives should be holistic and include performance, cognitive, and affective learning domains.
3 Performance objectives relate to movement skills. Cognitive objectives relate to knowledge and decision making about tactics, strategies, rules, and skills. Affective objectives relate to mental skills, attitudes, and values. To enhance athlete learning, include all three domains of learning in every training session.
4 Objectives should be written as outcomes with descriptions of the task to be learned and the situations under which the task will be performed.
5 Based on the objectives, the best way for athletes to learn should be considered before choosing your coaching method.
6 Planning requires a consideration of different ability levels, the organisation of learning activities, equipment, and instructional aids, safety implications, and appropriate progressions.
7 There are two aspects to managing an effective learning environment: maintaining appropriate behaviour and providing optimal time on task.

8 Positive management involves reinforcing desired behaviours and ignoring negative behaviours.

9 Athletes should contribute to creating the rules and expectations as part of the development of team culture.

10 When a negative training environment pervades, athletes' achievement is poor.

11 A managerial task is a non-instructional episode that includes organising athletes, gathering and dispersing athletes, and time athletes spend waiting their turn.

12 To increase time on task, coaches should plan routines to decrease time in organisational matters such as gathering and dispersing athletes, arranging groups, distributing equipment, or listening to the coach.

CHAPTER 5

CREATING A POSITIVE ENVIRONMENT

This chapter covers

- Positive approach
- Communication
- Motivation
- Self-control

There are numerous facets to a positive environment, some of which have been mentioned in Chapter 4. Before detailing what coaches can do to be positive, communicate effectively, and enhance the motivation of their athletes, we will first briefly identify five other important facets of a positive environment. The environment should:

1 *Be supportive* – a positive environment offers accessible support when needed. Support can come in many forms (Rees & Hardy, 2004). Positive reinforcement can increase athletes' self-worth, feelings of competence, and motivation. Informational support comes in the form of advice or suggestions. Tangible or instrumental support can be in the form of equipment, transportation, or facilities. Social support provides affiliation and enhances feelings of self-worth. A lack of social support, although undesirable, is not the worst scenario. Social disapproval is worse than no social support. Ridicule indisputably has a negative effect on individuals. Disapproval, whether demonstrated by the silent treatment, sarcasm, or outright rage, is obviously not present in a positive environment.

2   *Allow self-determination* – self-determination was mentioned in Chapter 1 as a major component of intrinsic motivation. If athletes are placed in an environment where they are always told what to do, when to do it, and how to do it, they fail to learn to think for themselves. When athletes have some sense of input or control (i.e., autonomy), not only do they increase their awareness and their abilities to think and to make decisions, they also feel less manipulated and, therefore, can learn to take responsibility for their actions (Mallett, 2005).

3   *Be familiar yet challenging* – familiarity is good in that it is comfortable and athletes know what to expect. Nevertheless, when things become too familiar (e.g., always doing the same drills in the same order), boredom sets in. New situations and new experiences provide challenge.

4   *Be safe* – the environment should always be structured in a way that minimises injury and harm. Attention needs to be paid to surfaces, equipment, protective clothing/equipment, as well as correct technique and warm-up. Consider beginning each session with a quick update on any injuries so you can be sure to keep athletes from participating in activities that may exacerbate existing conditions. (See Chapter 10 for equipment safety.)

Figure 5.1 A positive environment needs to be safe

5   *Allow for individual differences* – when athletes know that it is okay to be different and that they do not have to be exactly like everyone else, it gives them the freedom to explore and try new things. Their self-esteem and self-concepts should be based on their own improvements rather than how they compare to others. As mentioned in Chapter 3, differences in individual physical characteristics, senses, personalities, experiences, and culture will influence how they learn and behave. Also, exposure to a variety of people can enhance the acceptance and appreciation of people who are different.

POSITIVE APPROACH

Because of individual differences in both athletes and coaches, no single prescriptive approach to coaching will be equally effective in all situations. Nevertheless, even with the individualisation of coaching approaches, an emphasis on the positive is warranted (Smith et al., 2007). A basic ratio of four positives for every negative is effective, but even more emphasis should be placed on the positive when first working with a person or team, or when introducing a new skill or strategy. If you are not sure how positive to be, at first err on the side of being too positive, then later adjust to individual and situational requirements.

What is the positive approach?

The positive approach is more than just telling your athletes that they are wonderful. The positive approach is a combination of providing information and rewards while being sincere and realistic within a supportive environment.

Rewards are an important aspect of the positive approach. Coaches should reward and encourage their athletes both verbally and non-verbally. Rarely are extrinsic rewards such as money, trophies, or other tangible objects needed. Over time extrinsic rewards tend to lose their value (Martens, 2004). Nevertheless, over-reliance on any one form of verbal or non-verbal encouragement can limit its value. Therefore, using a variety of verbal and non-verbal forms of reinforcement is ideal.

93

Provide five additional examples of verbal and non-verbal encouragement.

Verbal	Non-verbal
1 'Well done!'	1 Thumbs up
2	2
3	3
4	4
5	5
6	6

It is important to be sincere when giving rewards or encouragement. An insincere or sarcastic 'well done' is obviously not part of the positive approach. Similarly, rewarding a poor performance (a behaviour sometimes seen in coaches who indiscriminately praise their athletes in attempts to be positive) can have a negative effect on self-concept and motivation. Athletes may think that if they are being praised for a poor performance, the coach must know they can't do any better. Rewards should be given immediately and contingently. It is no good saying, 'That kick you had two weeks ago was well controlled.' To be effective the reinforcement needs to be given only when deserved and as soon as possible (Martens, 2004).

Unfortunately it is usually outcomes and results that get rewarded. A concerted effort should be made to reinforce technique, performance, effort, and other factors that the athlete can control. Athletes cannot control outcomes. If Sharon is swimming in lane 4, she can only control what happens in lane 4. She has no control over what happens in lanes 1, 2, 3, 5, 6, 7, or 8. Similarly, in softball Earl cannot control the score because he cannot control what everyone else on his team or the other team does. Coaches should reward controllable factors (e.g., technique, effort, punctuality, encouragement of a teammate).

Another aspect of the positive approach is to have realistic expectations of your athletes (Mageau & Vallerand, 2003). If Toni currently swims the 50m free in 45 seconds, focus on improving her performance to 44 or 43

94

seconds. Better still, focus on developing techniques that will help her have a stronger kick or a more efficient pull. Some coaches argue that they do not want to restrain their athletes by limiting expectations in any way and thus expect that their athletes can do anything and everything. Expectations that are unrealistic, however, only serve to set the athletes up for failure. Expecting Toni to be able to swim the 50m free in 30 seconds would probably result in her complaining, dropping out, and/ or developing low self-esteem.

Similarly, telling Rick that he has great potential as a sailor is not always a positive move. Potential can become a heavy weight for an individual to carry. If Rick believes that he continually fails to reach his 'potential', he will probably lose confidence, not only in himself, but also in his coach and his training programme. Each error he makes becomes an example to him of how he is a failure.

Positive coaches provide feedback in a positive manner and are constructive in the debriefing of previous performances or competitions (see Chapter 6 for further information about feedback). A useful formula to follow is 'good, better, how'. The coach indicates what about the performance or technique was good, what could be better, and most importantly how the athlete can improve. Ideally coaches will encourage athletes to do their own 'good, better, how' analyses. Too often athletes and coaches skip the step of recognising what has been done well (the good). In addition, when correcting technique there often is a tendency to point out what was wrong instead of focusing on what needs to be done to progress. Athletes need specific strategies about how they can improve their performances.

Example

Giving positive instruction for an athlete working on backcourt skills in volleyball:

Good: 'You read the ball well and made good court position.'

Better: 'You need to react more quickly when the ball is hit.'

How: 'Keep your weight on the balls of your feet.'

Provide two examples of 'good, better, how' for common errors made by athletes in your sport:

Good:
Better:
How:

Good:
Better:
How:

An important aspect of providing feedback is to word things positively. Coaches can be enthusiastic and supportive of their athletes, but then reduce their effectiveness by wording statements negatively. For example, a common error in beginning backstrokers is that they bend their arms during the recovery phase of the stroke (when the arm is out of the water). The automatic inclination for many coaches is to tell the swimmers not to bend their arms. As coaches we quickly see that something is being done incorrectly, and instinctively tell athletes not to do it. Instead, we should take the extra bit of time and work our brains a bit harder and tell them what it is that we *want* them to do.

If athletes are told not to bend their arms, the first thing they think about is bending their arms. Some athletes will actually picture themselves bending their arms and will therefore be mentally practising exactly what you do not want them to do. Thus the instruction to keep their arms straight, rather than not to bend their arms, gives them a positive visual image on which to focus.

ACTIVITY

Reword the following instructions so they are phrased positively, focusing the athletes' attention on the desired behaviour.

Don't bend your elbow.   Keep your arm straight.
Don't serve into the net.
Don't have your weight on your heels.
Don't drop the ball.
Whatever you do, don't false start.

Video yourself for an hour during a training session. Play the video back and count the number of times you worded something in the negative. For every negatively worded statement, write down how it could have been stated in the positive. After a few weeks of working on using positive language, test yourself a second time.

Why use the positive approach?

The positive approach does not guarantee winning. Nevertheless, the positive approach to coaching does influence athletes' attitudes. Coaches who use more reinforcement, encouragement, and instruction, and fewer punitive behaviours, are liked better and are seen as better teachers than negative coaches. Athletes with positive coaches also like the sport and their teammates more than do athletes of negative coaches. In addition, athletes with positive coaches express a greater desire to continue participating in their sport, and overall are more likely to genuinely enjoy taking part (Barnett et al., 1992).

What about punishment?

Punishment is sometimes necessary to temporarily stop detrimental behaviours. Reinforcement does not always work perfectly by itself. Therefore, coaches need to be able to use punishment effectively. Punishment is most often called for when athletes' behaviours are dangerous to themselves or others. When the following guidelines are observed, punishment (i.e., consequences for misbehaviours) can be part of the positive approach (although just a small part).

- Use punishment in a corrective manner to stop a behaviour. It is the behaviour that is being punished, not the person. Once the punishment has been served, the athlete is back on an equal footing with everyone else.
- Be impersonal when punishing. Punishment should be imposed calmly. When coaches yell or use comments that belittle an individual, the punishment can easily be perceived as revenge or a desperate attempt by the coach to show who is in charge.

97

- Be consistent across time and across athletes. Everyone should receive the same type of punishment for breaking similar rules. Similarly, if a particular behaviour is punished early in the season, the same behaviour should be punished later in the season.
- Be careful in the selection of punishments. If you use a punishment that makes you feel guilty, that guilt will overshadow your relationship with the athlete far into the future. Use punishment that is realistic (i.e., punishment you can and will apply when required). For example, if you say the person won't be able to travel with the team on the weekend, but the team will forfeit without that athlete, then you probably would not follow through with the punishment. Be sure the punishment you select is actually perceived as punishment and not a reinforcer. For example, when an athlete is made to sit out of a learning activity for being disruptive, the athlete may perceive that as a reinforcer if the particular activity is disliked.
- Never use physical activity as a punishment. This guideline is usually the hardest for coaches to accept because, in the short term, running laps can be an effective method of altering behaviour. Coaches, however, should be aware of the long-term message that is being sent. Using physical activity as punishment indicates that physical activity or exercise is unpleasant, something to be avoided, and something only to be endured when one has misbehaved.
- Avoid using punishment as a tool to correct technique. When punished for poor skill execution, athletes develop a fear of failure. For example, if athletes are punished for dropping the ball, athletes will be worrying about dropping the ball and expending their energy trying not to drop the ball instead of focusing on catching the ball correctly. Such punishment also decreases the athletes' motivation to take risks or try new techniques.

COMMUNICATION

Effective coaching is dependent on effective communication (Gilbert & Trudel, 2004). Communication is a two-way process. We'll first mention the sending of messages (the aspect of communication on which most coaches traditionally focus). Later we will discuss two

98

often ignored components of communication – non-verbal messages and listening.

As a coach, having all the knowledge in the world about your sport is worthless to your athletes if you cannot convey it to them. If coaches want athletes to listen, they should avoid delivering their messages with sarcasm or threats. Making negative comparisons of your athletes with others is a good way of ensuring that they will stop listening (or stop coming to training altogether). Using the positive approach, however, is only a small part of effective communication.

ACTIVITY

For each of the following scenarios, determine the aspect(s) of sending messages that could make the coach more effective. What should each coach do to improve as a communicator?

1   Andre knows a lot about his sport and tries to get all that information across to his athletes at every opportunity. As a result, his athletes often are overloaded with information.

2   Rachel is concerned about hurting the feelings of her athletes. So when she has to drop people from her team she tries to maintain their self-confidence by telling them that they are in fact quite skilled or dedicated. These athletes end up being confused – why were they dropped if they are so good?

3   Greg is coaching his child's team because he felt that if he didn't, no one else would. He doesn't really know that much about the sport and without realising it often says things that aren't quite right.

4   Rosemary expects her athletes to be on time to training, follow good nutritional advice and get plenty of sleep. She is often found rushing to morning training sessions while munching on a pastry and looking as if she has just woken up.

5   Juan used to compete at the top level of his sport. He is now coaching a team of novices and often uses terminology (jargon) that they don't understand.

6   Cheryl feels she gives her athletes lots of feedback. She is constantly telling them when they are performing well and when their performances just aren't good enough. The athletes are getting frustrated because they don't know what they should do to improve.

7   Kevin provides his team with useful information and carefully plans his training sessions. His athletes, however, feel that he is unapproachable and that he doesn't understand how they feel.

8   Linda is worried that her team doesn't respect her and that they think she doesn't know what she is talking about. Therefore, she never admits to being wrong because she feels that if she did she would lose whatever credibility she has.

Now, using the aspects of sending messages you listed above, write down your own communication strengths and weaknesses.

Strengths	Weaknesses

What might you do to improve a communication weakness?

Non-verbal communication and listening

Two aspects of communication that coaches usually need to work on the most are their non-verbal communication skills and their listening skills. Non-verbal aspects of communication (or body language) include mannerisms, movements, touching behaviours, voice characteristics, how much space you allow between yourself and others, body positions (e.g., arms crossed in front), and facial expressions. Non-verbal skills can become even more important when talking one on one with athletes. An easy way to remember some of the basic non-verbal skills is to remember to **ROLL** with your athletes.

R Remain relatively *relaxed* with your athletes as you interact with them. Being relaxed indicates you are confident in what you are doing. It also helps the athletes relax, which is particularly important if athletes are nervous, anxious, or stressed.

O Face your athletes and adopt an *open* posture. An open posture tells the athletes you want to be non-defensive and that you are available to work with them.

L *Lean* towards the athletes at times. You probably do this naturally when talking with a good friend. Leaning emphasises your attentiveness, basically showing them that you are interested in what they are saying.

L *Look* at your athletes when communicating with them. Maintaining eye contact without staring shows that you are focused on them and their concerns.

Figure 5.2 ROLLing

Get together with two other people who are interested in enhancing their communication skills. Take turns playing the roles of coach, athlete, and observer. Have the athlete relate to the coach his or her goals and expectations of her or his participation in sport. After two or three minutes have the observer give the coach feedback about how well she or he ROLLed with the other person. Focus on the non-verbal aspects of communication, but also consider issues such as whether the coach dominated the conversation, whether appropriate questions were asked, or if the coach was animated or had a dull, flat-toned voice. Try to use 'good, better, how' (see p. 95) to provide constructive feedback. After the observer has given feedback, allow the athlete to comment. Be sure each person gets an opportunity to play each role.

As mentioned above, most coaches need to improve their abilities to listen. Usually coaches are good at jumping straight into a situation and giving advice. Unfortunately, when people go directly into advice-giving mode, they are seldom entirely clear on the situation. Listening is a greatly underrated skill.

To begin to reflect on your listening skills, for the following scenarios indicate the key experience, behaviours, and feelings or emotions generated by the person. Obviously, because this activity is not a recording, but rather a written statement, you are not actually listening. The point, however, is to attend to what is being said, rather than solve any problem. Try to see the situation from another person's point of view. Write down what messages are being sent. There is no single correct response to each scenario. Just make your best judgement.

Example   A 17-year-old school volleyball player has been selected for a national junior team. To be able to attend the various training sessions and tournaments, the player needs to find a significant amount of money. He has started a part-time job in addition to his volleyball and school commitments. He is having trouble balancing his life.

Key experiences	Training, school work, additional work, social life
Key behaviours	Falls asleep in class, limited intensity at training, not playing well
Feelings or emotions generated	Excited to be selected, but tired and anxious

1　An athlete in her teens is concerned about her levels of anxiety during major competitions. She has always performed well at the local level, but national and international competitions scare her.

Key experiences	
Key behaviours	
Feelings or emotions generated	

2　An athlete in his mid-20s has been married a little over a year. He has just quit work to train full time. He is having trouble with his marriage. He is having second thoughts about quitting his job and training full time.

Key experiences	
Key behaviours	
Feelings or emotions generated	

3　A 16-year-old athlete, who has been told she has great potential, is feeling stressed because she wants to do as well as possible in sport. She realises that a career in sport can be relatively short and therefore wants to be sure to gain entrance into a university. She does not know if she can keep training as much as expected and still get the grades in school that she needs to be able to study at a university.

Key experiences	
Key behaviours	
Feelings or emotions generated	

By trying to determine the key experiences, behaviours, and emotions, the emphasis is on understanding the specific situation rather than solving problems. In many instances the athletes themselves are not entirely clear about what the issues are. By trying to clarify the situation for yourself, you may help the athlete clarify it as well. If you compare your responses to the above scenarios with somebody else's, you will probably find a few differences. This inconsistency does not mean that either of you is wrong. Often the situation that is first presented to us lacks clarity. Unintentionally we tend to fill in the gaps based on our own expectations or experiences. Problems arise when our interpretations of situations are notably different to what is really happening.

The next step is to communicate your understanding of the situation to the athletes concerned. For example, try to paraphrase what you believe the athletes are saying. If your understanding is correct, communication will be enhanced, because the athletes will believe you really grasp what they are experiencing. If your initial understanding is incorrect, communication will be enhanced by the athletes clarifying the situation. Your sincere attempt to understand what athletes are experiencing will encourage them to clarify the situation.

ACTIVITY

For the next scenarios, list two different ways in which you could try to express understanding to the individual involved. An example is provided.

Example   A parent is concerned that her son will get hurt participating in sport at the more advanced level. The child is talented, but the parent feels that the child's health and safety are more important than any performance.

    1   So you're worried that if your child keeps competing, he'll get hurt.

    2   You believe that it is better for your child to stay at the lower level than to compete at a more advanced level where there is a greater chance he might get hurt.

A A fellow coach is losing sleep because he can't make the final decision about which athletes to include in his representative under-18s team. He has selected most of his team, but the final two spaces are down to four athletes. He spends all his time weighing the pros and cons of these four athletes and how they would fit in the team. He is incredibly stressed about it.

1

2

B An athlete you coach approaches you to complain that you treat the star player differently from everyone else. This top athlete gets away with being late to training and missing some training sessions entirely. Nothing is said when this happens, but if anyone else did the same thing they'd get pulled up in front of the whole team.

1

2

C The administrative body of your sport demands to know why your athletes have not won more. They believe that with the talent you have available to you, you should have obtained more impressive results.

1

2

It was probably more difficult to come up with expressions of understanding in the last two scenarios. Two things need to be stated here. First, communicating that you understand what someone else is experiencing is not the same thing as agreeing with the person. Second, demonstrating that you understand what the other person is experiencing in a confrontational situation can help diffuse anger and therefore increase the chances of eventually dealing effectively with the situation (Turner, 2007). Although a self-defence mode may be the automatic response to a confrontation, it often leads to increased tension, turning a comment into an altercation.

If possible, role-play the above situations with another coach. At first your responses may seem stilted and uncomfortable, but with practice they will become more natural. Keep in mind that these expressions of understanding only take a few seconds. One does not continue in this mode for a long period of time. The point is to clarify the situation before attempting to solve any problems. Listening is the key element of effective communication, and the basis for understanding (Parvis, 2003). Without active listening, any actions that follow may be less than ideal. Instead of immediately justifying your own behaviour or doling out advice, first be entirely clear about the situation.

MOTIVATION

Sometimes coaches complain that a particular athlete is not motivated or they worry about the decreased motivation of an entire team. Motivation is a commonly used term, but is not necessarily an entirely understood concept. We have already discussed in Chapter 3 how athletes are motivated by different incentives, and that most athletes have more than one motive for participating in sport. Research in sport motivation considers factors such as perceived competence, achievement goal orientations, attributional style, self-determination, and motivational climate. There are entire books written on the topic (e.g., Roberts, 2001). Rather than having a great theoretical discussion about motivation in this book, we will stick to the basics. First, you should know that there are few unmotivated people in the world. It might be problematic for you if you have athletes who are motivated to play video games or go to the movies instead of going to training, but the individuals themselves are not devoid of motivation.

Before continuing this discussion, it is useful to consider what motivation actually is. Motivation is made up of three components: direction, intensity, and persistence. Direction refers to where we choose to invest our energy. You may choose to go to the movies, the opera, training, or home. We all have lots of choices when it comes to direction. If you want your athletes to choose the direction of training, you might consider how to make training inviting and enjoyable.

The second aspect of motivation is intensity. Intensity refers to how much effort an individual puts in to the chosen direction. You've probably experienced the situation where many athletes have chosen the direction of training, but they participate at different levels of intensity. Most coaches want their athletes to try hard at training and feel that the more intensity athletes demonstrate at training, the better. Too much intensity, however, may have a negative effect on the third component of motivation, persistence.

Persistence is sticking with something over time. Sometimes when athletes train with high levels of intensity they experience problems with staleness, overtraining, or burnout. Too much intensity may lead them to quit. If we want our athletes to persist, we need to be careful about maintaining appropriate levels of intensity. More is not always better. If your athletes are tired or irritable, have a drop off in performance, get sick, or just look bored, the intensity level may be too high.

Increasing enjoyment

As mentioned above, making training sessions enjoyable will increase the chance of athletes choosing the direction of training. Similarly, just as coaches can be intrinsically motivated to coach, athletes can be intrinsically motivated to train. A person engages in intrinsically motivated behaviours to feel competent and self-determining (Ryan & Deci, 2000). Coaches can enhance athletes' intrinsic motivation by providing them with opportunities to feel competent and self-determining.

Structuring the environment so there is a reasonable probability of success can increase athletes' feelings of competence. By matching task difficulty with ability levels, learning activities can be organised to meet the needs of the individuals (see Chapter 4). If the activity is too difficult, athletes will perceive themselves to be failures, causing intrinsic motivation to decrease. On the other hand, if the activity is too easy, intrinsic motivation is not enhanced because successful completion of a simple task does not indicate competence.

ACTIVITY

Select two learning activities or drills commonly used in your sport. Describe how you could make each task easier or more challenging so that it could be matched to the ability levels of different individuals.

Learning activity	Easy version	Difficult version
1		
2		

Increasing each athlete's perceived significance to the team also can influence feelings of competence. When athletes have clearly defined roles, they are likely to recognise their contributions to the team (Bray et al., 2005). These roles should be openly discussed (see Chapter 3).

Intrinsic motivation also can be enhanced by letting the athletes make some decisions. They might make decisions about what time training will be, how long training will last, or what learning activities might be done. This strategy relates to the self-determination aspect of intrinsic motivation.

Allowing experienced athletes to have input into what strategies or tactics will be used in a particular competition serves to increase their self-determination. (See box for Recent Research on the application of self-determination theory to the coaching of elite athletes.) Players also can feel empowered by leading some segments of training. For example, they might take turns leading warm up or designing games or activities.

Individuals are likely to choose directions that they feel will give them what they want. Therefore, it is imperative to focus on their reasons and motives for participating in sport. If they primarily are involved because they want to play with their friends, then dividing a large group into ability levels that causes them to be separated from their friends would decrease their enjoyment. It is worth discovering the motives of your athletes (see Chapter 3).

Lastly, making participation fun will increase enjoyment. Avoid specialising players into positions or roles (or even sports) at an early age (Coté et al., 2009). Let participants play different positions and try different skills. What is or is not fun depends on the viewpoint of the participants. Many individuals feel that the following activities can be fun: training in a different place, learning something other kids don't know, playing music at training, trying something a bit daring, having a chance to really scream and yell, getting a special treat, trying out original strategies or tactics, and playing games.

ACTIVITY

Ask your athletes what they think is fun. Record the 10 most popular answers on the left side of the following table. Then, on the right side of the table, decide how you can incorporate their ideas of fun into training or competition.

athlete development

What is fun	How to include it
1	
2	
3	
4	
5	
6	
7	
8	
9	
10	

APPLYING SELF-DETERMINATION THEORY TO THE COACHING OF ELITE ATHLETES

Coaches affect athletes' motivation through their influence on perceptions of self-determination (autonomy). Individuals with high levels of self-determined motivation have been shown to perform better, persist longer, try harder, and cope with stress better than those with low levels. Mallett, a registered psychologist and qualified coach, applied his knowledge of self-determination theory in preparing Australia's men's track and field relay teams for the Athens Olympics. Developing an autonomy-supportive (i.e., self-determining) coaching environment evolved over a two-year period.

The athletes were given choices in areas such as uniforms, training times, venues, and content. Even when it came to the Olympic finals of the $4 \times 400m$ relay, the athletes were provided with relevant information and two possible options regarding the running order. The coach made the decision (with sound rationale) for the composition of the team for the final, but he gave the athletes the responsibility for deciding on which of the two running orders they would use. Mallett felt that he may not have had full commitment from the athletes if he had decided upon the running order, which would have had the potential to undermine performance.

The coach also used a problem-solving approach in place of traditional instruction. For example, the athletes watched videos of performances and then worked together (with suitable questions from the coach) to consider options and develop appropriate race tactics. Autonomy was also created in training. For example, when working on baton exchanges, two athletes would execute the skill, consider the strengths and weaknesses of the exchange, obtain feedback from the other members of the team who had been stationed in various places to observe different aspects of the exchange, observe the performance on video, and then discuss the performance as a group. The coach asked facilitative questions, and only gave his own feedback after all other sources of input had been provided.

Although the performance results of the athletes cannot be singularly attributed to the creation of an autonomy-supportive environment, both the 4 × 100m and 4 × 400m teams performed well using both norm- and self-referenced data. For example, the 4 × 400m team ran the Olympic final faster than their previous season best time and faster than their Olympic semi-final time. Ranked thirteenth prior to the Athens Games, the team placed second in the final.

In summary, the application of self-determination theory to elite coaching resulted in excellent performances. In addition, the coach found the autonomy-supportive environment to be intrinsically rewarding.

Source: Mallett, C.J. (2005). Self-determination theory: A case study of evidence-based coaching. *The Sport Psychologist*, 19, 417–429.

Goal setting

An effective technique for maintaining or enhancing motivation is goal setting. Setting goals can enhance all three components of motivation: direction, intensity, and persistence. Goals give direction by providing a target; people can see what they are aiming for, what they are trying to achieve. Goals also can enhance intensity in that they provide reasons for our behaviours. When we are asked to do something that we believe has no value or purpose, it is likely that we will not put much effort into that activity. Athletes find value in completing training activities that they believe can help them achieve their goals. Similarly, coaches find value in actively changing how they coach if they believe it will help them achieve their goals. We all put more effort into activities that we believe serve a purpose. Intensity levels increase when we are striving to achieve goals rather than just going through the motions of coaching or training.

Goals also help with the persistence component of motivation. Persistence is aided in two ways by goals: reinforcement for success, and perseverance when success is not readily achieved. Achieving goals makes us feel that what we are doing is valuable. We are likely to continue doing something when we feel that by doing so we will achieve what we want. Reaching goals increases our confidence and boosts our motivation. If, on the other hand, we have a goal that we are struggling to achieve, we will persist by finding new strategies if we believe the goal to be worthwhile. If we want to attain a particular goal, we will find additional ways of achieving it. If there is no goal, however, we will likely quit. Unfortunately, although many athletes and coaches set goals, they do so in a manner that is not as effective as it could be.

Long-term and short-term goals

One common problem in goal setting is for people to set only long-term goals. At times, a long-term goal can seem so far away that the individual gives up before getting there. A series of short-term goals that lead to the long-term goal can provide reinforcement along the way. Once the first short-term goal is achieved, individuals will have improved self-confidence and motivation that will in turn encourage their achievement of the next short-term goal. Without the attainment of short-term goals, people don't get the message that what they are doing is working. It is difficult to maintain motivation towards a task when the benefits of doing so are questionable.

Controllable goals

Setting a series of short-term goals with the final aim of achieving a long-term goal is only one aspect of goal setting. In addition, goals need to be related to performance or technique rather than outcomes. If individuals set goals related to an outcome (e.g., winning), then they will be thinking about the outcome rather than what it is they need to do to achieve the outcome they want. Winning is great fun; almost everyone enjoys winning. But if we focus on nothing other than winning, we will actually be decreasing our chances of winning. You have probably seen examples of athletes or teams who have been focused on outcomes, been noticeably ahead during competitions, thought they had them won, slackened off on their performance, only to be beaten at the end. Similarly, performance decreases when athletes have outcome goals and perceive that winning is not possible. The thinking then seems to go along the lines of, 'Well, I can't win, so I might as well give up.' If you want to win, or achieve a particular placing, fine – but then focus your attention on what you need to do to increase the chances of achieving that outcome, and set goals related to that process.

POINT TO PONDER

Further decreasing my times was the major incentive for me to do well.
(Shane Gould Innes, multiple Olympic gold medal swimmer)

Setting outcome goals is also problematic for other reasons. For example, if all swimmers in an event had the goal of winning, everyone would fail except for the one person who won. Even a swimmer with a personal best time who came in second would be a failure if the only goal was to win. Swimmers can only control what happens in their own lanes.

Performance or technique goals encourage swimmers (and all athletes) to focus on what they can control. Coaches need to remember that their goals should also be controllable. It is easy to fall into the trap of setting the goal of having athletes you coach being selected for representative teams or achieving a particular level of performance. These are outcome goals and you cannot control them. Achieving these goals relies on the politics of your sporting organisation and on what your athletes do. Setting goals that require other people to do things is immediately putting the achievement of the goals outside your control. If you want your athletes to achieve a particular level of performance, your goals should be related to what you can do to structure an environment conducive for learning and practice.

Challenging but realistic goals

Effective goal setting requires a balance between challenge and realism. Some individuals are so concerned about succeeding and being able to say they achieved their goals, that the goals they set are actually endeavours they have already accomplished. They are guaranteed to achieve their goals, but doing so will not enhance their performances or change their behaviours because they have not challenged themselves in any way. Other individuals tend to go to the opposite extreme. They feel that setting realistic goals is restrictive and argue that by expecting the impossible from themselves they avoid setting any limits on themselves. Although technically this may be true, in reality they usually just set themselves up for failure. Repeated failure to achieve goals often reduces motivation, self-confidence, and confidence in the programme and other people.

Positive goals

As well as correcting errors as part of the positive approach of coaching, it is necessary to state goals in positive terms. If goals are worded negatively, individuals are thinking about, planning for, and possibly doing exactly what they do not want. If your goal is not to think about pink elephants, you won't be able to help thinking of pink elephants! Phrasing goals in the positive encourages people to think about, plan for, and achieve what they desire.

Specific and measurable goals

A common error in goal setting is being vague about what one wants to accomplish. The goal of being a better coach, a fitter athlete, or a more knowledgeable individual does not allow a person to know if or when success has been achieved. How does one know when one is better or fitter? For goals to be effective they need to be specific and measurable. The easiest way is to make them numerical.

Objective measures such as distances, weights, repetitions, or times can easily become specific goals. For goals where objective measures cannot be used, previously established subjective rating scales may be beneficial. For example, if someone tends to be negative and is often swearing and remembering past mistakes instead of being positive and constructive, setting a goal of increasing positive and constructive self-talk would be useful but virtually impossible to measure objectively. Creating a subjective 10-point rating scale where 1 means the person's self-talk was entirely negative and 10 means the person's self-talk was entirely positive and constructive is a means of trying to make subjective goals measurable. Of course it is important to define all the numbers on the scale, not just the endpoints. If the numbers are not defined prior to working towards the goal, the scale often changes as the behaviour changes, with behaviour originally rated as 6 being rated as 3.

ACTIVITY

Rewrite the following goals to make them specific and measurable. Be sure they remain positive.

Vague goal	Specific goal
I want to be faster in the 100m sprint.	I want to improve my personal best in the 100m sprint by 1.4 seconds.
I want to be a more consistent scorer in basketball.	
I want to have a tougher serve in volleyball.	
As a coach I want to improve the planning of my training sessions.	

Sometimes when athletes and coaches are told that outcome goals are to be avoided, they have difficulty determining useful performance or technique goals. Goals can be set in a variety of areas. Athletes can set goals in the areas of physical fitness (strength, power, speed, flexibility, endurance, agility), physical technique (dependent on the sport), mental skills (e.g., self-confidence, arousal control, imagery, concentration, self-talk), tactics and strategies, general health (e.g., nutrition, sleep), as well as numerous other domains such as attendance at training, being on time, looking after equipment, and communicating with others. Although coaches may want to set similar goals as athletes (particularly in relation to stress or time management), they might also consider the areas of knowledge, planning and management of training sessions, and instructional techniques. Goal setting is not just for athletes, it is an effective strategy for coaches as well (Sousa et al., 2008).

ACTIVITY

Thinking and introspection are required for individuals to set appropriate goals. Using whatever reference points you choose, answer the following questions:

1   Where are you now (where do you see yourself as a coach)?
2   Where do you want to be in one month's time (again, in reference to coaching, as opposed to 'on a beach in Tahiti')?
3   Where do you want to be in six months? What changes would you like to see in your own coaching?
4   Where do you want to be in two years? (Allow yourself to dream a little!)
5   List three strengths and three weaknesses you have as a coach (remember, these can relate to any area of your coaching performance):

Strengths	Weaknesses
(a)	(a)
(b)	(b)
(c)	(c)

6 Review what you have written above. Now select an area on which you want to work. Some coaches choose to strengthen one of their weaknesses, others choose to take greater advantage of one of the strengths. The choice is yours. You may wish to refer back to something you wrote regarding where you want to be in the future.

7 In the area that you have chosen, set a long-term goal with a target date. Think along the lines of what you want to achieve in your selected area in the next six months to two years. When you write the target date, be sure to write the actual date. Many individuals make the mistake of saying, 'In one year I will achieve X.' The problem arises when six months down the track they reread their goal and it still says, 'In one year ...'

8 Once you have set your long-term goal, set a series of short-term goals that will lead you to it. Use the time frame of one to four weeks for your short-term goals. You may find it helpful to consider the short-term goals as a staircase to get you where you want to go. At the moment you are at the bottom of the stairs. Each short-term goal is a step that brings you closer to the top of the stairs (your long-term goal).

9 Check that your short-term goals (particularly the first one or two) are challenging, realistic, positive, specific, measurable and controllable, and that they have target dates. If your goals do not meet these requirements, rewrite them so they do.

10 Some people make the error of thinking they have completed the goal-setting process at this point, but they have failed to determine what they are going to do to achieve their goals. Strategies need to be outlined for achieving the short-term goals. Ideas and suggestions from others are useful at this point. Determine at least four strategies to aid the achievement of your first short-term goal. You may not use all the strategies, but it is useful to have a backup in case the original plan doesn't work.

(a)

(b)

(c)

(d)

Now it is time to get even more specific. Write down exactly what you are going to do during the next two weeks that will help you achieve your goal. Be sure to address when, where, and how you will be applying your strategy or strategies.

116

Goals must be evaluated on a regular basis. It does not help to outline specific goals, target dates, and strategies just to find them buried under a pile of magazines six months later. When the target date for a short-term goal arrives, evaluate whether or not you have achieved the goal. If you have, great! Celebrate! Often the achievement of the goal is reward enough, but you may want to reward yourself with a special treat. Achieving the goal will give you belief in your strategies, and maintain or enhance your confidence and motivation that you then need to apply to the next goal (the next step).

If, however, the target date arrives and you have not achieved your goal, there is no need to commit hara-kiri. Instead, reflect on why the goal was not achieved. Perhaps you got sick, injured, or bogged down with work and were unable to make progress towards your goal. If this was the case, set a new target date. Perhaps the size of the step was too big. In that case, set a new, more realistic short-term goal with a new target date. You may still believe the goal to be a good one, but the strategy you selected was ineffective. Set a new target date, but then apply different strategies.

For goal setting to be most effective, the goals need to be recorded in a manner that allows you to remind yourself on a regular basis what it is you are trying to achieve. You might record the goals in a training diary or planner that you use regularly. Alternatively you might record your goals (with background music if you like) and then play them back on an iPod or MP3 player before going to sleep or while on your way to training or competition. Another possibility is to make a poster of your goal, where you can shade in your improvement or achievements as you go. Some individuals choose to display these posters in a public place (such as the changing room) because for them making their goal public enhances their motivation. Others, however, would see the public display of their goals as a source of unneeded pressure, and prefer to keep their goals private.

The goal-setting process outlined above is effective, but often athletes and coaches need to be thinking about achieving goals in more than one area. Using a form such as the one provided in Figure 5.3 can be useful. The example provided in the figure is designed for athletes. The categories can be changed if the form is to be used with coaches.

Goals	Target dates	Strategies
Fitness		1
Long term		2
Short term		3
Technique		1
Long term		2
Short term		3
Mental		1
Long term		2
Short term		3
Tactics		1
Long term		2
Short term		3

Figure 5.3 Sample goal-setting form

Remember, this goal-setting process is useful for both athletes and coaches. You can lead your athletes through a similar process to that listed above. Keep in mind that athletes need to set their own goals. Setting goals for them may be simpler, easier, and less time consuming for you, but the athletes will have much more commitment and energy for goals they set themselves. Coaches, however, can be a good source of ideas for strategies. It is imperative to recognise that the goal-setting process is exactly that, a process. Just sitting down once at the beginning of the season and setting a few goals does not mean that you can tick 'setting goals' off your list of things to do. Goals need to be continually revisited.

SELF-CONTROL

Competition (whether immediately before or during) is not the time to overload athletes with information or the place to introduce new strategies or techniques. Although opportunities for coaching input vary by sport, the coaching that actually can be done during competitions is minimal. Even though athletes can learn from competition, the competitive situation is not the appropriate place for vast amounts of instruction.

As mentioned in Chapter 3, athletes' anxieties increase when importance is placed on the outcome and/or when they feel uncertain

118

about their abilities, training, places on the team, or any other aspects of performance. One of the most common competitive coaching errors is to place great importance on the outcome of specific competitions. It is not unusual to hear comments such as, 'This event is what you have been training all year for', 'The upcoming game is the most important game of your life', or 'Remember, the selectors will be watching this weekend, be sure to perform your absolute best.' Even young children recognise the importance of elimination matches, grand finals, and selection trials. Reminding them only serves to place greater pressure on them, usually resulting in increased anxiety and self-doubt, and poorer performance.

Some coaches feel compelled to pull out all the stops when it comes to a grand final or an unusually important competition. Instead of sticking with routines and behaviours that worked to get the players or competitors to where they are, they decide that fancier methods are required. No major changes should be made immediately before or during major competitions. Athletes need to know that the coach has faith in the existing plan and in them. Things should remain as familiar as possible. Even if a particular behaviour is less than optimal, suddenly changing (or trying to change) that behaviour before a competition usually has worse consequences than persisting with the original course of action. For example, if athletes are junk food junkies, changing their diet to healthy meals and snacks would be a beneficial change in the long run. Nevertheless, if the change was made immediately prior to a major competition, those concerned not only may have physiological reactions to the change in diet, they also may feel out of sorts because things are different. They are no longer in their comfort zones and feel that things are not quite right.

Coaching during competitions can be frustrating because coaches have limited control at this stage in terms of how their athletes perform. In reality, coaches can often do more harm than good during competition. The previous paragraphs mentioned the anxiety of athletes, but it needs to be noted that coaches get anxious as well. The main difference is that coaches' anxieties can be compounded by their sense of having little or no control. It is not unusual for the heart rate and blood pressure of coaches on the sidelines to exceed that of the athletes out running around.

Just as athletes need to focus on controlling the controllable, coaches should do the same. Athletes (especially children) react to coach (and parent) reactions on the sideline. Techniques for activation control are introduced in Chapter 8. Although when coaching you may get frustrated and be tempted to lose your temper, maintaining self-control and remembering to implement the positive coaching behaviours mentioned earlier will be beneficial for your athletes. If you are nervous or anxious, your athletes will pick up on that nervousness and anxiety and become more like you. On the other hand, if you are calm, focused, and positive, your athletes will tend to be the same. In short, emotions and attitudes are contagious. Be sure yours are ones you want your athletes to catch!

POINT TO REMEMBER

You have done all you can do to prepare your athletes for competitions. If you have not, then it is too late to prepare them during competitions. Enjoy the competitions and learn from what occurs. The positive approach is for competition as well as training.

Figure 5.4 When coaches lose their tempers they lose the positive approach

For this reflection you will need to have videos of yourself coaching during competitions. Observe yourself coaching during competitions. The following reflective questions are designed to help you determine how your behaviours and attitudes affect your athletes.

- How confident do you appear to be of your athletes?
- Do you demonstrate any signs of anxiety?
- Do you remain positive even when your athletes are not performing as well as you may have expected or hoped?
- Does it look like you are enjoying yourself and that you really want to be there?
- Do you provide your athletes with cue words or phrases?
- Have you avoided the pitfall of information overload?
- How enthusiastic do you seem?
- Does your frustration show, or were you able to control it? Are you smiling?
- What comments did you make during the competition? Were they effective? Why or why not?

Now select two behaviours that you could improve during competitions. State specifically what you are going to try to do that is different from what you are currently doing.

Behaviour	Specific improvements/changes
1	
2	

SUMMARY

1   A positive environment is supportive, familiar yet challenging, and safe; it allows for self-determination and individual differences.
2   The positive approach is a combination of providing information and rewards while being sincere and realistic within a supportive environment.
3   Encouragement can be verbal and non-verbal.

121

4 Feedback should be given using 'good, better, how'.
5 All instructions should be phrased positively, indicating what you want the athletes to do.
6 Coaches need to be able to communicate effectively with their athletes.
7 Non-verbal communication skills can be improved by ROLLing with your athletes: be Relaxed, have an Open posture, Lean towards them, and Look at them.
8 Listening and understanding are the first two requirements for effective communication. Many coaches need to improve their listening skills.
9 Motivation is made up of direction, intensity, and persistence.
10 Athletes are likely to choose the direction of training if they have a reasonable probability of experiencing success, feel they have some input into the programme, and think training is fun.
11 An effective technique for maintaining or enhancing motivation is goal setting.
12 Athletes and coaches should set controllable, challenging but realistic, positive, specific, and measurable goals.
13 Goals need to have target dates and strategies and should be evaluated on a regular basis.
14 During competitions, coaches need to maintain self-control and remember to implement positive coaching behaviours.

CHAPTER 6

LEARNING SKILL

The human being is a complex, dynamic system (Renshaw, 2010), therefore learning any kind of movement involves many inter-disciplinary factors, integrating aspects from the task, environment, and individual. A useful current way of looking at learning skill is through a constraints-led approach (Davids et al., 2008). A constraints-led approach focuses on the dynamics of movement, recognising that skills cannot be learned in isolation, but that task, environment, and individual constraints must be taken into account to acquire a particular skill (see Figure 6.1). This dynamic, constraints-led approach is an alternative to the traditional technique-based, structured, skill acquisition approach (see box for Recent Research on a constraints-led approach). In essence, the constraints-led approach suggests that the manipulation of constraints (task, environment, and/or individual) enables individuals to self-organise and problem solve optimal movement patterns in specific, realistic contexts. Based on this notion of dynamics of movement, a coach's role is to provide opportunities to practise in match-like situations so that transfer to competition itself is seamless and realistic.

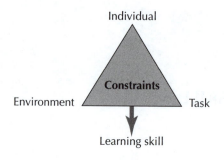

Figure 6.1 The constraints-led approach to coaching
Source: Renshaw (n.d.)

SELF-ORGANISING USING DYNAMIC SYSTEMS FOR SKILL ACQUISITION

An explanation of Teaching Games for Understanding (TGfU) from a motor learning perspective was presented in this research article through a non-linear (multidimensional) approach, highlighting the dynamic movement systems and the interactive roles of key constraints (performer, task, and environment) within a sport setting. Previous research in motor learning has focused on lab-based linear studies (one-dimensional, unilateral) to explain skill acquisition. Using non-linear pedagogy (interactive nature of movement) of key constraints, a case study on women's water polo in Australia was used to demonstrate the dynamic nature and decision-making capabilities needed in an elite-level sport. A shooting intervention using small-sided games (with two or three players per team, depending on the game) and practices was used to improve shooting ability and decision making in attack. The aim was to use games (a dynamic practice) to increase the ability of the players to adapt to unexpected game play, moves, and perturbations from teammates. The research team introduced various task constraints to change the nature of the movement effects in the training of shooting. These task constraints were in the form of equipment (pool noodles and other obstacles) to explore alternative coordination patterns as well as differing water polo ball weights to elicit variability in the learning process. The water polo players found the constraints approach quite challenging, but meaningful to the real game situations they encountered.

124

The intervention enabled the researchers to further theorise the conceptual framework of a dynamic systems, constraints-led approach and suggest practical examples for coaches to work on athletes' complex neurobiological systems using TGfU. 'It has been observed that changes in movement behavior do not necessarily follow a linear progression and sudden and abrupt changes in system organization might arise as a result of the dynamic interactions that occur in a learning context …' (p. 134). By focusing on the authentic context of actual game play movement, athletes are able to organise and coordinate movements and gain perceptual signals that enable them to read the game and respond to varying, dynamic situations of game strategies they may encounter in competition.

The authors concluded that the non-linear dynamics perspective supports the intention of TGfU as a means to manipulate task constraints within the game to enhance learning of tactics and skill (e.g., changing the equipment, adding or removing players). There is a need for further research about non-linear pedagogy to increase the empirical support from the motor learning field.

Source: Chow, J., Davids, K., Button, C., Renshaw, I., Shuttleworth, R. & Uehara, L. (2009). Nonlinear pedagogy: Implications for Teaching Games for Understanding (TGfU). In T. Hopper, J. Butler & B. Storey (Eds), *TGfU … Simply good pedagogy: Understanding a complex challenge* (pp. 131–144). Ottawa: Ottawa Physical Health Education Association.

Teaching Games for Understanding (TGfU) has become a popular approach to learning movement, because using games enhances skills, techniques, and tactics and transfers practice into match-like situations (i.e., creates an environment conducive to learning). TGfU was originally developed by Bunker and Thorpe (1982) and has been studied, adapted, and published as other names (e.g., Game Sense and Play Practice; Launder, 2001). Though all have slight differences, the principles of learning through playing meaningful games are the essence to the approach, and a valid, conceptual foundation to the function of TGfU is underpinned by the skill acquisition theory of the constraints-led approach (Chow et al., 2009). Games set realistic problems that athletes have to solve. The idea of TGfU is for coaches to develop purposeful games so athletes can enhance performance through intrinsically motivating activities that involve decision making and tactics, thus attending to the dynamic nature of human movement. Coaches design practice sessions that are related to the specific sport itself, so athletes can practise in a real context.

For athletes to learn skills, feedback can help to guide their execution. To decide on what kind of feedback to provide, coaches need to be able to observe and analyse. Some of the challenges faced when observing and analysing are knowing how to observe the skill, selecting what to look for, and finding the best ways to help athletes enhance skill. Considering the dynamic nature of movement, there is much to observe and analyse, and many environmental, task, and individual constraints may influence athletes' performances. Often instant decisions must be made as to how to manipulate a skill or game to enable the learning activity to be relevant so that the athletes can learn effectively. To be effective observers and analysers of skills, coaches must determine the factors that affect performances, including the moods or levels of the athletes (individuals); the weather (environment); the state of the facilities and equipment (environment); the rules, techniques, and tactics (task); and then manipulate these factors as well as provide sound advice (feedback).

In this chapter, we first discuss and explain the recent dynamic systems approach, then offer some practical tips for coaches to develop TGfU games that work on movement and successfully observe and analyse athletes' performances so that worthwhile feedback can be given. Finally, the purpose of feedback, and guidelines on how to develop feedback strategies, are outlined in this chapter.

A CONSTRAINTS-LED APPROACH

Using the idea that a practice environment and the ability to learn skill is a complex, dynamic process, we discuss how coaches can use constraints to help athletes acquire skills. This constraints-led approach suggests that athletes have a number of ways to learn and solve movement problems. The constraints defined here are boundaries or limitations that affect the decision-making process that enables understanding of

126

the skill in context (Renshaw, 2010). Newell (1986) suggested three constraints that influence performance at any time:

1   Task constraints include the rules of the sport, available equipment, player numbers, and the relative state of the game. For example, if defence is the purpose of the game, then the coach might provide points for the defensive team when they force a turnover. Or a condition might be given that there are 30 seconds left in the game and the score is 10–3.
2   Individual constraints include athletes' physique, mental (cognitive and psychological) and social skills, such as self-efficacy, emotional control and motivation; technical skills; and fitness level, all of which can influence decision-making behaviours.
3   Environmental constraints include weather conditions, the laws of physics and nature (e.g., gravity, altitude), or practice facilities. These environmental constraints also include the social experiences of the individual (e.g., social constraints such as family, peer groups, the culture of a sport club, previous access to high-quality, developmentally appropriate coaching; Davids et al., 2008).

Coaches need to understand these constraints so they can observe a learning activity and the constraints that might occur in that practice environment. Through this understanding, coaches then manipulate constraints to enable athletes to learn about that particular situation realistically. For example, if an athlete is standing watching a learning activity and not engaged, that is an individual constraint that must be changed so the athlete is included. The coach might alter the task to overload one team or change the scoring system and purpose so that all individuals can participate.

The three constraints often overlap and are interactive, making the learning approach complex. Due to the nature of this interactivity, it is sometimes difficult to classify any one of the constraints as unique and unilateral (Davids et al., 2008). For example, if a game has been designed to work on a particular tactic, an individual may gain an understanding of a technique in a fatigued situation as well as a perceptual component based on the tactic to be learned. The environment has created the ability for the athlete to feel fatigued and the conditioned game (task) has enabled the individual to acquire a skill or tactic while fatigued and under pressure.

127

The nature of the constraints-led approach relies on problem solving and how interacting constraints enable learning. Athletes do not fit into a 'one size fits all' way of executing skills. The dynamic conditions affect how athletes learn and develop. Coaches should not force all athletes to try to fit into a perfect movement template often highlighted in many textbooks as the one way of performing a movement (Renshaw, n.d.). Coaches have the responsibility to enable their athletes to solve problems in ways that are best suited to their own individual constraints, using the environment and the task to better meet their learning needs. The key point for coaches is, therefore, to encourage athletes to solve problems using methods that are most suitable to them individually. TGfU provides a mechanism for all these constraints to interact so that athletes can learn and solve problems. In TGfU, decision making and perception (reading the game) can be gained through the dynamic environment of games.

TEACHING GAMES FOR UNDERSTANDING

The purpose of having a section on TGfU in this book is to introduce a valuable learning approach. As noted previously, there are several other terms for a games approach, but for this book we have decided to introduce the original concept of TGfU (Bunker & Thorpe, 1982). For further development of a games approach, there are other resources that focus on the theory, application of theory, and provision of specific games that are useful to readers (Butler & Griffin, 2010; Griffin & Butler, 2005; Launder, 2001; Mitchell et al., 2006).

TGfU was developed as a result of Bunker and Thorpe (1982) observing children in physical education classes and noting that they learn well in game situations. Developed from educational gymnastics and originally designed for children, TGfU has been adapted by many coaches to suit various levels of many different sports, from children through to high performance teams. TGfU challenges the traditional training programme where the game is often saved for the end of a training session (and often used as a reward for good behaviour). Instead, purposeful games are the essence of the training programme. TGfU is an approach that enables athletes to learn about the game and practise movement within the context of a game rather than separate from it. Learning in context provides a sound understanding of the game and better opportunities to apply movement and decision making (a skill that is consistently considered desirable for athletes; Kidman & Lombardo, 2010b). When athletes are allowed to play or practise uncluttered by coaches telling them what to do and where to go, they are productive in terms of learning in context, enhancing motivation through challenges, interacting socially, and making decisions (Thorpe, 2005). For example, watch a group of children on the playground. They seem to enjoy their time and all are involved and participating. They design their own rules and nobody stops to tell them what to learn. They learn for themselves. There is a great message for adults here. Children learn and participate without continual coach interruption (Cooper, 2010).

To the contrary of some pessimists' views of 'allowing' athletes to have choices, coaches are still important. Their roles should be to design meaningful games that contribute to athletes' learning and enjoyment. The games can be designed using the constraints-led approach, so that the game fulfils the purpose of developing what the athletes need to perform better (Renshaw, 2010). When implementing the games, a coach's role is to make decisions on what constraint to put on the game, or what questions to ask the athletes so they can learn about a particular aspect of their performance. The ability to take this role is an art in coaching. The 'art' is being able to design purposeful games that work on options and situations, and knowing when to stop and problem solve with the athletes and when to just let them continue, so they learn on their own. Thorpe (2005) emphasised this 'art':

> When speaking to coaches, I often use the phrase, 'You can play games well/badly.' What I mean is that I watch people with relatively poor techniques totally engrossed in [playing] a game of badminton. They have good tactical understanding, are totally absorbed, dash about the court and leave the session satisfied and want to come back next week. So? The toughest call for a coach is to decide 'not to do anything'. I know I could make them better players, but is it the right time to step in? Will I have enough time to ensure that my input will be positive? The coach who steps in and explains what a player is doing wrong, or shows a 'better' way is having a very negative effect if they do not have the time to spend or the player does not have the ability to incorporate a

lasting improvement into their 'fun' game. This said, some would argue that the traditional lessons that do this are not well taught, which results in poor responses to lessons by children, rather than the approach [as such] being incorrect.

(Thorpe, 2005, pp. 236–237)

Well-structured games are designed to provide options that help athletes arrive at tactical understanding for themselves. Thorpe (2005) suggested:

Teaching Games for Understanding was literally an approach in which we wanted children to understand:

- the game they were playing;
- what they were trying to do;
- why they might select a particular move/action;
- that you could play games with varying degrees of competitiveness;
- that there were no universal right and wrong answers (the phrase of TGfU is 'it all depends': it depends on the opponent's move, it depends on your position on court, it depends on how much skill you have, it depends on the situation, etc.);
- why they might want to learn and practise skills; and subsequently
- that success was there for everyone, but depended on them not the teacher or coach who could only help.

(pp. 233–234)

Intrinsic motivation is also enhanced with the TGfU approach. TGfU enhances the affiliation motive to participate (see Chapter 3) because there are always situations where athletes are playing with their teammates and interacting. Through games, athletes share success and failure, they learn how to trust each other, and to know each other's ways of competing and making decisions, thus enhancing team culture. Achievement is also enhanced because TGfU enables athletes to do something well, to problem solve, and take ownership for their own learning. Of course, enjoyment is definitely enhanced because games are fun (Kidman & Lombardo, 2010b).

When introducing this approach to coaches, often a comment such as 'Well, where is the technique practice, doesn't this approach encourage incorrect technique?' is heard. The answer is that the technique is developed through the games. Using the constraints-led

130

approach, a constraint can be added into the game to work on an individual's technique. Technique is practised, understood within the context, then worked on individually as the need arises (Chow et al., 2009). Individualised instruction is thus enhanced because the rest of the team continues to participate while the coach works with one athlete. Athletes are still encouraged to learn the fundamentals of the sport, but are provided with interesting ways to practise these fundamentals through games. Nevertheless, those who are involved in the game understand what they are trying to do and thus are motivated to learn the skill or technique needed to play the game. There are many examples of athletes who are motivated (at many ages) by games, spending time perfecting movements on their own and outside of training time (Kidman & Lombardo, 2010b). Game-centred learning helps athletes to learn skills using variable practice, which enhances memory retrieval of movement patterns (Davids et al., 2008). Coaches who have isolated skills or techniques from a game in a structured, drill-like environment often make comments such as, 'Why can't you apply that to the game? We just spent an hour practising that skill.' The reason is that often the isolated skill or technique practised does not directly transfer to the game. It is important for athletes to gain long-term learning. Isolated practice of skills and techniques might work well in one training session, but because of the lack of variety or application in realistic contexts the learning may not be carried into the next session.

TGfU is advocated as an approach with an emphasis on tactical learning and decision making. Children are motivated to learn through this approach and can be encouraged to work on skills and techniques within the context of a real game situation. The approach is about providing meaningful, purposeful games that have goals and foci, not rolling out the ball and playing the full game of the sport. The key for coaches is to design games that work on particular situations within the larger game (Thorpe, 2005).

VOLLEYBALL EXAMPLE USING TEACHING GAMES FOR UNDERSTANDING

Purpose	To find the gap in the opposition and get the ball to drop to the floor on their side of the court (placement work).
Players	Two on one side of half the court, two on the opposite half of the court.
Rules	Service starts by throwing the ball over the net. Every time the ball hits the floor, the play starts again from the service. Basic volleyball rules apply. No spiking, only passing or setting.
Questions for athletes' awareness	What did you look for to get the ball to hit the opposition's floor?
	Where were opposition players when you returned the ball over the net?
	What could you do to ensure you get the ball to open space?
Possible constraints to manipulate	**Environment:** Increase or decrease court size.
	Task: Add more players to the game or overload one side (e.g., 3 *v.* 2).
	Individual: Allow them to spike.

ACTIVITY

Design a purposeful game for your next training session. Ensure you consider the needs of the team/individual and the specific situation of the group or season.

Purpose:

Players:

Rules:

Questions for athletes' awareness:

Possible constraints to manipulate:
   Environment:
   Task:
   Individual:

FEEDBACK

One way to correct or maintain performance is through feedback. Feedback is defined as the information that is available during or after a performance (Schmidt & Wrisberg, 2004). It is provided, intrinsically or extrinsically, to enhance athletes' learning. Without feedback, it is difficult for athletes to understand and make decisions about their performances. Athletes who obtain some form of feedback tend to perform consistently (Davids et al., 2008).

Observing and analysing

To obtain or provide effective feedback of athletes' performances, athletes and coaches must be able to observe and analyse performance or movement patterns. Observing and analysing athletes' sporting performance is complex. To understand these complexities, coaches need to gain an indepth knowledge of the task, environmental, and individual constraints that influence the learning setting (Davis & Broadhead, 2007). Numerous factors influence the nature of the movement and all must come together to enable a coordinated event to occur. To find this optimal coordination, coaches need to be able to manipulate the constraints to promote learning. For coaches to manipulate the constraints, they need to be able to observe all three aspects of activities, then make decisions on whether to step in and offer feedback, or leave the athletes to shape their own ways of performing (Southard, 2007). Manipulating the task, environmental, and individual constraints is important for the development of physical, psychological, and cognitive performances. Observing and analysing the constraints can be done with the entire team/squad or with an individual athlete performing a skill. When observing and analysing the team or squad, coaches are partly concerned with such questions as 'Did the athletes understand my explanation and demonstration?', 'Were the learning activities at an appropriate level of difficulty?', or 'Are athletes given decision-making opportunities to enhance skills/games?' Information about how to ask questions is provided in Chapter 7.

An effective observer and analyser is able to focus on a small number of parts of the task, environmental, or individual constraints that are important in a particular situation. To enhance your observing and analysing strategies, identify constraints of the athletes and their movements and decide what is important, why it is important, and where improvement can be made. For example, if a coach is planning to teach a drop kick in rugby, he or she should list all the parts of the task, environmental, and individual constraints and be able to manipulate them to effect learning. The coach should list the task (e.g., distance, spacial awareness), environmental (e.g., noisy crowds, windy conditions), and individual (e.g., vision, strength) constraints that could influence the kick. In another example, if coaches are teaching a two-on-two game of basketball, it is important that they break down the multitude of options of that skill, such as space, width, concentration, and needed strength. This information will enhance the coaches' analyses of what will guide particular athletes to enhance performance. Ultimately, the athletes should choose and take responsibility of what to change, but guidance from coaches is crucial.

Using video for observing and analysing

When observing and analysing athlete performance, video footage provides an objective tool to help determine aspects that can be measured (Hughes, 2008). Video footage can also show aspects that may be difficult to measure, such as the mood, environment, or individual constraints (Davids et al., 2008).

Video analysis has become a major tool in coaches' toolboxes to help analyse performance and enhance feedback with athletes (Hughes, 2008).

There are several systems available (e.g., *SportsCode*; Sportstec, n.d.) that are expensive and difficult to obtain for most coaches. With these coding systems, coaches can not only analyse skills, games, and training sessions, but also look at the opposition and predict their play.

Even though most coaches don't have access to these coding systems, using basic video analysis is a powerful tool. Video recordings can help athletes to see their movements and coaches to observe and analyse key situations and athletes' performances. Using video, coaches and athletes can view performance execution in slow motion, view it as many times as needed, and assess relevant constraints. Another benefit of video analysis is that athletes can sit and view their own performances with or without their coaches or they can analyse them together.

The first step in live observation or video analysis is selecting a constraint on which to focus so that too much information does not hinder learning. Observe or watch the video as many times as needed to gain enough information to make an accurate analysis. Be sure to look at constraints that may be affecting that particular performance.

After making an initial observation, try to move (or move the camera) around to gain several different vantage points to enhance the analysis. The observation position depends on the movement being performed, but you should assure you are in an appropriate place to see various phases of the movement. Coaches are notorious for standing in one place to observe.

At the beginning of training sessions athletes are generally fresher and therefore may process skills or techniques better than later in the training sessions. In determining when to observe or video, also consider how warmed up the athletes are. Coaches should perhaps observe skills or techniques before athletes are too tired to execute them effectively, or they may decide that the athletes need several attempts before observing or videoing the performance.

Just as athletes must practise their performances, coaches should practise their observing and analysing strategies. Experience increases the effectiveness of coaches' observation and analysis strategies. Trial and error play a major role in determining what works best for each athlete. Nevertheless, by analysing and identifying constraints, coaches will be able to enhance their coaching strategies and provide athletes with insights and knowledge to effectively develop skills and techniques.

Figure 6.2 Video analysis is a useful tool

ACTIVITY

1   Select a situation to video.
2   Which constraints will be the focus for this situation?
3   Where will you position the camera to see the performance?
4   When in the training session will you record the movement?

Providing feedback

During observation and analysis, coaches often need to decide how athletes will benefit from these analyses through various forms of feedback. Feedback fulfils two main functions: informational and motivational. Informational feedback provides athletes with knowledge about how the movement was performed. Motivational feedback provides athletes with verbal or non-verbal cues from the coach, or intrinsically from the experience itself, to encourage or discourage ongoing attempts of the skill or technique. Although the two functions can be independent, they also can be outcomes of each other. For example, informational feedback can be motivational in and of itself. A tone of voice or a non-verbal gesture combined with information of the performance can be motivating or demotivating (Martens, 2004).

There are two types of feedback: intrinsic and extrinsic (Martens, 2004). Athletes receive intrinsic feedback as a natural consequence of their performances. Intrinsic feedback comes via kinaesthetic, tactile, visual, and auditory sensory systems, for example the feel of the ball as it leaves your hands, the sound of the ball hitting the racquet, or the sight of the ball going through the net. Extrinsic feedback is that which is given from an external source such as the coach, other athletes, parents, and spectators. Extrinsic feedback can be verbal or non-verbal and can help or detract athletes from improving their performances. Extrinsic feedback can supplement intrinsic feedback.

Intrinsic feedback

Intrinsic feedback is the key to athlete self-awareness, the ability of individuals to make decisions about their performances based on their own interpretations (Chow et al., 2009). Intrinsic feedback comes from athletes using their senses to determine how they have executed movements as individuals or within a team. Athletes can determine if a catch or pass is good, for example by the sound of the ball hitting the fingertips or the sound of the ball entering the right place in the glove. In racquetball a good hit can be determined by the sound of the ball hitting the strings. In canoeing, an athlete knows what the feel of the paddle entering the water should be. Athletes can also feel how muscles are reacting while performing different movements. When athletes comment that 'it felt good!' they are reflecting positive intrinsic feedback. Athletes can also tell a successful or unsuccessful performance through the sense of touch. In diving, for example, athletes can evaluate dive execution according to how they enter the water. Coaches can, however, play a role in enhancing intrinsic feedback by asking their athletes how the movement felt or sounded (Cassidy et al., 2009). Athletes can see how well they perform using mirrors or videos to watch themselves. Intrinsic feedback develops athletes' self-awareness and abilities to determine how well they performed particular movements.

Using intrinsic feedback, athletes can determine their own errors and strengths of their performances. It is important to give them many opportunities to be able to judge their own performances. You may recall some surprises and elation when, upon seeing themselves on video, athletes could finally understand what you had been telling them. A coaching strategy to give athletes opportunities to analyse their skills has been suggested by Hadfield (1994) and is known as the query theory.

Basically, the query theory recommends that coaches encourage improvement in movement through athlete self-awareness. This self-awareness is gained by providing ways for athletes to solve problems about the performances by themselves, rather than telling them what to do and how to correct it. For example, if you are trying to get athletes to determine the correct pass to make in football, give them a situation and get them to work out the correct answer. The purpose of using self-awareness as athlete feedback is that until athletes can kinaesthetically understand what movements feel like, they cannot make the necessary adjustments. If athletes cannot feel movements or understand them, they cannot change them. A cricket example is presented from Hadfield's (1994) query theory:

> I was coaching a group of youngsters in a net and was trying to help one lad rid himself of a very common technical error – moving the back foot towards the leg side (i.e., backwards) just as the bowler was delivering the ball. ... Many coaches of young cricketers have spent a considerable amount of time trying to correct the fault. I was following my normal routine of identifying the fault ('you're moving your back foot to leg as the bowler bowls, Ned'), explaining why it wasn't a good idea and suggesting a correction ('Keep your feet still, with the weight on the balls of your feet, until the ball is released, Ned'). As usual, it seemed the lad had great difficulty in changing what he was doing. Seeing a demolition brick lying at the foot of the nearby clubrooms, I had a stroke of inspiration. I got the brick and placed it behind the young batsman's back heel – the one that was causing the problems with backwards movement. I then instructed him to bat as normal. The bowler ran in and let the ball go and as usual, the young batsman went to shift his foot backwards. This time however, his heel ran into the unyielding mass of the brick and came to a rapid halt. The lad was so surprised that he didn't even attempt

138

to hit the ball and turning to me with a look of astonishment and amusement on his face, said something like 'Crickey you're right Dave! I am moving my back foot aren't I?' At the end of the session, he had stopped moving his back foot.

(Hadfield, 1994, pp. 16–17)

The cricket example above demonstrates a method that allows athletes to work out problems by themselves, with a bit of assistance from the coach, such as the constraint of a brick in this instance, or even a question or two. Self-awareness is a key to improving athletes' performances. Coaches need to ask the right questions (more information about asking meaningful questions is presented in Chapter 7). The 'right' question is dependent on athlete understanding and needs, and depends on the individual, the environment, and the task at that moment. As coaches, we want to promote athlete curiosity rather than the judgement of athletes. The query theory helps to create independent athletes, individuals who are self-aware and take responsibility for their learning. As Whitmore (2002) suggested, coaches hold back their knowledge to gain feedback from the athletes' perspectives. For example, rather than saying, 'Watch the ball', a better way to enhance athlete awareness is to ask, 'What did you notice about the ball?' Instead of 'Bend your knees', coaches could use a rating system (e.g., 'On a scale of 1–10, 10 being very bent, rate how bent your knees are'). Rather than saying 'Pass to the striker', coaches could ask, 'Who is available?' Rather than 'They are beating us down the right side. Simon, you've got to get back to cover the striker', coaches could say, 'Where are they beating us? Who's going to take care of that?'

As Thorpe (2005) pointed out:

> TGfU's intention is to use games as fantastic learning opportunities, whereby athletes become self-aware and the games provide a problem solving mechanism. Many coaches and teachers, though well intentioned, spoil that learning opportunity by telling the athletes how they should play the game, or what tactic they should use. This way of teaching and coaching limits not only those learning opportunities, but intrinsic motivation as well, as the athletes stop to listen to the 'words of wisdom' reducing their own input and thus their ownership of learning. Ensuring athletes are provided with opportunities to solve problems themselves and understand why certain situations occur is the key to TGfU.

(p. 239)

Figure 6.3 The query theory

Extrinsic feedback

Coaches who give too much external feedback are often problematic. With an emphasis in this book on non-traditional ways of enabling learning, coaches need to rethink how verbal guidance can facilitate the learning process (Davids et al., 2008). Athletes and coaches can over-evaluate movement, rather than leaving athletes to feel movement (Galwey, 2009). Thus, coaches need to consider the implications of offering extrinsic feedback before doing so. In coachable moments (i.e., those moments where athletes show a readiness to learn) coaches need to determine whether to offer feedback or not. Before jumping in and offering feedback, consider whether athletes have self-awareness and are able to use intrinsic feedback. Is the movement efficient for the individuals, and at their ability levels, considering their physical, psychological, and cognitive constraints? The purpose of coaching is to enhance athlete learning and performance, so it is key to be able to read and understand the athletes (Kidman & Lombardo, 2010a).

Once deciding that extrinsic feedback is appropriate for a task, environment, and individual, providing appropriate and timely feedback to athletes is a strategy that coaches should practise and review. The basic premise to extrinsic feedback for coaches is 'good, better, how' (what was *good* about the performance, what can be done *better*, and *how* can the athlete make it better?). Athletes should be able to understand the feedback and from it modify the movement. To ensure feedback is understood, use coaching cues to remind athletes about parts of the skill or technique to perform, without giving too much direction. After giving the coaching cues, observe subsequent performances to determine if the feedback was understood. Stand back and watch for a while so the athlete can work out the information.

There are times when providing general evaluative feedback is useful, but it is important to provide athletes with specific information about how to improve, or what was correct. General feedback such as 'Good', 'Well done', and 'Good on ya' provides sources of positive feedback that nurture the caring environment, but do not specify what was good or why it was well done. Specific feedback contains information and tells athletes what they need to know to improve or continue to perform. Athletes benefit from obtaining specific information from coaches or others about skills and techniques.

The nature (positive, neutral, or negative) of feedback is an important element in the provision of effective extrinsic feedback. Positive feedback provides encouragement to athletes and may enhance their self-esteem. Everybody likes to receive praise, especially if it is sincere and honest. Negative feedback does not encourage or motivate athletes to perform, and sarcasm from coaches is counterproductive to athlete motivation and may cause them to give up easily (Nakamura, 1996). Coaches are notorious for recognising and correcting errors more often than noticing correct aspects of movement. One of the most commonly used forms of negative feedback is the word 'Don't'. If you said to an athlete 'Don't think about how hard the ball is', you may have created fear for the athlete. What do you think of when someone says 'Don't worry'? Negative feedback can hinder athletes' learning. Be cautious in how and when you use negative feedback. Neutral feedback has no positive or negative connotations. It usually provides a prompt, such as 'Remember to use one hand for balance.' Coaches often use neutral feedback when athletes are first learning skills, to remind athletes of important points to the skill or technique.

Immediate feedback is more useful than delayed feedback because it provides the athlete with information just after the performance (Lawrence & Kingston, 2008). Often coaches remind athletes of ways to perform skills or techniques several minutes after they were performed. Athletes cannot remember or feel exactly how they performed if the feedback is too delayed.

Whether the feedback is congruent or incongruent is also important (Martens, 2004). Congruent feedback focuses on the coaching cue verbalised or demonstrated to the team/squad. Congruent feedback corresponds to the idea just presented to athletes. The feedback provided should relate specifically to what athletes are practising. If a lacrosse team is working on creating space after making a pass, it is important to focus only on the notion of space. Feedback on other aspects of the pass is incongruent feedback and would distract athletes from focusing on the original goal – finding space. Incongruent feedback may load athletes with too much information. By planning the learning activity, coaches can focus on one or two aspects of the skill at one time.

POINT TO PONDER

When I first began to realise that I was unequally distributing feedback was when one of my hockey players (a 12-year-old) asked why I always talked to those who could not perform the skill well. I hadn't realised that I wasn't giving positive feedback and further encouragement to those who were doing well. I always felt that the players who needed to develop their skills were the ones who needed the most feedback. I was wrong. The higher-skilled players need as much feedback as the lower-skilled players or they won't continue to develop.

As mentioned several times in this book already, every athlete should be given equal attention. Often coaches tend to favour particular athletes. Some favour the brightest, some favour the most attractive. Similarly some coaches favour higher-skilled, some lower-skilled athletes. Some coaches may provide more feedback to boys, some to girls. Ensure that you are providing equal attention or feedback to your athletes. From one of your coaching videos, analyse the feedback you provided for your athletes using the following reflective questions:

- Which (if any) athletes did not receive attention or feedback from you? (To determine the amount of feedback, write down all the athletes' names on a piece of paper and tick their names when you discuss their performances with them, then designate whether the feedback was positive (+), negative (−) or neutral (0).)
- Which group did you tend to favour, for example the highly skilled or the more personable athletes?
- How did you promote athlete self-awareness through feedback?
- How did your athletes respond to any feedback given?
- Was the feedback you provided sincere? Why or why not?
- Was your feedback given immediately? Give some examples.
- List the feedback questions you used. Analyse their effectiveness.

POINT TO PONDER

I watched a coach turn into a different person after viewing himself giving feedback. He commented, 'I always bark at the kids. I'm so negative.' To change, he began getting the athletes involved in the learning process by questioning them about how the skill felt. The kids were surprised at first, but then really started enjoying the session because they were helping themselves learn.

SUMMARY

1 The human being is a complex, dynamic system and, as such, learning any kind of movement involves many interacting factors.
2 A constraints-led approach is a skill acquisition theory that suggests that the constraints of task, environmental, and individual factors can be manipulated to enable learning to occur.

3 Teaching Games for Understanding (TGfU) is an approach where coaches design games to develop athletes' learning within the context of the sport.

4 Acquiring technique through realistic games provides athletes with a context so that they understand the reason for the technique.

5 TGfU increases the motivation of athletes because they feel achievement and affiliation.

6 To provide athletes with information about their movement, coaches should develop effective observing and analysing strategies.

7 Feedback serves informational and motivational purposes and provides athletes with information and reinforcement to correct and/or maintain performance.

8 Intrinsic feedback comes from athletes themselves and is a natural consequence of skill and technique performance. Extrinsic feedback is obtained from external sources such as the coach and should be used sparingly.

9 The query theory is a self-awareness strategy whereby athletes discover their own strengths and weaknesses of movement performances.

10 Coaches need to consider the implications of offering extrinsic feedback before doing so. Look for coachable moments.

11 General feedback provides athletes with no specific information or direction of focus. Specific feedback provides athletes with precise information about their skills and techniques.

12 Extrinsic feedback is classified as positive, negative, or neutral. Coaches, in general, give too much negative feedback.

CHAPTER 7

COACHING STRATEGIES

Do you remember the teacher you had when you were in school who loved to talk? Does the following sound familiar? 'Good morning, boys and girls. Today, we are going to work on learning the capitals of the world. I think it is important to learn the capitals of the world because then we can keep up with current events. I learned the capitals of the world when I was young. In fact, we used to have contests to see who could name the most. Do you guys do that now? [No time for an answer.] Well, it was pretty special. I was very good at it and could name about 40 of them without stopping ...'

By this time you were probably asleep and, about five minutes later, you were startled awake by the teacher who said, 'Chris, why aren't you working?' How many coaches have you had who may have displayed similar behaviour? Think about how much you actually learned from such a coach.

From a different perspective, think about a time you explained and demonstrated a skill and the athletes could not perform what you expected. You thought that the explanation was superb, and the demonstration was excellent, yet you faced blank faces after the instruction. Why did this happen? Another, possibly more effectual approach is to question. When coaches ask questions, athletes must find answers, which in turn increases their knowledge and understanding of the purpose of particular skills and tactical plays in the context of competition. As educationalist John Dewey said, 'Thinking in itself is questioning.' Questioning stimulates athletes' thinking, providing them chances to be creative and make decisions. It is also a powerful means to inspire in athletes an intrinsic motivation to learn.

In this chapter, we introduce explaining, demonstrating, and questioning coaching strategies that, when performed effectively, can enhance athlete learning. The goal of using various coaching strategies is to ensure the athletes understand and at the same time do not get bored from over-instruction. Often there is limited time allocated for training and every moment is precious to the athletes. This time is their chance to improve and perhaps demonstrate that they are worthy of competing in the next competition. They want to be involved in learning, solving problems, and practising skills and tactics as much as possible, not listening to coaches telling their life stories. Sometimes learning takes time, but because problem solving enhances learning, questioning enhances long-term learning.

POINT TO PONDER

I hear, I forget
I see, I remember
I do, I understand

(Ancient Chinese proverb)

DEMONSTRATIONS

'A picture is worth a thousand words.' This saying is old, yet so important in learning sport skills. The purpose of demonstrating is to increase athletes' understanding of skills and tactics by providing a model. If coaches can provide pictures suitable for their groups of athletes of what is to be practised, athletes should be able to acquire images as a focus for the appropriate practice of sport skills and tactics. Coaches are sometimes afraid to demonstrate a skill because they lack confidence to do so or they have not performed the skill for years. Alternatively, coaches who used to be (or still are) elite athletes may provide demonstrations to novices

146

that may appear unachievable and/or attributed to the experience of the demonstrator. There are many ways to demonstrate an accurate skill without the coach having to do it all the time.

Modelling (copying a picture) and observational learning (Davids et al., 2008) are effective learning tools that use images of the skill to be performed. A model provides a guide for athletes to observe so that they can get a general understanding of what they are trying to perform. Social learning theory (Bandura, 1977) provides a basis of understanding of modelling that recognises that athletes learn from observing and copying respected (the respect comes from the athlete) role models (Purdy & Jones, in press). They also learn consciously and subconsciously from their social environment, which can contribute to the learning of skills in a sporting context (Smith, n.d.). Therefore, demonstrations need to be modelled in real contexts and presented in different forms (e.g., live situations, television) to help athletes gain blueprints in their heads.

Visual demonstrations are beneficial, but not for everyone. Demonstrations will be useful when they are meaningful to the athletes. The individuals will use the information that applies to their ability levels (physical, cognitive, and emotional). If the demonstration is perceived to be too difficult, motivation to attempt the skill may wane because athletes don't have the confidence to perform the movement. The most important reason for the demonstration is for athletes to gain a general movement idea and then adapt it to suit their needs. For example, many basketball players are motivated through observing Kobe Bryant perform a dunk. We see many players attempting to dunk at training sessions to copy Kobe Bryant but all have different abilities. If athletes have a desire to copy that movement they will work out how to perform an approximation of that movement. Therefore observational learning, either through demonstrations at training or outside of training, is a key for athletes to understand movement.

Demonstrations are a valuable tool in a coach's toolbox, but coaches need to ensure that they are valuable for the individual athletes they are coaching. In many training sessions, coaches introduce new movements or tactical plays and they should plan how to present them. In planning a demonstration, consider the following questions: *Who* will demonstrate? *How* will the movement be demonstrated? *How* will you ensure that it most approximates the movement in the game or competition? *What* equipment will you need to provide an effective demonstration? *Where*

147

will the demonstration take place? How will you know *whether* the athletes understood the demonstration? *When* should the demonstration be provided? We will consider these factors below.

Who

There are several options as to who can demonstrate. Take into account the difficulty of the demonstration and who is capable of performing a demonstration relevant to the athletes' abilities. If you, as the coach, are going to demonstrate, remember that realistic demonstrations are essential. If you feel comfortable, demonstrate. You should not be afraid to admit, however, that you cannot demonstrate a particular movement. By you making this admission, athletes will be able to understand how difficult and how much time it takes to become proficient at such a skill. If coaches can admit that they are not perfect, they tend to create an atmosphere of respect. By promoting a respectful atmosphere, athletes can understand it is all right if they are not perfect.

If athletes are to be chosen to demonstrate, first examine their personalities and decide if they are capable of getting up in front of a group. Once athletes have been selected, practise the movement with them in advance to ensure a clear demonstration.

Consider, also, the process of selecting athletes to demonstrate. Do you tend to pick the same high-skilled athlete to perform demonstrations? How do the other athletes feel about that person who is always in the limelight? Everyone on the team/squad can demonstrate something. Look for the contribution that each athlete can make. If there are some who are shy, think about using two or more athletes to demonstrate, so the quiet ones get equal limelight opportunities.

Some coaches are lucky in that they have access to video recorders and may be able to effectively demonstrate a skill or technique from a video. Ensure that the recording is shown as near to the time of the training session as possible and preferably that the athletes(s) who demonstrate on the video are similar to those being coached. When using video, provide verbal cues of what the athletes are going to work on during the training session. These cue words can remind athletes what to focus on when they practise the movement.

Another option is to have a guest come to a training session to demonstrate. Ensure this person is a good role model, one who athletes can look up to, and one who promotes the philosophy of fair play. Athletes can be motivated to perform the skill or technique when they see such a demonstration. Nevertheless, when choosing such a person, remember that some athletes might see the demonstration as easy for an expert, but too difficult for them.

How

It is important that athletes give their full attention to and can see the demonstration. Plan the most effective formation, so that all athletes can observe the demonstration with no obstructions. For example, at a diving pool, you only may be able to line up two divers to see the entry into the water. Arrange the others on both sides of the pool, then rotate the divers to different points of observation to take in the skill or technique from different perspectives.

What will you require to perform this demonstration? What equipment will you need to be able to demonstrate the whole skill, or part of the skill? Will you need a partner, for example? Will you require goal posts or witches' hats/cones to be able to make certain points about the skill or technique? Will you need modified equipment initially or can the athletes understand using regular equipment? Consider how to provide the most suitable picture to the athletes.

What

Generally, physical education teaching literature suggests that coaches should demonstrate the whole skill or technique first, and then break it into parts (Graham, 2008). The first demonstration should be an actual model of the movement. For example, if a diver is learning a pike dive, the actual pike dive should be performed at normal speed. Then, the coach can break down the skill or technique into parts.

It might be useful for complex skills to be viewed in slow motion, so that athletes can focus on particular aspects of it. When showing slow motion movement, use verbal cues to point out aspects of the skill to be practised. For example, you could break down the pike dive on the pool deck where athletes look at the pike position. Before the pike dive is demonstrated, you could use verbal cues to focus on the part that you want the athletes to look at, for example 'Look at how she is kissing her knees when touching the toes.'

To observe effectively and process cognitively how to perform a movement, athletes should view it from different angles, such as back and front or right and left. These types of viewings may remind athletes about a previously learned skill and enhance their understanding of the movement.

Remember that if there are right- or left-handers (or -footers) on the squad, show athletes the mirror image on both right and left sides. If concentrating on certain aspects of the skill, be sure to provide verbal cues so that both right- and left-handers can understand what to attempt.

Where

The location of the demonstration is also an important consideration. When planning, think about the location of the sun, how many athletes you have, and how many different perspectives of the skill or technique athletes need to see, such as right *vs.* left, front *vs.* back. The location is just as important as the other considerations because, if athletes cannot see, they will not get an accurate picture from which to begin the learning process. One way to determine if all can see is by observing the group. Can you see all of the athletes' eyes? If not, rearrange the athletes so that you can.

Checking for understanding

The best way to check for understanding is to get the athletes to perform the movement and observe what they are practising. Another effective way is to ask questions such as 'Ramon, how would you touch your toes in the dive?' or 'Why were Angela's hands pointing that way?' If you ask the athletes 'Do you understand?', what do you think their response will be? They will be excited to try the new skill and will probably just say 'Yes' or nod their head in anticipation. Also, few people want to publicly acknowledge they do not understand something.

When

There are several stages during the training session in which effective demonstrations will be useful. An obvious time to have a demonstration is when athletes are learning a new skill or technique. The demonstrations will provide an image to athletes about how to execute the movement. Remember that athletes may be at different stages of learning, so repeating the demonstration or part of it may provide them with answers to questions that arise. If the athletes attempt the skill or technique and one or two have difficulties, rather than calling everyone back in to demonstrate, provide the demonstration to those who may not have understood the first time. Coaches can provide a demonstration as a reminder of skills worked on in a previous training session. Athletes often forget from week to week and a reminder demonstration is effective. Another useful time to provide a demonstration is at the conclusion of a training session, where it acts as a final reminder of what they may need to practise.

These guidelines will help to create an effective demonstration. Remember that each of the components must be planned and also that a brief demonstration is a good demonstration. Try not to spend more than one minute demonstrating before having the athletes themselves attempt the movement.

ACTIVITY

Plan a demonstration for a performance objective that you designed in Chapter 4. When planning, ask yourself who will demonstrate, what task will be demonstrated, and when and where you will provide the demonstration.

EXPLANATIONS

An explanation is often an important component of a demonstration. It may also be delivered to athletes as a learning aid without an accompanying demonstration. An explanation is when the coach talks and the athletes listen. Their full attention should be gained and maintained. Explanations should be planned, brief, and they should contain key points. An explanation should lead directly into physical practice, which provides the opportunity for maximum development and learning (Graham, 2008).

As with a demonstration, the explanation phase of the training session is a strategy that should be planned and practised. It is important for coaches to have a space or location where all athletes meet upon a signal such as a whistle. By having such a routine (see Chapter 4), the time for instructions is reduced and practice time increased. If you are planning to introduce a new skill, how will you introduce it? Will you provide the demonstration, the explanation, or both? What kind of language will your athletes understand? What will the key points of your message be? On which part of the skill do you want the athletes to focus? In which part of the training session will you plan to have this explanation? When introducing or reviewing a skill or concept, first tell the athletes why it is important to learn the concept or skill, and follow it up with an explanation and a demonstration.

Explanations and demonstrations complement each other as long as coaches remember not to talk during the physical demonstration. Athletes will have a difficult time focusing simultaneously on both the picture exhibited and the sound of talking. Nevertheless, if coaches provide a verbal cue before the demonstration, athletes can apply the verbal cue to the picture. Remember to check for athletes' understandings of an explanation or demonstration.

Figure 7.1 Avoid long-winded, complex explanations

152

Explanations need to be simple (matched to the developmental level of the athletes) and brief and should include reminder cues, words or phrases to help recall the idea and to provide a picture of what is to be performed. When explaining skills or techniques, try to get athletes to focus on one concept at a time. For example, if a rowing coach wants athletes practising the stroke in the water, the coach should not then begin to discuss information about the coxswain's responsibility at the same time. Athletes should only focus on one skill or tactic at a time, practise it, let it become automatic, then change to another. Ensure your explanation complements your demonstration or vice versa.

EFFECTIVE EXPLAINERS

- Make brief and clear statements during the early stages of a training session about what skills and tactics are to be learned, when to use them and how to do them.
- Provide opportunities to practise what was explained.
- Simplify or 'chunk' the information to avoid confusing the athletes with too much information.
- Direct (and redirect) attention to the important parts of the skill or tactic.
- Question athletes to determine their understanding of the explanation and remind them of previous learning.
- Question athletes to get them to make decisions and comparisons that aid their learning.
- Help athletes to understand by creating images and cue words that they can use to build on previous experiences and skills.
- Avoid explaining during the demonstration.

ACTIVITY

Based on the performance objective you used to plan your demonstration (see previous activity), develop an explanation to provide information to your athletes about the skill or technique. List key coaching points to help you remember essential information to cover in the explanation.

Plan and implement a training session that focuses on the coaching strategies of demonstrating and explaining. Once again, you will need to video yourself coaching. While looking at the recording, answer the following questions in reflection:

- How did you arrange your athletes to demonstrate and explain the activity? What was the routine established so that athletes knew where to meet?
- Did you provide any demonstrations at the beginning of practice for a particular skill? Did you provide any demonstrations during the practice of a skill? Why or why not? List specific examples from your video recording.
- What or who provided the demonstrations? Were these effective? Give specific examples from the video recording.
- When demonstrating, did you provide the whole skill, parts of the skill or both? Please provide specific examples.
- Did your athletes understand the demonstration? How did you determine whether they understood?
- What cue words or phrases (including imagery) are used with the demonstrations?
- How clear and concise was your explanation?
- How well did you accommodate different developmental levels of the athletes? How clear was your language for the athletes' ability levels?
- Were you able to offer the explanation simply and in minimal time? Why or why not?
- Did you elaborate on only one idea, or did you tend to go off on tangents? Explain.
- Was there anything you'd like to improve in your demonstrations or explanations? Explain why.

QUESTIONING

For athletes' learning to occur and for cognitive objectives to be met, it is important to ask meaningful questions. Often, coaching is ineffectual without a high level of questioning and clarifying to generate answers from the athletes. Athletes learn well and have higher retention rates if

154

they are given opportunities to work out for themselves what to do and how to do it (Hadfield, 1994). As part of becoming successful coaches, we need to learn to ask meaningful questions and apply effective questioning techniques at training sessions, to enhance athlete learning.

When coaches pose questions athletes will try hard to solve a problem if given the opportunity. The solution they generate is theirs and thus athletes will take ownership and remember, understand and apply the content more effectively than if they were told what to do, when and how to do it. Solving problems through coach questioning encourages high-level thinking where athletes explore, discover, create, and generally experiment with a variety of moving and tactical processes of a specific sport.

Sport and physical activity are superb ways to involve athletes in high-level thinking. Coaches need to trial their questioning strategies in each particular situation and adapt them to meet the purpose of the training session and athletes' needs and expectations. Coaches are often surprised and excited by how much athletes really do know and how easily they self-learn.

Implementing a questioning approach may be uncommon and, to some, may feel unnatural. Athletes may initially be surprised that they can have input into solving problems and thus their immediate response may not be favourable. Nevertheless, if questioning becomes part of a coach's repertoire and the coach focuses on questioning well, then athletes will enjoy solving problems and be successful.

Among advocates of a direct coaching approach, there is a perception that coaches who ask questions do not know the answers themselves. Indeed, coaches may find it difficult, and at times daunting, to design questions that generate high-level thinking. Yet to create situations where athletes learn best, by listening to their responses, then redirecting, prompting or probing for better or more complete answers, coaches must have an indepth understanding of the material they are asking about and the context in which it will be applied.

As Wayne Smith (rugby coach) suggested:

> … ensure that they [athletes] have fun and use questioning for them to become self-aware … I believe at the elite level, the questioning approach really tests your [the coach's] knowledge and in particular your eyes and technical nous.
>
> (Kidman, 2005, p. 204)

155

The following is a five-stage structured framework with important considerations in the questioning process that serves as a guideline to help coaches ask meaningful questions (see Table 7.1). The five steps of the framework (i.e., (a) prepare the question, (b) present the question, (c) encourage athlete responses, (d) process athlete responses, and (e) reflect on the questioning process) are discussed below.

Table 7.1 Framework for questioning

Stage 1: Prepare the question

- Identify the purpose
- Determine the content focus (according to athlete needs)
- Understand the cognitive, physical, social, and emotional levels of athletes
- Formulate the question for the athletes' levels of understanding

Stage 2: Present the question

- Indicate how athletes can respond (e.g., raise hands to answer)
- Ask the question, then step back and let athletes formulate answers
- Select athlete or athletes to answer

Stage 3: Encourage athlete responses

- Use wait time to determine whether to encourage responses
- Assist athlete(s) to respond (if necessary)
- Use athletes' cues to encourage responses

Stage 4: Process athlete responses

- Listen carefully
- Pause following athletes' responses
- Provide appropriate feedback (according to athletes' responses)
- Expand responses
- Encourage athlete reactions and questions

Stage 5: Reflect on the questioning process

- Analyse questions asked
- Reflect on which athletes responded and how
- Evaluate athlete response patterns
- Examine coach and athlete reactions

Adapted for coaches from Walsh & Sattes (2005)

Stage 1: Prepare the question

Formulating meaningful questions is a key element in establishing a great questioning environment (Walsh & Sattes, 2005). Planning the questions for the training session is the most important step, especially if questioning is a new part of your coaching repertoire. Wayne Smith (rugby coach) encouraged such planning:

> On my practice plan, I have questions, general questions that I would be asking them. Like the decision, where I saw [someone] in an attacking situation that didn't pass the ball, 'What did you do, what did you see, why didn't you pass it?' – basically to get feedback and ensure they were developing self-awareness about skill execution and tactical understanding.
>
> (Kidman, 2005, p. 194)

To plan meaningful, clear, and coherent questions, a coach:

■ considers the nature of the content to be mastered and the athletes' readiness to contribute;
■ rehearses the questions for the next training session by writing them down;
■ ensures there is a variety of questions;
■ plans the questions to lead systematically to a planned answer (and knows the answer);
■ formulates questions appropriate to the athletes' levels of learning (e.g., 'What flight angle will be most appropriate to get the ball through the goal post?' may not suit young athletes);
■ practises by reading the questions aloud.

For example, a coach's goal may be for the athletes to learn the footwork involved in tenpin bowling. The coach would like the athletes to find out what the steps might be. Before starting to question, the coach determines the number of steps to where the ball is released. Then the coach begins to create the questions. The first question might be, 'As a right-handed bowler, if you were to release the ball at the boundary line, which foot would have to be in front?' Once the athletes have worked out the answer, the coach might ask, 'How many steps would it take to get to the line where you release the ball?' The next question might be, 'So if it takes three steps to the release line, what should your foot position be at the start?' The athletes will give many different answers, but each of them will work

157

out the answer in their own way. By the end of the set of questions, athletes will have solved the problem about their footwork, with no direct instruction from the coach.

It is important to be flexible in both developing the questions and timing the questions. Among coaches who are new to questioning, it is common to ask the planned questions but not to move beyond those questions in the training session. The real art of questioning is to read the athletes, look at what is happening, and ask relevant questions when the athletes are ready or need to solve a problem. For example, coaches will plan general questions, then in training formulate further meaningful questions based on the situation as they read it.

Low-order and high-order questions

The goals of effective questioning include actively involving athletes in the learning process, and enhancing their task mastery and conceptual understanding. Another goal is to promote both simple (low-order) and complex (high-order) thinking (Sadker & Sadker, 1986). These two forms of thinking require different types of questions.

When athletes need to remember specific ideas or concepts, simple or low-order questions are appropriate. These questions serve as reminder cues that might be important to a learning sequence. Low-order questions are often 'what' or 'where' questions asked during drills. Low-order questions are factual, generally with only one possible answer. Examples of low-order questions used in coaching are:

- 'What part of the foot do you use to kick a goal?'
- 'Where should you aim when shooting in basketball?'
- 'What is the lunge in fencing?'
- 'How many points is a try?'

Research indicates that coaches tend to use low-order questions and certainly in some instances low-order questions are appropriate (Walsh & Sattes, 2010). Coaches, however, should strive to ask high-order questions to extend athletes' opportunities to self-evaluate and make informed decisions.

158

High-order questions require abstract or higher-level thinking processes. These questions challenge athletes to apply, analyse, synthesise, evaluate, and create knowledge (Anderson & Krathwohl, 2001). They are generally suitable for analysing tactics and complex skills. 'Why' and 'how' questions enhance athletes' abilities to make decisions. Although both children and elite athletes respond well to high-order questions, it is advantageous for coaches to create the questions according to the athletes' developmental needs. Designing high-order questions and a questioning sequence is appropriate when encouraging independent learning, where athletes are required to think in greater depth about the subject matter or context and can search for multiple answers. Examples of high-order questions in sport settings include:

■ What did you notice about the balance of people on that side of the court?
■ How many different ways could you get past the defensive player?
■ What option might you use here?
■ Where should you open up after your pike dive?
■ What strategy might you use to get past a cyclist in front of you?

Tactical questioning and technique questioning are two specific kinds of high-order questions that can be helpful to a coach. Both strategies are detailed below, before consideration is given to a third strategy that forms a useful part of high-order questioning: movement responses.

TACTICAL QUESTIONING

Questions that call for decision making and problem solving with respect to the strategies of the competition are tactical questions. Prescriptive coaches often direct and decide on the competition plan. Yet unless athletes understand why the game plan exists and take ownership of it, coaches will find it difficult for athletes to accept and implement it. To increase tactical awareness and decision making, coaches should use high-order questions that allow athletes to create and develop their ideas.

In training, coaches can set up tactical situations as problem-solving exercises. They should ask 'how' and 'why' questions for athletes to solve tactical problems and enhance understanding. Examples of some useful questions might be, 'Given a three-on-two situation, where is the space? Why?' or 'How would you finish the race in the last 100 metres?' It is important for the athletes to perform the actual movement as they solve problems, seek solutions through practice, and try various alternatives, and thus build a better understanding of possible situations.

TECHNIQUE QUESTIONING

Formulating questions for athletes to become aware of their technique gives them purposeful feedback. Through this mechanism, coaches prompt athletes and compare their actions to an ideal model of performance. Hadfield (1994) introduced this method as the query theory (see Chapter 6), which involves coaches asking athletes questions about their technique (see box for Recent Research about using questioning for feedback). For example, a question such as 'What happened to your hips when you played the shot?' is based on the athlete's knowledge and understanding passed to their brains by their proprioceptive sensors. The purpose of the query theory is to increase kinaesthetic (body and sensory) awareness of appropriate technique execution so that athletes are able to make decisions about what strengths to keep and what weaknesses to fix (and how to fix them).

To aid athletes in learning technique, a coach asks 'what', 'where', 'why', and 'how' questions (e.g., 'What did your arms do when you released the ball?', 'Where was your head when the hockey stick contacted the ball?', 'Why is it important to have a follow-through?', 'How did your legs move to complete the handspring?'). Such questions should help athletes become aware of their body movements in executing a skill. If athletes are still unaware of what their bodies are doing, the coach can reformulate questions (e.g., 'What did the demonstration show you about using your legs?', 'How did you use your legs?').

QUESTIONING THAT REPLACES DELAYED FEEDBACK CONTRIBUTES TO IMPROVED TECHNIQUE AND SUBSEQUENTLY TO A FASTER RACE TIME IN SWIMMING

Motor learning research highlights the effectiveness of augmented, immediate feedback for athlete performance, but many studies have failed to determine the effects on relatively permanent changes in performance over time. Chambers and Vickers argue that one of the possible reasons that previous research showed the effectiveness of extrinsic, constant feedback was because athletes may have cognitively relied on that constant, external coach information. Over the long term, however, athletes do not process the information, only respond to it.

The effects of a coaching intervention involving bandwidth feedback and questioning (BF-Q) on competitive swim times, practice swim times and technique were determined for competitive youth swimmers. Twenty-four swimmers (with one to three years' experience, ages 14–17) and two coaches volunteered for this study. Control and BF-Q groups were created and swimmers participated for a four-month season. Both groups had the same frequency and duration of swim training. After establishing baseline feedback and questioning behaviours (using videos) of the coaches, the BF-Q coach was given a two-hour instructional programme and a BF-Q booklet (designed by one of the authors). The control coach was put into a swimming instructional programme, but not trained in BF-Q. The intervention was six weeks out of the four-month swimming season. The period after the intervention was the post-transfer period. The swimmers were timed in 400m freestyle during practice and in a competitive event before, after, and post intervention. Their technique was also analysed in the same periods using a video coding system.

▼

161

Compared to the control group, the BF-Q group displayed greater gains in technique during the intervention period and greater improvement in competitive time during the post-transfer period. The long-term, positive effects of questioning were evident from the study. Swimmers who had the BF-Q coach took more responsibility for and awareness of their learning. Chambers and Vickers also claimed that the research supported the enhancement of coach–athlete relationships. Coaches who use questioning methods may have the power to effect positive advances in performance and overall development of athletes.

Source: Chambers, K.L. & Vickers, J.N. (2006). Effects of bandwidth feedback and questioning on the performance of competitive swimmers. *The Sport Psychologist*, 20, 184–197.

ACTIVITY

Think of a skill in your sport that your athletes could discover themselves. Write the answer at the bottom of this activity and plan your questions to arrive systematically at the answer you have determined. The number of questions will vary, so use the outline below only as a guide.

Questions:

1 _____

2 _____

3 _____

4 _____

5 _____

Answer (skill or part of skill): _____

_____

_____

162

After planning the questions, read them out loud and determine whether they are clear and appropriate to the athletes' levels of learning. Come to training prepared – know what the answers are, formulate the questions at the levels of the athletes, and ensure the questions are clear and coherent. After implementing the questioning strategy, coaches should evaluate the lesson (see Self-reflection on questioning, p. 172) to help improve questioning skills.

Next the athletes execute the technique using their knowledge and kinaesthetic awareness. The coach should allow the athletes to experience the technique several times before asking another question. The purpose of such sequences is to enable the athletes to become self-aware of the technique and to take responsibility for making decisions. When they are performing the technique in a competition, the athletes will understand how to perform it and when it feels right.

MOVEMENT RESPONSES

Although questioning has always been considered a mental strategy, athletes can learn much through problem solving and questioning using movement responses. A movement response requires an answer that involves a physical demonstration.

A typical example of a problem that requires movement response is, 'Show us how to control the ball most effectively', or 'Show me how to grip the racquet.' Even though the coach does not express either of these statements as a question, the athletes must provide answers by showing the coach what they understand.

Posing movement questions is an effective tool to enhance physical skill learning. In providing movement responses, athletes can identify faults or determine correct skill technique. Consistent with the query theory (also see Chapter 6), if athletes have input into correcting skill performance, with appropriate self-awareness, they tend to retain the information they have discovered. Through this mechanism, some athletes may determine the correction they need for a technique that their coach has been trying to correct in them for years.

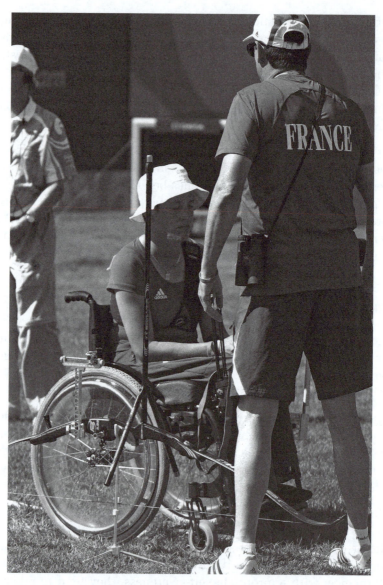

Figure 7.2 Coach, how about sitting at my level?

athlete development

Stage 2: Present the question

Coaches need to choose the moment of athlete readiness to ask questions. The ability to pick this moment is considered a key aspect of effective coaching. There is no formula for the right time to ask questions. The answer is 'it depends'. It depends on fatigue, coachable moments, individual differences such as intrinsic motivation, and whether the athletes are capable of solving the problem by themselves. A coach should read or analyse each situation to determine the athletes' needs to solve a problem at that time and in that situation. Frequently coaches jump in because they feel like they are not doing anything and need to advise. Often well-coached athletes can determine their own mistakes and fix them because of their own decision-making abilities and self-awareness. When an athlete makes a mistake and obviously knows it, there is nothing so stressful as being reminded of it by a significant other.

All athletes are aware. Coaches should allow them to determine their own needs and have faith in their abilities to solve problems. As René Deleplace (mentor to rugby coach Pierre Villepreux) said, 'There is no point in coaching unless the teaching you do helps the student to overtake you.'

The first strategy when presenting a question is to ensure that all athletes are quiet and listening and ready for the questioning sequence. To this end, a coach could get the athletes to make rules to encourage attention, for example by asking the question, 'How can we make sure everyone hears?' The athletes will take responsibility for ensuring the rule is followed if they have ownership of the rule.

Gain the athletes' attention

An important management strategy in questioning is to ensure that all athletes are quiet and listening to the questioning sequence. To this end, a coach may create rules to encourage attention. Useful examples of rules include, 'When one person is talking, everyone else listens' or 'Raise your hand and wait to be called on.' Notice that to contribute to a supportive environment, both rules contain positive words, rather than negative words such as 'don't'.

Once the coach has the attention of all athletes, everyone can hear the questions. The coach can then make appropriate eye contact, present the question and look for non-verbal signs of misunderstanding or

165

excitement among the athletes. At this stage, the coach can begin the planned segment of the coaching session using questioning strategies.

Leading and rhetorical questions

Coaches should avoid using leading and rhetorical questions. A leading question is one that a coach might ask that has the answer in it. For example, 'Don't you think you should have bent your knees there?' or 'If you had gone left, wouldn't you have beat the defence?' A leading question takes away the ownership from the athlete and insinuates that the coach does not believe in the athlete's response choice. The trust relationship is in jeopardy between coach and athlete when this happens.

A rhetorical question is one that coaches do not expect athletes to answer or that coaches answer themselves. An example is, 'Can you please pick up that baton?' The response might be, 'No, I can't ...' Other examples are when the coach asks 'Will you please sit down?' but is actually giving a direction, or asks 'What is the best way to pass to another player?', then gives the answer, encouraging the athletes to be passive.

Stage 3: Encourage athlete responses

It is important for coaches to allow athletes to think about questions and help and encourage them to answer. If athletes are having difficulty with the answer, a coach can redirect or rephrase a high-order question so they can think carefully about what has been asked. The coach should never give the answer itself, because it takes ownership of the problem-solving process away from the athletes. Be careful with the 'why' question. Depending on your tone when asking, athletes could become defensive in their responses and think you are criticising their execution of skill.

With high-order questions, there are no wrong answers because the athletes generally interpret the questions at their own levels of understanding. Coaches need to listen closely to the answers, interpret the significance, and use the athletes' answers to respond accordingly. Often athletes come up with answers that coaches may find useful to elaborate and apply within their game plans. By listening, coaches can learn much from their athletes.

One reason for gaining and maintaining athletes' attention is to provide wait time for athletes to consider their responses to the question. Increasing wait

166

time enables athletes to formulate better responses and encourages athletes to give longer answers because they have had the opportunity to think. When given this thinking time, athletes are more likely to respond and tend to volunteer better answers. They are better able to respond to high-order questions because they can speculate more. With longer wait time, athletes tend to ask more questions in turn. If they do not understand or they need more information, athletes feel they have been given an opportunity to clarify the question. With longer wait time, athletes exhibit more confidence in their comments and those athletes who may be relatively slow learners offer more questions and more responses.

Wait time is quite difficult for coaches when they are first learning to question. Many times, coaches tend to become impatient or answer their own questions when a wrong or incomplete answer is given. Counting three to five seconds before making any comment is a useful strategy to encourage wait time. Be careful not to call an athlete's name immediately after posing the question. Once you identify an athlete to answer the question, the other athletes tend to relax and stop thinking and become disengaged. Coaches will find that athletes benefit more from questioning when there is wait time than they do if the coach calls on them for immediate responses.

Reinforcement

As athletes offer solutions, either verbally or through a movement response, a coach should encourage their innovative ideas, no matter how silly or inadequate the coach may perceive those ideas to be. If athletes find no sincere support (either verbal or non-verbal) for answers, they will be less likely to respond next time they are questioned. The art of questioning is to encourage athletes to continue to try for a solution, even though they may appear to be a long way from it.

It is important to establish an environment in which athletes feel confident to volunteer responses. When a coach is deciding how to handle an inadequate answer, it can be difficult to determine whether the athlete is off task or deliberately trying to be silly. If the response is off task, the coach should refocus or ignore it, then reinforce the athlete's next attempt to respond. Sincere positive reinforcement will likely motivate athletes to respond enthusiastically to later questions. Different individuals respond to different types of reinforcement.

167

For effective reinforcement, a coach should:

- praise based on the athlete's answer – for example, 'That's an interesting answer, can you tell us why you said that?';
- praise with the focus on reinforcing the athlete's response;
- praise honestly and sincerely;
- give non-verbal reinforcement such as eye contact, thumbs up, smiling, nodding, and clapping hands – all extremely useful as forms of praise.

Stage 4: Process athlete responses

Coaches will notice that some athletes cannot wait to answer the questions while others prefer to remain anonymous in the background. The athletes who volunteer readily are probably the most confident in their skills and their cognitive abilities. Research in teaching suggests that teachers tend to neglect the students at the back. This tendency is found in sport settings as well. Coaches must make a conscious effort to include all members of the team/squad in problem solving.

Coaches should allow equal time for all athletes to contribute to the discussion. Through skilful directing and distributing of discussion, they will provide a fair environment where athletes can contribute equally. Directing questions to athletes in a non-threatening way can encourage those who may not be likely to participate. If a reluctant participant responds to a question, the coach should praise this answer and use the content of the response in further discussion.

Really listening and accepting athletes' responses to questioning and problem solving is essential for coaches to gain and maintain athletes' trust. Paying attention to the meaning of the athletes' answers will help coaches to formulate the next question and enable the athletes to take responsibility for the solution. As Whitmore (2002) reminded us, 'we are told to listen at school, not trained to or coached to' (p. 49).

Prompting

With prompting, coaches use cues to remind athletes of something that they have learned and help them to answer a question (Graham, 2008).

Examples are, 'What did you determine about using a fake on offence?' or 'How have you been putting the shuttlecock on the floor? Think about the racquet swing.'

It is important that, in giving cues, coaches do not give athletes the entire answer. The purpose of prompting is to encourage athletes to provide a response. Prompting can help them gain the confidence to answer the question.

Probing

Probing is a questioning strategy in which a coach asks follow-up questions so that athletes can extend, amplify, or refine their answers (Graham, 2008). Here the coach should avoid using 'uh-huh' or 'okay' because such comments show limited interest in athletes' responses.

The following is an example of an effective probing sequence.

Coach: How can we get the ball down the court?

Athlete: Dribble it.

Coach: Is there a way you can get it down faster? **[probe]**

Athlete: You could run faster.

Coach: That is a good answer. What other skill have we been learning to move the ball around? **[probe]**

Athlete: Passing.

Coach: Great. Now what is it about passing the ball that gets the ball down the court faster? **[probe]**

Athlete: When you pass the ball to a person, the speed of the ball is faster than when you dribble.

Coach: Now you are getting the idea. If the ball is faster when passing, what does that mean when you are being defended? **[probe]**

Athlete: The defender has less time to recover when you pass the ball to someone else. When you dribble, the ball is moved more slowly and therefore the defender has more time to catch up.

Probing, prompting, and reinforcing promote learning through extending current thought processes and encouraging athletes to respond.

Guided discovery of a new skill or technique

Many coaches believe that they must tell and show their athletes exactly how to perform a correct movement. In contrast, athletes learn skills, techniques, and tactics through guided discovery and through self-awareness (Metzler, 2005). Guided discovery involves coaches giving guidance with a series of meaningful questions about athletes' skills or tactics (while recognising that athletes are capable of participating in sport without being taught the perfect technique). Athletes then learn by discovering how to do the tactics or skills themselves, in a process similar to the query theory, which focuses on feedback after executing the skill or tactic, rather than learning a new skill or tactic.

Techniques or skills do not have to be taught explicitly because athletes at all levels can often figure out the approach needed. A good example is found by observing children in action in the playground, where they are very capable of discovering how to perform a game without being told by someone else.

To use guided discovery as a coaching tool, it is useful to plan the line of inquiry. The coach should first decide and plan the answer or ultimate skill or technique, then arrange the questions for the athletes to discover the answer. Athletes then provide demonstrations of the techniques or skills as they discover the solution.

This process is illustrated through the following example, in which athletes discover how to find the open space after a dribble in football.

Coach: In a three-on-three situation, what is the best way to get the ball to your teammate? Let's try it.

[Athletes pass all kinds of different ways.]

Coach: What happens if you pass the ball behind your teammate? Let's try it.

[Athletes pass to partners and aim everywhere. Some athletes have to turn around and run for the ball, some are going forward nicely.]

170

Coach: Now, if you want to make sure that your teammate goes forward (towards the goal), where do you want the pass to go?

Johnny: They should go behind the person.

Coach: Great, let's see how that works, Johnny. All go out in your threes and try to pass behind the person.

[The athletes try this approach.]

Coach: Did that work?

Athletes: [In unison] No!!

Coach: Why didn't it work?

Athletes: Because we had to keep coming backwards.

Coach: So how shall we do it this time?

Kirsten: We should pass it to the front of the player.

Coach: Great, let's try what Kirsten said.

From this step the coach might get the athletes to practise in a game, concentrating on passing forward or passing to the place where the athletes are headed. Once the athletes have mastered the concept, the coach might call them in again and try the same sort of discovery for passing and running to a space. An example might be, 'Now that we can pass it well, what do you think the player who just passed the ball should do?'

Notice that in the above example, the coach never provides an explanation or demonstration. Instead, the athletes figure out for themselves how to pass forward. With any method where athletes have to figure out how a technique or skill is performed, they will not only retain and understand that technique more fully, but also get more practice opportunities and take control of their own learning. Athletes tend to remember more because they are doing it, rather than watching a coach explain and demonstrate.

Step 5: Reflect on the questioning process

After implementing the questioning strategy, coaches should evaluate the session to improve their questioning skills. To this end, they may write down questions they used and determine their relevance, or get someone on the sideline to evaluate these questions.

Plan and implement a training session that includes the coaching strategy of questioning. After practising the questioning strategy, video a training session. Observe and analyse your use of questions from the video. Answer the following questions with regards to your questioning technique. Continue this practice or process until you are comfortable with using questioning skills.

EFFECTIVE QUESTIONING

Enjoy your questioning session, it will be rewarding. Please do not give up if the session does not work the first time; your athletes may not be accustomed to answering questions. The use of effective questioning will further enhance your coaching process and promote athlete learning.

- How clear and coherent were the questions that you asked your athletes?
- When asking questions, how did you gain the athletes' attention?
- How many seconds did you generally wait for an athlete response?
- Did all the athletes have a chance to answer questions? Why or why not?
- What reinforcement strategies did you use for athletes' responses? Were they effective? Why or why not?
- How well did you listen to and accept athlete responses?
- After listening to the answers, were you able to probe to extend the athletes' understanding? List examples of your probing questions and analyse them.
- List the questions that you asked during the session. How many were high-order questions and how many were low-order questions? Was the ratio effective? Why or why not?

Now that you have used questioning, how did it go? Were the athletes quite willing to solve the problems you posed? What were the athletes' reactions to becoming part of this session?

SUMMARY

1 Effective coaching strategies are essential to enhance athlete learning.
2 An effective demonstration is a coaching strategy that provides athletes with an image of what a skill might look like in a realistic situation.
3 To plan an effective demonstration, consider who will demonstrate what, and how and where the skill or technique will be demonstrated.
4 An explanation is a coaching strategy that is used directly by the coach to introduce, provide or expand on information to be learned. An explanation often accompanies a demonstration.
5 Coaches should check for athletes' understanding of a demonstration and/or explanation by asking specific questions about the information given, or watching how they execute the task.
6 Questioning is a coaching strategy that enhances athletes' learning by putting the learning into their hands.
7 Having a questioning framework guides coaches in their questioning techniques.
8 Questioning is an important coaching strategy. Educational research has shown that the real struggle is making the change from a directing to a questioning approach.
9 Low-order questions require athletes to remember specific ideas or concepts. Low-order questions generally have a specific answer.
10 High-order questions challenge athletes to apply, analyse, synthesise, evaluate, or create new knowledge. High-order questions have multiple answers.
11 Questioning in sport includes the use of movement responses that enable athletes to answer questions through physically demonstrating the answers.
12 Listening to and using athletes' responses enhances their ownership of the problem they are solving and their trust in the coach.
13 Guided discovery is a questioning strategy to guide athletes to answers. In guided discovery, you never give answers, the athletes discover them.

173

CHAPTER 8

ENHANCING PERFORMANCE WITH MENTAL SKILLS

This chapter covers

- What are mental skills?

- How to include mental skills training with physical training

- Developing a pre-competition routine

- Developing a competition plan

One of the primary roles of coaches is to help athletes improve their performances. When improvement occurs, athletes tend to find participation enjoyable. Improved performances also can lead to increased self-esteem, motivation, confidence, and belief in the training programme (including belief in the coach). Performance enhancement, however, is not just improving a personal best or an individual's top level of performance. A large part of performance enhancement is increasing the consistency of performance. Instead of having the quality of performances fluctuate, with high peaks but low troughs, athletes should be able to maintain a consistently high level of performance. Many aspects of performance enhancement relate to physical techniques and tactics that are specific for each sport, or even particular positions or events within the same sport. Coaches should check sport-specific sources for these contributions to performance. Physical fitness will also contribute to performance, but it is not the purpose of this book to explain exercise physiology. This chapter instead focuses on how mental skills can help both you and your athletes achieve better and more consistent performances.

174

WHAT ARE MENTAL SKILLS?

Few athletes dependably produce high-quality performances time after time. Various factors can affect performance consistency. For example, when physical training programmes are designed to have athletes peak at a particular point in time, physiological factors may prevent athletes from achieving their best during other phases of training. Many athletes will also have below par performances when ill or injured. But even taking these more obvious considerations into account, there are still many athletes (and coaches) who do not consistently perform at the levels they are capable of achieving. So why are people inconsistent in their performances? The following activity should help you answer this question.

ACTIVITY

For each of the situations in the following list, note whether you believe it is 'A' – something that contributes to the inconsistent performance of your athletes – and/or 'C' – something that contributes to your own inconsistent performance as coach.

☐ Thinking about work or study

☐ Being distracted by spectators

☐ Worrying about winning (thinking about the outcome)

☐ Being uncertain about own abilities (self-doubt)

☐ Worrying about the performance of teammates

☐ Being indecisive (changing your mind halfway through an action)

☐ Struggling with a new technique early on in a competition

☐ Having no plan

☐ Being too anxious

☐ Feeling too much pressure from others

☐ Thinking you have won

☐ Thinking the competition is a lost cause

☐ Thinking about the next round of competition (while still involved in the current round)

- [ ] Worrying about what others might think
- [ ] Being concerned about other people's performances
- [ ] Thinking about what someone said or did to you before competition
- [ ] Skipping the normal pre-competition routine
- [ ] Feeling like being somewhere else (mind wanders)
- [ ] Feeling burnt out
- [ ] Having unrealistic expectations
- [ ] Dwelling on mistakes
- [ ] Having doubts about physical preparation or equipment
- [ ] Falling in love
- [ ] Trying too hard
- [ ] Participating in a competition below your ability level
- [ ] Participating in a competition above your ability level
- [ ] Spacing out (visiting another planet)
- [ ] Thinking about a previous or existing injury
- [ ] Being self-conscious performing in front of others
- [ ] Disagreeing with officials
- [ ] Losing your temper
- [ ] Thinking about what it is you do not want to do
- [ ] Being distracted by the opposition
- [ ] Thinking about the weather, venue
- [ ] Having no reason for being there
- [ ] Realising the competition is running late
- [ ] Doing unexpectedly well
- [ ] Doing unexpectedly poorly
- [ ] Being bored between events/games
- [ ] Thinking about what effect the outcome of the competition might have

176

☐ Swearing at yourself

☐ Focusing on the media

☐ Having to reach preset criteria/having to qualify

☐ Performing in front of selectors

☐ Having ongoing arguments with others

☐ (Add your own) _____

Of the hundreds of athletes and coaches with whom we have worked, all of them have believed that many of the above statements related to them. Assuming that you are the same, and at least some of the situations listed in the above activity contribute to inconsistent or poor performances for either yourself or your athletes, the good news is that developing mental skills can help. How individuals react to the situations listed above relates to cognitive or behavioural factors that can be controlled with practice. The second section of this chapter will give examples of strategies that can be used to help control or cope with some of these situations.

Athletes generally state that between 40 and 90 per cent of their performance depends on psychological factors. Although most athletes agree that mental skills account for at least 50 per cent of performance, much less than 50 per cent of training time is spent on developing specific mental skills. Although we are not suggesting that you spend half of your training time on the development of mental skills, we do recommend that mental skills be incorporated into your training programme.

Mental skills tend to be ignored by coaches and athletes for four main reasons: (a) individuals do not know how to develop mental skills; (b) individuals believe that people either have the mental skills or they do not; (c) coaches don't think there is enough time to include anything else into training sessions; and (d) people feel there is something wrong with them if they try to work on mental skills (Weinberg & Gould, 2007). They may feel that admitting that their mental skills can be improved is confessing that they are mentally ill.

Mental skills help athletes and coaches perform to the best of their current levels of ability, help people enjoy their participation in sport, and can help athletes and coaches develop skills for use in situations other than sport. Mental skills are not designed as a treatment for individuals with clinical psychological issues.

Mental skills influence performance and, just like physical skills, they can be improved through practice. Mental skills do not take the place of physical skills and physical fitness, but they do contribute to the overall sporting experience. Just as there are numerous physical skills, there are diverse mental skills. Examples of some of the mental skills that successfully can be included in sporting programmes follow, with specific suggestions about how to develop the skills provided later in the chapter.

Concentration and attention

During training and competition both athletes and coaches should be focused on what is currently happening. Performance will not be optimal if individuals are worrying about the argument they had with someone before training or thinking about what they are going to have for dinner when they get home. Performers need to be in the present, in the here and now. Individuals need to decide what they should focus on and then develop plans accordingly. People can use cues to focus on technique, strategy, attitude, or effort. Developing concentration and attention skills helps people focus on important cues and ignore irrelevant information or distractions (Moran, 2010). A discussion of different attentional styles was presented in Chapter 3. The processes of developing cue words and controlling self-talk, skills that improve concentration and attention, are described later in this chapter.

Optimal activation

Individuals vary in their levels of activation, from sleep to hyperactivity. Athletes differ in their abilities to calm down when they are feeling uptight, and to pick themselves up when they are feeling flat. Performances can be less than optimal if activation or arousal levels are too high or too low. Under-activation most frequently occurs during training sessions (particularly when training is perceived to be irrelevant or boring) or when participating in a competition below one's ability level. Over-activation usually occurs when feeling anxious, pressured, or stressed. Over-activation in sport can result in choking, when performance just seems to disintegrate. Coaches are not immune to over-activation. Coaches can make poor decisions when anxious, pressured, or stressed.

178

There is no fixed optimal level of activation. The optimal level will vary with sports, positions, and individuals (Weinberg, 2010). Generally, a higher level of activation would be expected for someone weightlifting than for someone putting in golf. In rugby, kicking a goal would generally require a lower level of activation than would packing a scrum. Within a specific sport, position, or event, however, there will be individual differences. Some people perform their best when feeling laid back, relaxed, and calm. Others need to be highly activated to perform their best and some even need to feel angry. An analogy can be made with the expression 'having butterflies in your stomach'. For some people the optimal level of activation involves having no butterflies whatsoever. Others may like a few butterflies flitting around. Some people may feel optimally activated when they have butterflies in their stomach but they are flying in formation; in other words, the individual has the butterflies under control. A few may even prefer having bats to butterflies! Whatever the desired state, individuals can learn to use mental skills to achieve their own optimal levels of activation.

ACTIVITY

On a scale of 1 to 10, with 1 being sluggish as if you had just woken up and 10 being the most activated you have ever been in your life (the adrenalin really pumping), estimate where on the scale you need to be to perform your best in the following situations.

Score   *Situation*

☐   Threading a needle

☐   Running to catch a bus or train

☐   Throwing a ball as far as you can

☐   Being interviewed for a job or a promotion

☐   Explaining to an official why you disagree with a call or ruling

☐   Walking across a balance beam that is only a few centimetres off the ground

☐   Walking across a balance beam that is 10 metres off the ground

You probably had different answers for the above situations, because most people would require a significantly higher level of activation to run to catch a bus than they would to thread a needle. Check, however, your responses to the last two situations. Although you probably would tend to be more anxious 10 metres in the air than close to the ground, the skill (walking across a beam) is exactly the same in both situations. Therefore, the level of activation needed to optimally perform that skill should be the same. If you compared your scores to somebody else's you would probably discover some variation because of individual differences mentioned earlier. With specific exercises (discussed later in the chapter) and practice, athletes and coaches can learn to control their activation levels, ensuring that they are optimal for the individual and the situation.

Imagery

Imagery, sometimes called visualisation, is the ability of a person to mentally recreate objects, persons, skills, movements, and situations (Morris, 2010). Although there is not complete agreement on how imagery works, it is generally accepted that imagery provides a mental and physical blueprint of the performance. Basically, our minds cannot distinguish between a vivid image and the real thing. The more we do something, the easier it is to do. By using imagery, we can perform a skill correctly many times, so that when we physically perform the skill, our minds think something along the lines of, 'Well, I've been there and done that, so this should be pretty easy.'

Imagery is valuable because it is not physically fatiguing. Some individuals want to have the experience of having performed a particular skill perfectly immediately prior to competition. Instead of physically tiring themselves before competition by performing the physical skill over and over, athletes can use imagery as a more effective alternative.

Injured athletes can maintain their technique by mentally rehearsing skills (although unfortunately imagery cannot maintain fitness). Imagery can be practised anywhere, anytime, such as while sitting on a bus on the way to competition or while washing your hair. The organisation and coordination of movement take place in the brain. Imagery accelerates the learning process because, when we image a movement, the requisite organisation and coordination are still taking place.

180

Figure 8.1 An athlete imaging her dive

Imagery can be used to help us set goals, control emotions, develop confidence, improve concentration, practise physical skills mentally, and even heal injuries and control pain. (See box for Recent Research on the use of imagery in building, maintaining, and regaining confidence.) There are two aspects of imagery, however, that must be developed for it to be effective: vividness and control (Vealey & Greenleaf, 2010). The more vivid an image is, the more likely our brains are going to think the image is the real thing. A silent, unfocused, black and white image will not be as effective as an image using technicolour and surround sound. When we are involved in sporting situations, we are not just seeing things. All of our senses are involved. Therefore, when imaging, all the senses should be incorporated.

THE USE OF IMAGERY IN BUILDING, MAINTAINING AND REGAINING CONFIDENCE IN SPORT

There is general agreement that imagery use is related to increased confidence. How athletes use imagery, however, may be dependent on whether they are building (i.e., trying to establish, strengthen or increase confidence levels), maintaining (i.e., trying to keep a strong sense of confidence), or regaining confidence (i.e., trying to recover confidence after it has been lost). Ross-Steward and Short (2009) investigated the content and effectiveness of images athletes use to build, maintain, and regain confidence.

The participants were 142 North American intercollegiate athletes, primarily from team sports. They completed the Sport Imagery Questionnaire (SIQ) (Hall et al., 2005), which has five subscales: cognitive specific (CS; e.g., 'I can consistently control the image of a physical skill'), cognitive general (CG; e.g., 'I make up new plans/ strategies in my head'), motivation specific (MS; e.g., 'I image other athletes congratulating me on a good performance'), motivation general–arousal (MG–A; e.g., 'I image the emotions I feel while doing my sport') and motivation general–mastery (MG–M; e.g., 'I image giving 100 per cent'). The athletes completed the SIQ three times, each time focusing on a different subfunction of confidence (i.e., building, maintaining, regaining). For each question respondents indicated how often they used the image to enhance the subfunction of confidence, and how effective they thought the image was for building, maintaining, or regaining confidence.

The MG–M subscale was used the most and perceived to be the most effective, and the MS the least used and least effective, for all confidence subfunctions. The MS subscale focuses on images of goal-oriented behaviour (e.g., winning a championship), which intuitively we might think would be beneficial for confidence. Nevertheless, the MS subscale images are mostly outcome related, and not focused on process. As mentioned elsewhere in this book, athletes can only control the process of their own performances, and not the outcomes. Therefore, focusing on outcomes (even successful ones) doesn't appear to be an effective strategy for developing, maintaining, or regaining confidence.

182

The CS, MS, and MG–M subscales were used more for building confidence than for maintaining confidence, and more for maintaining than regaining confidence. The MG–A subscale was used most for maintaining confidence, but was perceived to be ineffective for all three confidence subfunctions. In addition to investigating subscale use, however, the authors also looked at the use of individual items. The MG–A subscale contains items related to anxiety and excitement (both components of arousal). It is not surprising that the items related to anxiety and stress were not used to help confidence, but that items about being excited were.

The subscales perceived to be most effective were used the most and those perceived to be least effective were used the least. The individual items perceived to be most effective were also used the most, but some of the individual images that were perceived to be the least effective were not used the least. The authors speculated as to why athletes might use images that they do not perceive to be effective. First, athletes who have had imagery training may have been instructed to use particular images. Second, athletes without imagery training may not have considered alternative images. Regardless, athletes (and coaches) may benefit from imagery training that considers the purposes of different images.

If coaches are considering having their athletes use imagery to build, maintain, or regain confidence, they should consider recommending 'I image giving 100 per cent' and 'I image my skills improving', because these images were considered to be the two most effective and were the most used for all three confidence subfunctions.

Source: Ross-Steward, L. & Short, S.E. (2009). The frequency and perceived effectiveness of images used to build, maintain, and regain confidence. *Journal of Applied Sport Psychology*, 21, S34–S47.

A vivid image by itself will not necessarily be effective. Images also need to be controlled. For example, Steve was a basketball player who could easily make free throws during training, but could not make a free throw to save his life during the pressure of competition. Steve had vivid imagery so he decided to image himself making free throws when the pressure was on. Although this strategy of using imagery was good in theory, in practice it did not work because Steve had no control over his imagery. In his images when he dribbled the ball before shooting, the ball would stick to the floor, never even giving him a chance to shoot. This lack of control only increased his anxiety when it came to shooting free throws in competition. Therefore, when using imagery with your athletes, it is important to help them develop vividness and control before expecting imagery to be a helpful tool.

Self-confidence and self-talk

Self-confidence is the realistic expectation individuals have about generally being successful, or the general faith in their abilities to perform (Vealey & Vernau, 2010). A person must, of course, be physically capable of performing the skills required (i.e., confidence alone will not mean you will be able to perform). Confidence is especially important in situations where adverse consequences are expected from a poor performance, for example competing in selection trials or elimination tournaments. Similar to activation levels, confidence levels can be detrimental if too low or too high. It is fairly obvious that if confidence levels are too low, athletes will doubt themselves, be hesitant, and generally perform poorly. Over-confidence, however, can also be a problem. Over-confidence is actually false confidence, and can lead people to have the attitude that, 'I'm so good I don't need to train or practise.'

The relationship between self-confidence and performance also can be considered as being circular or spiral, each component influencing the other. If you have a slightly off performance, you may begin to doubt yourself, which will contribute to another poor performance and so on. This downward spiral can be broken either by improving performance or improving self-confidence.

Confidence is related to anxiety as well as to performance. Anxiety and self-confidence have an inverse relationship. As confidence increases,

184

anxiety decreases. Similarly, as anxiety increases, confidence decreases. Techniques that help decrease anxiety also can serve to increase confidence.

Negative self-talk often enters the picture when self-confidence is taking a bit of a dive. Negative self-talk impairs performance and creates stress. Usually when we are having bad performances and feeling stressed, we are not enjoying ourselves. Realistic and constructive positive self-talk, on the other hand, can help us focus our attention and increase our confidence (Van Raalte, 2010). Once we control that little voice in our heads, we begin to control our self-confidence.

> **POINT TO PONDER**
>
> Nobody can make you feel inferior without your consent.
> (Eleanor Roosevelt)

Additional mental skills

Motivation can be developed and enhanced. Goal setting is a useful skill to help with the maintenance and enhancement of motivation (see Chapter 5). Mental techniques can also be developed to improve organisation and control skills such as communication (Chapter 5), time management (Chapter 10), team building (Chapter 3), overcoming jet lag, dealing with the media, conflict resolution, and psychological rehabilitation from injury. See Hanrahan and Andersen (2010) for additional information about these and other issues.

HOW TO INCLUDE MENTAL SKILLS TRAINING WITH PHYSICAL TRAINING

The main objective of developing mental skills is to help individuals control the controllable. Goals help control motivation levels. Relaxation and stress management skills help control activation levels. Controlling self-talk helps develop self-confidence and attentional focus. Imagery helps individuals control physical skills and emotions. Appropriate forms of concentration help control attention.

Many people waste an incredible amount of time stressing out about things they cannot control. They worry about what other people do and say, things that happened in the past, the weather, and an entire range of other matters that they cannot control. Instead of wasting our energy stressing about the uncontrollable, we would be much better off focusing our energy on the factors we can control.

Self-awareness

The first step towards knowing what skills need to be developed is self-awareness (see also Chapters 6 and 7). How do we know what to correct if we do not know what we are currently doing? Although there are multiple approaches to self-awareness, two will be addressed here. The first is using self-evaluation forms, and the second is individuals determining their own unique optimal mental states for peak performance.

In Chapter 1, a simple self-evaluation form was presented. Just as self-evaluation forms are beneficial for coaches, they are also beneficial for athletes. To help your athletes become aware of themselves (and also to help them remember some of the information you give them), it is useful to create a self-evaluation form for them to complete. Even young athletes can benefit from simple forms, for example using drawings of faces that range from a big grin to a big frown to evaluate how they are performing. Although young athletes may not differentiate between trying hard and performing well, rating their performances helps them become aware of what they are doing.

The skills, characteristics or elements that you include on a form serve as reminders of the points on which you want your athletes to focus. Experienced athletes can benefit from being involved in the creation of the form. The more advanced the athletes, the more detailed the form needs to be. In addition, rather than having responses to scales range from '1 = poor' to '5 = excellent', more precise information can be included. For example, if you were interested in having athletes rate their peripheral vision, you could have the rating scale range from '1 = tunnel vision, unaware of surroundings' to '5 = reads play, very aware'. The factors to be included on a self-evaluation form are only limited by your own and your athletes' imaginations. Examples of elements that could be included are:

186

- aspects of fitness (e.g., speed, strength, power, endurance, flexibility)
- sport-specific technical skills (e.g., blocking, serving, kicking)
- mental skills (e.g., confidence, concentration, activation control)
- social skills (e.g., leadership, team harmony, communication)
- game play (e.g., anticipation, decision making, sticking to the game plan).

Once again, the younger or more novice the athletes, the simpler the form needs to be. Only a few minutes should be needed to complete the forms. Most of the questions should involve circling a rating. Including a couple of open-ended questions, however, can be useful. For example, a question about what they want to remember for the next training session or competition may help them recall an important coaching point. Asking them to state one thing they did well that day can help them focus on the positive. When self-confidence is lagging, reading back over all the great things they have previously accomplished is uplifting.

ACTIVITY

What were the three things you most wanted your athletes to achieve or remember as a result of your most recent training session?

1

2

3

Now for each of those factors/elements, describe poor and good execution or performance.

Factor/Element	Poor	Good
Example: Batting placement	Found fielder	Found space
1		
2		
3		

Continuing this process, you can begin to create an athlete self-evaluation form for your sport. Figure 8.2 provides an example of a self-evaluation form for an experienced volleyball team.

Player: _____		Date: _____		Venue: _____

Skill	Elements	Key		Rating
Serving	Preparation	Rushed	Deliberate	1 2 3 4 5
	Accuracy	Frequent errors	Hit target	1 2 3 4 5
	Tactics	No plan	Selected options	1 2 3 4 5
	After serve	Too slow	Quickly in position	1 2 3 4 5
Reception	Anticipation	Not ready/late	Early position	1 2 3 4 5
	Footwork	Nil/clumsy	Smooth/balanced	1 2 3 4 5
	Arm position	Late preparation	Good platform	1 2 3 4 5
	Movement	Jerky/disjointed	Smooth/coordinated	1 2 3 4 5
	Touch	Tense/hard	Soft/smooth	1 2 3 4 5
	Accuracy	No control	Consistent to target	1 2 3 4 5
Setting	Footwork	Late/off balance	Under ball/balanced	1 2 3 4 5
	Body position	Back to net	Square to target	1 2 3 4 5
	Touch	Hard/tense	Soft/smooth	1 2 3 4 5
	Accuracy	Sprays sets	Consistent zone	1 2 3 4 5
	Set selection	Guess/no plan	Selected best option	1 2 3 4 5
Hitting	Contact point	Low	High	1 2 3 4 5
	Power	Weak	Strong	1 2 3 4 5
	Success rate	Lots of errors	Lots of kills	1 2 3 4 5
	Reading block	Not aware	Good vision	1 2 3 4 5
Blocking	Anticipation	No idea	Read play well	1 2 3 4 5
	Hands	Soft	Hard/thumbs up	1 2 3 4 5
	Penetration	Hands off net	Good reach	1 2 3 4 5
Defence	Attitude	Wimped out	Committed	1 2 3 4 5
	Anticipation	Guessed	Read play	1 2 3 4 5
	Court position	Out of position	In position	1 2 3 4 5
	Body position	Too high/on heels	Weight forward	1 2 3 4 5
Mental	Confidence	Easily intimidated	Believed in ability	1 2 3 4 5
		Tentative	Decisive	1 2 3 4 5
	Concentration	Easily distracted	Remained focused	1 2 3 4 5
	Determination	Gave up	Hung in there	1 2 3 4 5
	Team values	Ignored	Demonstrated	1 2 3 4 5

Keys to remember for next time: 1 _____
                                2 _____

Highlight: _____

Figure 8.2 Self-evaluation form for an experienced volleyball team

188

Providing a few minutes at the end of training sessions for athletes to complete self-evaluation forms indicates to your athletes that you believe it is an important activity. If you just ask them to complete the forms sometime before you see them next, they will perceive that you do not think the forms are important because you are not willing to use training time for their completion. In addition, the longer they wait to complete them, the less accurate their responses will be.

Another technique for increasing self-awareness is to help athletes determine how they need to be to perform their best (i.e., their optimal states). Do they need to be relaxed, excited, thinking about their technique, focused on the feeling of movement, or nervous? Thinking back to past performances can provide an estimation, but a more accurate understanding can be obtained by keeping diaries.

If you are just familiarising athletes with this concept, have them think about two past performances: one where they individually performed well and one when they did not perform as well as expected. Avoid selecting performances that were influenced by illness, injury, or major equipment failure. Then have them write down everything they can remember about what they were thinking and how they were feeling before and during each performance. Most athletes will discover that their thoughts and feelings were different for the two performances.

ACTIVITY

Think back over your performances as a coach. Avoiding situations when you may have been sick or injured, select a time when you think you performed well as a coach and another when you did not perform to your expectations. Write down a few facts that will remind you of the specific situations, for example where you were, when it was, or anything memorable that occurred. Then write down everything you can remember about what you were thinking or how you were feeling both before and during those two performances.

Positive experience	Negative experience
Description:	Description:
Thoughts and feelings:	Thoughts and feelings:

Write down any differences you find between the positive and negative performances in terms of what you were thinking and how you were feeling.

Most of us perform our best when we are focused on what it is we are doing and we are feeling confident, in control, and at our optimal levels of activation. Individual differences, however, do exist. Some people may perform poorly when feeling too confident because their overconfidence is really false confidence, such as the feeling that 'I'm so great I don't need to try.' As mentioned earlier in this chapter, some people need to feel relaxed and others need to feel nervous. Similarly, some individuals need to focus on specific aspects of technique or strategy, and others prefer focusing on the feeling of movement or looking at the big picture.

A more accurate reflection about thoughts and feelings can be obtained if they are recorded immediately after performances instead of days, weeks, or months after the fact. Whether recording the thoughts and feelings in a diary or recalling performances, the aim is to determine how each individual should be thinking and feeling to obtain consistently good performances. With practice, individuals can learn to control thoughts and feelings.

Setting goals

The goal-setting process (see Chapter 5) should not be a procedure that is entirely removed from training. If you are aware of your athletes' goals, you can try to incorporate some of their strategies for achieving their goals into the design of your training sessions. In addition, athletes can improve their concentration and levels of effort in training activities if they set specific goals for each session or even for specific activities. Coaches often set goals for their athletes during training by saying that a certain number of successful attempts need to be made before moving on to the next activity. Getting the athletes to set these goals themselves will make them more committed to the activity. You also can benefit from setting and working towards specific short-term goals about your own coaching behaviours during training sessions and competitions.

190

Watch 30 minutes of a video of one of your training sessions and answer the following questions:

- Which of your athletes' goals did you have in mind when planning this section of training?
- How did you refer to their goals during the session/how did you question your athletes about how activities related to their goals?
- How did you incorporate goal setting into any particular activities? Did you set the goals or did you allow your athletes to set the goals?
- What goals did you have for your own behaviour during this session? What other strategies could you use to achieve these goals?
- How might you better incorporate goal setting in your future training sessions?

Controlling activation

Earlier in this chapter you did an activity that asked you to rate your optimal level of activation for various activities. You used a scale of 1 to 10, with 1 being sluggish as if you had just woken up, and 10 being the most activated you have ever been in your life. Familiarise your athletes with the scale and get them to think about where on the scale they need to be for different technical skills or activities. Then, during training sessions (and competitions), you can periodically ask them where they are on the scale. If their ratings are lower or higher than they should be, they then can learn to raise or lower their activation levels.

There are many techniques that can be used to control activation levels (Williams, 2010). Space limitations do not allow for an indepth description of this area. Nevertheless, to give you some ideas about what can be done, examples of techniques for increasing and decreasing activation levels are provided.

Increasing activation

Athletes (and coaches) can use simple techniques to raise their activation levels. Under-activation can be a problem at training sessions, particularly if they are early in the morning or late in the day after a full day of study or work. Often just increasing activity levels helps wake people up and makes them feel more like training. Incorporating fun (and sometimes silly) games at the beginning of training can be an enjoyable way of increasing activity levels. For example, different versions of tag are often more engaging than simply running laps to warm up. Depending on where you train and the age of your athletes, you also might consider having team screams as a way of increasing activation. Having everyone yell at the top of their lungs for 15 to 20 seconds definitely wakes them up. Another option is playing fast-paced and relatively loud music at the beginning of training. You can use the privilege of selecting the music as part of your reward system. If individual athletes seem a bit slack in their attitudes towards training, reminding them of their goals can increase their intensity.

Decreasing activation

A multitude of relaxation methods exist. Abdominal breathing is a technique that can help with relaxation as well as concentration. The easiest way for you (and your athletes) to learn the technique is to lie down on your back with your legs uncrossed (if you have back trouble, put your feet and lower legs up on a chair). Place one hand on your stomach, just below your belly button, and then rest the other hand gently on top.

■ Inhale so that your stomach and hands rise as you breathe in.
■ Exhale so that your stomach and hands fall as you breathe out.
■ Try to spend the same amount of time breathing in as you do breathing out.
■ Try to make the transition between the two as natural as possible as if your breathing has a mind of its own.
■ If other thoughts come into your head, just let them float on through, and then refocus on your breathing.
■ Continue breathing in this manner, but now every time you exhale repeat the word 'relax' silently to yourself.
■ If other thoughts come into your head, refocus on your breathing and saying the word 'relax'.

You may want to replace the word 'relax' with a different concentration word or cue. Trevor, a coach, used the cue 'temper' to remind himself to keep his cool because he had the tendency to lose his patience when coaching.

athlete development

Yvonne, an athlete, used the word 'rhubarb'. Rhubarb has nothing to do with her sport, but there was a joke in her family about rhubarb and thinking about it made her relax and reminded her to have fun. Cherie, a volleyball player, used the cue 'thumbs up' when she was in front court to remind her about correct blocking technique. As you can see, the options are unlimited. The only requirement is that the cue is meaningful to the individual.

At first spend about six to 10 minutes on this exercise each day. Eventually decrease the time to three to five minutes. You should also change your position from lying down to sitting, to standing, and then eventually to a position that is relevant to your sport. For example, Jerry, a surfer, practised abdominal breathing using his cue word as if he were straddling his board. No matter what your sport is, you have to breathe while you participate. With the possible exception of underwater hockey, using breathing with a cue word can be applied at any time during training or competition.

ACTIVITY

To help your athletes discover cue words that might be useful, provide four words for each topic listed in Figure 8.3 that might be relevant for your sport.

Speed	fast	dash	quick	fly
Strength				
Timing				
Power				
Form				
Movement				
Rhythm				
Persistence				
Quality				
Concentration				
Emotion				
Other				

Figure 8.3 Cue words

Self-talk/Self-confidence

The cue words used to help control activation levels also help to control self-talk. That little voice in our heads cannot be reminding us of our past mistakes if we are engaging that voice in repeating cue words. The easiest way to control self-talk is to have something positive or constructive to think about.

In addition to cue words, we can also use affirmations to control our self-talk. Affirmations are just positive self-statements that can remind us of our strengths and abilities. Examples of affirmations include statements such as 'I am well prepared for this training session'; 'I am persistent, I always keep trying'; 'I am quick'; and 'I can adapt to changing conditions.' If we are thinking about what we are capable of doing, we cannot at the same time also be thinking about our weaknesses or doubts. Affirmations are only useful if we can agree, at least in part, with the statement. There is no point in saying something to yourself that you immediately identify as untrue. For this reason, it is imperative for individuals to create their own lists of affirmations. As a coach, you can create your own affirmations. After all, coaches need to be confident too. At the same time, encourage your athletes to write their own affirmations.

ACTIVITY

Write down 10 affirmations. If you have trouble thinking of positive statements, think back to the last time you did something that made you feel good about yourself or the times when others have complimented you. If you do not perform a particular behaviour 100 per cent of the time, you can still turn it into an affirmation because, if you have done something even once, you know you have the ability to do it again. For example, if you have tended to lose your temper in the past, but are learning to control it, you could use the affirmation 'I am capable of controlling my emotions.'

MY AFFIRMATIONS	
1	6
2	7
3	8
4	9
5	10

194

Now check the list you have written and ensure that all the statements are worded in the positive. For example, use 'I can control my emotions' instead of 'I don't lose my temper.' Also, check that all of the statements are about you – your characteristics, abilities, skills, or competencies. For this activity to be most effective, you should now make an audio recording of your statements. You may require four or five takes until your voice sounds convincing and believable. Some athletes prefer recording their statements over background music that they like to listen to before competition. The recording can then be played before competition or at times when a confidence boost is needed. Obviously, the recordings should always be the personal property of the individual for personal use rather than public address systems.

Applying strategies that have been discussed previously can also enhance self-confidence. For example, setting and achieving goals, attaining an optimal level of activation, and reviewing highlights, either from videos or from self-evaluation forms, can all strengthen self-confidence. Imagery also can help develop self-confidence.

Using imagery

Athletes can use imagery to see and feel themselves performing the way they want. Using imagery to remind themselves of previous good performances can enhance their confidence. As mentioned earlier in this chapter, imagery can also increase how quickly athletes learn new skills. Nevertheless, for imagery to be effective, it needs to be controlled.

You can help athletes control their imagery by developing imagery scripts. Writing (and then recording) scripts that indicate what a skill should feel like when being performed correctly allows athletes to follow your suggestions. Until athletes develop control of imagery, it is difficult for them to just close their eyes and instantly create appropriate images of skills or situations. When creating an imagery script, include as many of the senses as you can, be sure you word everything in the positive, and finish the script with a statement similar to 'and now repeat the image in normal time'. Images need to be repeated in normal time because it takes longer to describe the performance of a skill than it does to actually do it. If athletes only create images in slow motion as when following a script, they may end up performing that skill in slow motion as well.

ACTIVITY

Choose a physical skill or strategy from your sport that athletes sometimes have difficulty performing correctly. Write an imagery script for that skill. It is useful to get feedback about your script from others who are familiar with your sport. Refining and revising scripts as well as adding to your repertoire can be an ongoing process.

Once your athletes have used a couple of your scripts, you can then get them to write their own scripts. In addition to using imagery scripts, you also can incorporate imagery into your training sessions by having your athletes create 'instant replays'. When athletes perform a skill correctly, have them stop and recreate in their minds exactly what they just did by focusing on the feel of the correct performance and instantly replaying it in their minds. It is as if they are making videos of the performances that they can then take out and play whenever they want. Without instant replays, asking athletes to remember how they performed skills the previous week is usually ineffective. Athletes often forget what they did differently to improve their skills. By using instant replays, even if they do not understand exactly what it is that they changed, they can remind themselves of the feelings of correct performances and increase the chances of repeating those correct performances.

Concentration/Attention

Some ideas for improving attention were presented in Chapter 3. The cue words discussed in this chapter, in addition to helping with optimal activation and self-talk, help individuals focus on relevant aspects of performance. Cues relating to technique, form, timing, or concentration help athletes focus on what it is they need to do to perform effectively.

Figure 8.4 Focused attention is imperative for good performance in sport

Another simple exercise that can easily be incorporated into training is 'Past, Present, Future'. This exercise involves calling out once or twice a session, 'Past, present, or future?' The idea is for individuals to stop right then and determine whether they were thinking about the past, the present, or the future. Ideally, athletes should spend the majority of training (and competition) thinking about the present, what they are actually doing at that point in time. Unfortunately, some athletes get less out of training because they are thinking about the past (the mistake they made 10 minutes ago, or the argument they had with a friend before training), or the future (what they are going to have to eat when they get home or an assignment they need to complete). The use of Past, Present, Future increases athletes' awareness of when they stray from the present, the first step towards spending more time in the here and now.

Simulations

Simulating competition conditions during training is an excellent method of preparing athletes mentally as well as physically (Vealey & Vernau, 2010). It is a great way of integrating mental and physical skills. The constraints approach described in Chapter 6 introduced the idea of using simulations when applying environment constraints for learning. Simulations can also be used to familiarise athletes with the use of each skill in different situations. Examples of simulations are:

- simulating a noisy crowd by playing a recording of crowd noise at training;
- simulating rainy conditions by training with the hose on or in the sprinklers, and/or using balls from a bucket of water;
- simulating competition times by training at the same time the athletes will be competing (e.g., late at night or early in the morning);
- simulating competition surfaces by training on a variety of surfaces;
- simulating competitive situations by practising coming from behind. Similarly, it can be useful to practise situations where the athletes are well in front, or where the competition is even;
- simulating specific offensive or defensive situations.

ACTIVITY

Plan how you could introduce three different types of simulations in training:

1
2
3

Although coaches should simulate competition conditions during training, in some respects the opposite should happen during competitions. Athletes usually feel confident and comfortable during training sessions. Therefore, when athletes can feel that the skills and circumstances of competition are similar to those of training, they tend to be relaxed and perform better. For example, when shooting a free throw in basketball in the final moments of a close game, athletes will usually benefit from reminding themselves that they have performed the exact same action thousands of times in training.

198

The simplest method to ensure that athletes approach performance in competition the same way as they do in training is to help them develop mental plans. Experienced, high-performance athletes have a consistent base to their performances and behaviours. They use well-learned and consistent routines that they execute each and every time they train. If athletes want to produce consistent, high-quality performances every time they compete, they need to have a consistent base from which to perform. This base includes consistency in technique, fitness, and psychological, or behavioural routines.

If athletes have a consistent base from which to perform, they feel confident and maintain control of timing, concentration, thought processes, mental rehearsal, reactions to pressure, and emotional states. If something happens that has the potential to distract their preparation or concentration during performance, they will be more likely to recover quickly and refocus if they have good mental plans. Well-prepared athletes find it easy to maintain focus on task-relevant, positive aspects of performance because they have a plan to guide them. Mental plans include both a pre-competition routine and a competition plan.

DEVELOPING A PRE-COMPETITION ROUTINE

Pre-competition routines strengthen feelings of being prepared and therefore increase athletes' confidence. Prior to competition, athletes and coaches should avoid self-defeating thoughts that tend to lead to worry, poor confidence, interference with concentration and less enjoyment. Pre-competition routines help athletes and coaches enter desirable pre-event feelings, activation levels, and foci of attention (Lidor, 2010).

As the coach, you can help athletes to create their own pre-competition routines by providing a basic structure that they then edit to suit their individual requirements. A pre-competition routine will include elements of both physical and psychological warm-up. Most people are familiar with aspects of physical warm-up, but unaware of what a psychological warm-up might entail.

A psychological warm-up usually includes a combination of structured self-talk and imagery, sometimes with the addition of music. Self-talk should take the form of realistic positive self-suggestions such as reminders of preparation, readiness, ability, adaptability, commitment, and intensity.

LEEDS TRINITY UNIVERSITY

Imagery can be calming or activating (depending on the required level of activation) and typically includes reminders of the competition plan, past personal bests, or good training sessions, and the feeling of executing the first few moves perfectly. Music is sometimes included as part of a psychological warm-up because certain songs may help create the desired pre-competition state of mind.

The final element of a pre-competition routine is a pre-start focus (the focus of attention just before the start of competition). The pre-start focus can include a brief reminder of the competition plan, final adjustment of the activation level, and the focus on the first few movements. The pre-start focus should also help the athlete be completely engaged in the present rather than thinking about the past or worrying about the future.

When athletes create pre-competition routines they can draw upon the feelings and thoughts that served them best in the past. An example of a generic pre-competition routine follows:

- Arrive at venue XX minutes before the start
- Check equipment
- Begin stretching and warm-up
- Think happy, relaxed thoughts
- Positively image upcoming performance
- Listen to coach's brief comments (no new information)
- Apply these comments to imagery and/or self-talk
- Engage in heavier physical preparation
- Use more imagery if needed
- Engage in quicker physical activity
- Ready self for the start – think of opening skills
- Cue word for the first skill.

ACTIVITY

Help your athletes create a blueprint that they can use to develop a pre-competition routine. If you coach young children or novices, the routine should be fairly simple. If you coach older or more experienced athletes you can make the routine more complex.

Having a structured pre-competition routine is only part of the mental planning required to produce consistent performances. Being properly

200

prepared for competition just gets athletes started. They also need to be able to maintain their focus during competition. A competition plan is the second facet of mental plans.

DEVELOPING A COMPETITION PLAN

A competition plan should help athletes focus on the most appropriate cues during the competition. The plan should also help athletes get back on track if they are distracted, make an error, or their attention drifts. Basically, competition plans are a compilation of cue words. The type of sport will, in part, determine the make-up of the plan.

For team sports such as rugby, football, or hockey, the competition focus plan should break down the sport into specific skills or critical situations. For example, there can be a team strategy about what to focus on just after the opposition has scored. Short races or routines such as those involved in sprinting, throwing, diving or gymnastics can involve sequential checkpoints that remind the athletes of specific technical cues (see Mallett & Hanrahan, 1997). Long events such as marathons can have general cues or reminders that can be used throughout the event whenever athletes need to maintain focus. For example, cues relating to technique, activation, or self-encouragement could be used when experiencing signs of fatigue, approaching a big hill, or after being passed.

The specific cues used in a competition focus plan will depend on the athletes' personalities, their levels of performance, their experiences, and the sport itself. When creating a plan, athletes need to decide how they want to feel, focus, and function during each phase or segment of competition. Words and phrases that appear in the self-evaluation forms you and/or your athletes created, as well as the activities earlier in this chapter regarding cue words and affirmations, can all be sources of cues for competition plans.

Two examples of competition plans are provided in Figure 8.5. Note how they can be sequential or situational. In addition, cue phrases that initially are lengthy can be shortened over time and continue to retain their full meaning.

100m sprint (track)

Segment	Cue	Purpose
0–30m	push	acceleration phase
60–60m	heel	maximum velocity stage
60–100m	claw	speed endurance phase

Volleyball

Situation or skill	Cue	Shortened cue
Serving	take your time	time
Receiving serve	want to be served to	want it
Setting	make position	position
Hitting	high elbow	elbow
Blocking	thumbs up	thumbs
Back court	on toes, weight forward	toes
Other team scored	ready for next serve	ready

Figure 8.5 Competition plan examples

ACTIVITY

Create a draft competition plan that could be used as an example for your athletes. Although individual athletes should alter the plan to suit their own idiosyncrasies, using cues that are personally meaningful, a draft plan can provide them with a starting point.

Situation or skill	Cue	Shortened cue

Once competition plans are developed, verbally reminding athletes of cues during competition is usually much more useful than providing a long-winded explanation of what the athletes should be doing. The shortened cues also can be laminated on cards that can be placed where they will be seen as regular reminders.

Routines and plans are not only for athletes. Coaches can benefit from having pre-competition routines and competition plans. For example, a tennis coach might have the following pre-competition routine:

- Choose a team space (claim an area for a team base)
- Verify opponents, courts, and times
- Check on practice courts (if available) and organise times
- Check that the players are happy and starting their own pre-competition routines
- Timetable pre-match talks at times that suit the players
- Hold pre-match talks and/or warm-ups.

SUMMARY

1 Mental skills can help athletes and coaches achieve consistently good performances.
2 Mental skills not only aid performance enhancement, they also help people enjoy their participation in sport and can be useful in many situations outside of sport.
3 Mental skills require practice.
4 Athletes need to learn how to focus on important cues and ignore irrelevant information or distractions.
5 Performance can be less than optimal if activation levels are too high or too low.
6 Imagery needs to be vivid and controlled to be effective.
7 Realistic and constructive positive self-talk can help focus attention and increase confidence.
8 The main point of mental skills is to help individuals control the controllable.
9 Self-evaluation forms help athletes become self-aware and can serve as reminders of the points on which coaches want the athletes to focus.
10 Determining how one needs to be to perform one's best can be achieved by reflecting on past performances – both good and bad.

11 The first step of activation control is for individuals to determine their optimal levels of activation for different skills and activities.

12 Music, yelling, and active games can help athletes raise their activation levels. Abdominal breathing can be used to lower activation levels.

13 Cue words can help control activation levels and self-talk as well as help individuals focus on relevant aspects of performances.

14 Using imagery as a reminder of previous good performances can enhance confidence. You can help athletes control their imagery with the development of imagery scripts.

15 Simulating competition conditions during training is an excellent method of preparing athletes mentally as well as physically.

16 When athletes can feel that the skills and circumstances of competition are similar to those of training, they tend to be relaxed and perform well.

17 Mental plans, including pre-competition routines and competition plans, give athletes a consistent base from which to perform.

18 Pre-competition routines should help athletes obtain desirable pre-event feelings, activation levels, and foci of attention.

19 Competition plans should help athletes focus on the most appropriate cues during the competition and help them get back on track if they are distracted.

20 Verbally reminding athletes of cues from their competition plans is an effective coaching strategy.

PART 3

FACTORS INFLUENCING COACHING

CHAPTER 9

PARENTS

We include a chapter on parents because parents often are influential and provide a source of support and/or stress for junior athletes (and coaches). We often hear negative stories about what parents have and have not done on the sidelines during competitions and even during training, but there is also evidence of positive parental behaviours that provide support necessary for children to participate in sport (Blom & Drane, n.d.).

Children begin participating in organised sport as young as five years of age (Horn & Harris, 2002). At this young age, parents are pivotal in decisions about their children's participation. Not many five-year-olds ask their parents if they can play organised sport. Therefore, parents play a major role in allowing, encouraging, or preventing children playing sport.

A comment made in a 2003 BBC News article about parents' sideline behaviours (http://news.bbc.co.uk/1/hi/education/3039553.stm):

> I am a little-league American football coach … I've been coaching for three years, and each year, we have had to have a parent escorted from the premises for being too loud and boisterous. We even had a father come out on the field last year after a game and attempt to punch out a coach. It's ridiculous, because it upsets the coaches and the kids as well.
>
> (Alex, Nebraska, USA)

Incidents like the one described in 'Point to Ponder' above highlight the need to define parental roles and expectations within youth sports. Parents need to be aware that their behaviours can have a negative effect on children's participation in sport. Negative behaviours and comments on the sidelines can cause competitive stress, inhibit sport performance and cause children to drop out of sport (Scanlan & Lewthwaite, 1988). One course of action taken in some children's leagues has been to ban parents from spectating (Farrey, 2008). This option is unfortunate because parental support can have a positive influence on children participating in sport. Generally parental behaviour is not a problem when the children perform well, but parents are humans and sometimes tend to be critical. Parents may unintentionally discuss athletes' mistakes in a critical and demeaning, rather than positive, manner (see box for Recent Research on reasons for sideline rage at youth football games). Parents naturally want their children to succeed, and may become emotionally involved in a harmful way (Andersson, 2000). There is a problem when inappropriate actions of the parents begin to be accepted by the children and both children and parents have distorted perceptions of youth sporting experiences. Parental encouragement and support significantly enhance children's experiences in competitive sport. Parents have an important role in the success of children's participation in sport (Horn & Harris, 2002).

PARENTS AND SIDELINE RAGE

There has been much media exposure and anecdotal evidence of parents' aggressive and violent behaviours at youth sport events. This research project's purpose was to determine the motivational orientation of parents who were likely to demonstrate these behaviours. The authors used a motivational framework based on self-determination theory and analogous research on road rage to explore the behavioural nature of parents' spectatorship. Previous research about violence and aggression of fans has focused on collegiate and professional sports, therefore the authors purposely focused on children's football events.

Based on a motivational model of aggression and anger, the authors focused on two causality orientations, namely autonomy and control.

Autonomy orientation is described as 'regulating behavior based on interests and self-endorsed values' (p. 1444). A person who is autonomy oriented is likely to have high positive correlations with self-actualisation, self-esteem, and ego development. Control orientation involves 'orienting toward controls and directives concerning how one should behave' (p. 1444). A control-oriented individual is one who demonstrates feelings of stress and tension and public self-consciousness. Previous analogous research on road rage showed that a control-oriented individual tended to display more anger as a response to other drivers' actions than an autonomous-oriented person. The control-oriented individual was associated with aggressive driving patterns and obtained more traffic citations.

The authors used a number of psychometric measures, first to identify the orientation of the 340 parents sampled and then to determine whether the parents who were control oriented displayed more anger and aggressive behaviours (e.g., yelling, obscene language) towards others (including referees and children) than autonomy-oriented parents. Additional instruments measured situational motivation (feelings of pressure and ego defensiveness), parents' perceptions of pressure (prior to the match), parents' ego defensiveness (perceptions of notable incidents that provoked aggressive and anger behaviours), sport parent anger (causes of and intensity of anger), sport parent aggression (causes of and intensity of aggression), aggressive actions (self-reported responses that provoked behaviours), types of events (that caused anger or aggression), and the target of the parents' comments (e.g., child's teammate, son/daughter, referees).

The results showed that when parents had strong feelings of anger, the more aggressive their behaviours became. The main reason for these behaviours was ego defensiveness with daily pressures influencing their increased levels of anger. The authors found that control orientation significantly enhanced this ego defensiveness, while automony behaviours reduced parents' ego defensiveness. Therefore the results provide strong support that control-oriented parents are more likely to display anger and aggressive behaviours than autonomy-oriented parents.

Source: Goldstein, J.D. & Iso-Ahola, S.E. (2008). Determinants of parents' sideline-rage emotions and behaviors at youth soccer games. *Journal of Applied Social Psychology*, 38, 1442–1462.

One way to help parents enhance the environment and decrease competitive stress is for coaches to take responsibility for educating athletes' parents (Kidman et al., 1999). People who can best deal with the parents and the different situations in sport are the coaches. This chapter provides some insight as to how coaches can influence parental behaviour. The issue of parental behaviours and their influence on children will be discussed.

Figure 9.1 Critical parent

Guidelines on educating parents to be supportive and encouraging will be highlighted. One of the essential principles is to communicate effectively, and what better way than to hold a coach–parents meeting to discuss the team's philosophy and expectations for the season. Such a meeting is a great place to demonstrate and explain anecdotes about situations that have been observed, so parents may recognise and understand the effects of negative behaviours. Coaches can then ensure clear lines of communication throughout the season.

A COACH–PARENTS MEETING

A coach–parents meeting should be held at the beginning of the season and all parents should be encouraged to attend (Kidman & McKenzie, 1998). One of the first questions coaches may ask is, 'How do we get the parents of our team to this meeting?' Imagine a parent saying no to this request: 'Mummy, we are having a parents' meeting for our t-ball team next Monday night. It is going to be a sausage sizzle and the coach is going to provide games for us to play. She said I can't go unless I bring you, so please, please, can we go? I promised Joseph that I would come and he is bringing his skateboard.' The coach also can contact parents by phone to discuss the importance of the meeting or send home a special note. We all like to hear positive statements, so phone the parents and tell them something positive about their children. The objective here is to support the parents so they can support the coach. Of course there will always be parents who have genuine timetable conflicts and cannot attend. Keep these parents in the loop by providing a handout that summarises the main points of the meeting.

Benefits of a coach–parents meeting

There are many advantages to having such a meeting. Even if the coach has met these parents before on other teams or during previous seasons, a meeting to reinforce the team's philosophies and objectives is valuable. The biggest advantage is the establishment of clear lines of communication. By attending this meeting the parents will have the opportunity to speak with the coach. One of the major concerns expressed by parents is that they are not informed. They are generally quite keen to hear information about programmes in which their children are involved. At the meeting, the coach should help parents to understand the team rules and procedures. The team's expectations for training should be outlined in the meeting, so it is clear to the parents the commitment that is expected of each athlete. If the team has established rules and boundaries and the coach presents them at the meeting, the parents will be clear about team expectations. The understanding of team rules should reduce potential conflicts. The meeting also will provide an avenue for the coach to understand parents' concerns.

The meeting will allow the coach to present the team's objectives for the training season. The parents will get to know the coach better. The meeting provides an opportunity to discuss differing views so parents can make informed decisions. If the parents are not happy with the coach's approach to the team, then they can look for alternative teams. For example, if the purpose of the team is to develop skills and there is a parent who is more concerned with winning, communicate the rationale for the team's philosophy and methods that will be used to adhere to this philosophy.

The parents also should be informed about the sport and its potential risks. A coach–parents meeting is a golden opportunity for the coach to discuss safety and implications of wearing protective gear. This issue is major because coaches are responsible for athletes' safety. Parents should be informed of the sort of protective gear required and the consequences of athletes not having the gear. If the lack of protective gear can cause serious injury, the parents should be informed that their children will not participate if they are not supplied appropriately on the day. A coach's first concern should be the athletes' welfare.

The meeting is a great opportunity to inform parents about the sport and its process. It is an occasion for an explanation or demonstration of the sport itself, so parents have an understanding of the competition while watching. In addition, the coach can find out which parents will be able to help conduct season activities, fundraise, or provide other forms of support. Many of the parents will have special talents and skills to offer the team. For example, a parent may have an ability to raise funds for uniforms, or be able to make a mascot for the team. The meeting is a good opportunity to encourage the use of these skills to support the athletes.

It is also essential the coach discusses his or her expectations of parents on the sidelines – what is acceptable behaviour and what is not. Often just holding a meeting shows how much the coach cares about the children, but an emphasis on fair play and positive expectations helps to create a successful season on the sideline.

Conducting a coach–parents meeting

One of the first considerations is when and where the meeting should be held. Ideally, choose a time when most of the parents can attend. Ensure it is as close to the start of the season as possible because the sooner coaches communicate with parents, the sooner a positive, supportive environment can be created. Encourage all parents to attend. If you personally invite them, they are more likely to come.

Once the meeting is scheduled, then plan the meeting. Try not to make the meeting more than an hour long, because parents (and coaches) are busy people. The location of the meeting should be somewhere accessible, well-lit, temperate, and with enough space for the entire team to fit. Ensure there is a screen on which you can play video. A video of parents' behaviours, athletes' behaviours, or even the sport itself is quite useful when making a personal statement. It would be appropriate to prepare name tags or have icebreaker activities so the parents can get to know each other.

The athletes should attend the meeting if you are comfortable for them to do so. Sometimes having the athletes there can help remind parents of the team's expectations. Some coaches believe that having their athletes there may inhibit the communication with the parents. If you coach young athletes, it may be appropriate to organise a game or activity they can do while you are meeting with the parents. If the athletes are older, they should be included in the process. It is entirely up to each coach whether or not to include the athletes.

Agenda

What follows are only suggestions based on some experiences that have worked, but the crucial point is actually to conduct such a meeting. One of the first items for the meeting should be an introduction. Welcome the parents to the meeting and introduce yourself. The introduction should include a bit of background about your job and then information about your previous coaching and sporting experience. Next, briefly describe the team's coaching philosophy (see Chapter 2). To help prepare the philosophy use your reflective techniques and consider the following questions:

- Why do athletes participate in the sport you are coaching?
- How will athletes benefit from participating?
- What emphasis will the team place on winning, having fun, and helping the athletes to develop physically, cognitively, psychologically, and socially? (See Chapter 4 for objectives.)
- What do you expect from your athletes (e.g., commitment, effort)?
- What does the team expect from the parents (e.g., kind of support, encouragement)?

This section should last for about 10–15 minutes (just a guideline).

For the next item on the agenda, provide a demonstration of some sort. Providing a video of the children practising can be valuable. It allows the parents to see how their children are behaving and performing and what sorts of skills they are learning. Also, you would be surprised how many parents do not know about the sport their children play. Another useful video is one that shows parental behaviours on the sidelines. This video provides a background for discussion about coaches' expectations of parents. There are several commercially made videos that may be available; contact your regional sporting organisation. Another possibility is to get the athletes to provide a live demonstration about

214

some aspect of a skill or strategic move that they have been working on at training. This section should last for 15–20 minutes.

A useful item for the next section would be a discussion about the demonstration. If you do not provide a demonstration, then perhaps going straight into a discussion about aspects of parental behaviours and why children play sport would be useful. Remember that the main reasons that children play sport are to have fun, to be with friends, to learn and develop new skills, and to experience the thrills that sport offers (Ewing & Seefeldt, 2002). Also, remember that some of the reasons children drop out are lack of fun, lack of playing time, too many criticisms, mismatched competitions, and excessive anxiety (usually caused by adults who overemphasise winning; Murphy, 1999). Questions to use for discussion include:

- Why do you think your children are playing sport? Have they ever dropped out of a sport? If so, why?
- How important is winning to children?
- How important is winning to you as parents? (To help answer these last two questions, it might be useful to have a copy of a book or research article or a list of references for parents about children and winning (e.g., Smoll & Smith, 2002).)
- How important is having fun?
- How important is developing skills?
- What is the most important thing in youth sport?

The next item for this section may be to discuss what the roles of sport parents are. The roles of parents may not be clearly defined, but you could spark some ideas by mentioning some of the good qualities of sport parents, such as keeping winning in perspective, having healthy attitudes towards sport, being good role models, encouraging but not pressuring their children, knowing their children's goals and providing support to achieve those goals, helping their children to set realistic performance goals (see Chapter 5), and putting their children's development ahead of winning (Bigelow et al., 2001). Some questions for discussion are:

- What do you think are the most important aspects of being supporting parents?
- What are ways that parents put pressure on children without realising it?
- How do you think parents could provide a supportive environment for their children to achieve goals and have fun?

215

Another important issue to discuss is the coach's relationship with the parents. Stress open, honest communication, with parents supporting the coach when appropriate and talking to coaches about problems when necessary. Some questions for discussion are:

- What should the coach communicate to you – and what should you be communicating to the coach?
- What do you think a model coach–parent relationship should be like?
- What do you expect of your children's coach – and what do you think the coach should expect from you?

One of the major goals of this meeting is to help parents do what they can to make sport fun, safe, and a valuable experience for their children. Your goal as a coach is to point the parents in the right direction – by encouraging but not pushing their children, keeping winning in perspective, keeping the fun in sports, building the children's self-esteem, and providing emotional as well as routine support. What makes sport a valuable experience for children is closely connected to parents' understandings of why their children like to play sport and their roles as supporting parents (Farrey, 2008). Be the initiator of maintaining a healthy relationship with the parents, but parents also should be encouraged to maintain a healthy relationship with the coach. Some questions to discuss are:

- If you are unable to attend your children's sporting competitions, is your first question to them, 'Did you win?' or 'Did you have fun?'?
- What are the ways parents could make sport more fun for children?

This discussion section should last about 15–20 minutes.

Before opening the floor for questions and answers, inform the parents about the logistics of the sport, and the expectations of the athletes. Some topics to consider include: training times, length of a season, competition details, how you will decide who plays and who does not, how frequently the team will travel, expenses for the season, fundraising, required equipment, safety implications, rules of the team, how you will discipline athletes, and other specific details you may need to discuss.

Now that you have organised and facilitated this important meeting, allow the parents to ask further questions. Be prepared for anything here, but encourage the communication. If you cannot solve an issue that is raised, open it up for discussion to reiterate a willingness to communicate. Be sure to mention how the parents can contact you if they need to speak with you. Once questions have been answered, close the meeting. Re-emphasise some major points that have been made, such as maintaining a healthy sport perspective, encouraging but not pressuring children, and communicating effectively with the coach.

COMMUNICATION DURING THE SEASON

Communicating throughout the season is essential for maintaining or developing a good working rapport with the parents (Kidman & McKenzie, 1998). Regular newsletters, telephone calls, or texts to inform parents of current events are useful. Another possibility for regular communication with parents is to set up a website for the team. There will be issues that arise throughout the season – some that are expected, some that are unexpected – but coaches need to be prepared to deal with them. Parents have a right to know how their sons or daughters are performing or behaving. They have a right to know when the competitions are, what time training is, if there are any last-minute changes, if training or competitions have been cancelled, if their children are doing well, if their children are not doing so well, if there are injury concerns, or if the coach sees any changes that may be detrimental, such as signs of competitive stress. Parents and coaches should communicate for the betterment of the children throughout the season.

Parents want to know that their children are achieving something. They want to be reassured that their children are on track. Some parents want to be a part of the team more than others. By keeping the lines of communication open, coaches help to create positive, supportive parents. If parents know that you care about their children, they will be happy and more cooperative. An important communication process here is letting them know good things about their children. Be honest, but give them information about their children's improvements and efforts. Let them know that their children are valued members of the team or squad.

Parents want to see how their children perform. Many parents come along to the competitions to watch their children in action. When their children do not participate, they begin to wonder and question the reasons their children are involved in the sport. Many modified sports have rules about the amount of time that athletes compete, but some coaches cut this time to the bare minimum. It is disappointing to parents as well as the children to participate for the smallest amount of time allowed. Fun is participating and children participate for fun. Therefore, if coaches have chosen not to include certain children, they must be honest and let the parents (and the children) know why. If the parents know why and are still disappointed, sort out the confusion. If parents are still unhappy, do something about it, but try not to let the problem brew.

Parents also come along to competitions for social reasons. They enjoy meeting and socialising with their friends in the community. Part of the socialisation process is being able to speak with the coach, so make an extra attempt to get to know the parents' names. By showing your empathy and caring, parents will be more willing to help and provide much-needed support.

As described above, coaches should hold coach–parents meetings at the start of the season where they communicate their expectations of parents. Once parents understand the team's expectations, it is the coach's responsibility to be consistent and follow through with administering the expectations. An example of a team's expectations was demonstrated by a rugby team in New Zealand whose coach administered the rule for parents to be supportive and encouraging on the sideline. He created a poster that had parents' rules listed. When a parent steered away from the rule by saying negative things, the coach was there pointing to the rules and saying, 'Remember our policy.' It worked well.

There is also an example of a story that we received via email about a youth baseball coach who advocated the three-strike rule for the season. He said that if parents were abusive or negative on the sideline, he would give them a warning (one strike). If the negative behaviour occurred a second time, the parent was asked to leave the game (two strikes). If a third negative behaviour was exhibited during the season, the coach banned the parent from coming back (third strike, you're out). Although this response sounds extreme, the coach communicated his expectations to the parents and was consistent in adhering to the expectations. No one was kicked out, although several warnings were issued. Consistency is the key to successful communication.

Another technique that has been used successfully by coaches is to video-record inappropriate parental behaviour on the sidelines, and then invite the parents to view the video. In more than one instance parents have been shocked by their own behaviours. They sheepishly admit that they became so involved in the game or the score that they were not aware their actions or verbal comments were so extreme. By providing the mirror for parents to see themselves as others do (including their own children), the parents often modify their own behaviours without any additional intervention.

Determine two forms of communication you will use with parents this season. To complete this activity, list all key points you want to communicate (e.g., training times, equipment needs, expectations of athletes). After considering the pros and cons of both forms of communication, select one and actually develop it. For example, if you decide to create a website, create the website. If you decide to formulate an email newsletter, gather all the email addresses of the parents and write the first newsletter. Ensure you highlight a success or positive outcome within the season thus far.

After the communication goes to parents, ask them for feedback about the information given. Also, ask them for ideas of what to do the next time you communicate with the parents.

Guidelines to a successful coach–parents relationship

A positive, supportive coach–parents relationship is an important component of an ideal sporting environment for children. The following are some guidelines that might enhance this relationship:

- Clearly communicate the team's expectations to the parents.
- Be supportive and encouraging, yet firm with parents.
- Be clear on the parents' roles for the team or squad.
- Be firm and tough if parents get out of line. (Remember sport is for the benefit of the athletes.)
- Set performance guidelines for parents.
- Coach the parents to be positive on the sidelines.
- Maintain self-control by keeping your emotions in check. When the coach is out of control, the goals and objectives that have been set become impossible to achieve.
- Include parents in supportive roles (e.g., video-recording games, keeping stats).

- Avoid conflicts with parents because it is detrimental to the children.
- Remember that parental behaviour rarely changes quickly. Be patient, consistent, persistent, and firm.

PARENTS' EXPECTATIONS OF THEIR CHILDREN

One of the biggest reasons parents have a negative influence in sport is the pressure that they place on their children. Parents may have different ideas and expectations to their children regarding sport. Some parents may motivate their children to do well because they may feel that they missed out when they were young. Others gain glory from their children's successes. Most parents do not understand their own motivations for their children to participate. Some parents seem selfish, but this selfishness is usually unconscious. Parental ambitions sometimes exceed those of their children, to a point where children participate in a particular sport as a duty rather than a pleasure. These are the children who may drop out of sport, or become behaviour problems when they feel they have to attend when they don't want to be there.

Figure 9.2 Parents frequently focus on medals and trophies rather than fun or development

220

Parents have important roles in the success of children's participation in sport. Research indicates that children who experienced greater parental pressure to participate were more likely to have pre-competition stress (Horn & Harris, 2002). Children who feel their parents and coaches are satisfied with their performances and perceive positive adult involvement and interactions in the sport context experience greater enjoyment than their counterparts with fewer positive perceptions. Coaches should be aware of these pressures and look for warning signs. The following is a list of pressures that parents sometimes place on their children:

- *Guilt pressures* – Sometimes parents motivate their children to participate through guilt, which increases pressure on children. An example is when athletes are made to feel guilty when they are not doing well or do not achieve the goals of the parents. In this example, parents tend to provide pressure by saying, 'That isn't good enough, you need to work harder.'
- *Financial or investment pressure* – This pressure comes from parents who consistently declare to their children that they have sacrificed much to provide the financial support for their participation in sport. The children are made to feel responsible for the amount of time, money, and energy parents have invested so that they might succeed.
- *Sacrifice pressure* – Parents claim that they have given up their happiness and lives to help the children become the best athletes. For example, parents sometimes spend family holidays at sports tournaments.
- *Tension pressure* – Some parents incorrectly assume that pressure is good for their children, so they purposely pressure the children to force them to work harder. If children are not participating because they want to, or are only attempting to please their parents, additional pressure eventually tends to result in the children quitting the sport (sometimes through injury), and often a disintegration of the relationship between parents and children.
- *Living through their children pressure* – This pressure is placed on children by the parents who would like to have their children succeed in sports or skills in which the parents did not. These sorts of parents are ones who may not have been good, or not achieved a sporting goal and want their child to do it for them.
- *Family identity pressure* – This pressure comes from having a family of great athletes. There is pressure to be as good as or better than the family members who achieved in the past, or there is pressure to be as good as or better than siblings.

- *Self-worth pressure* – This pressure comes from parents who take away love and affection when certain goals are not achieved. An example is a mother saying to her child, 'I won't love you if you don't get a home run.' Self-esteem is essential to all human beings, so a parent can seriously damage a child by equating self-worth and performance in sport.

(Andersson, 2000)

This list of pressuring behaviours is provided so that you, as coaches, can look for signs from parents who are placing undue pressure on their children. To enhance safety and a positive sporting environment, it is essential to monitor the athletes and determine if there are excessive pressures being placed upon them. Some signs of competitive stress are irritability, tiredness, lethargy, and/or constant injury. If athletes have changes in personalities, attitudes or behaviours, competitive stress placed on them by parents may be the cause.

POINT TO PONDER

I've seen pushy parents in every sport and the results are generally bad. The kids that are pressured to play sport usually get sick of it and are disgusted with it for that reason. They decide to do something else.

(Arnold Palmer, PGA player)

POINT TO PONDER

Part of the problem with sport today is that the parents want the kids to be what they weren't and are trying to live through them. There's a difference between encouraging and standing behind versus pushing, and when the kids get old enough to make a choice, they give it away because they've been pushed so hard.

(Heather McKay, Australian squash player)

Should parents coach their own children?

We believe the answer to this question is most equivocally 'no'. There are several reasons why coaches should not coach their own children. The two most important are: (a) coaches could be seen to favour their own children

222

in managing behaviours, selecting teams, and other important factors in sport; and (b) coaches think that other people feel that they are favouring their own children and therefore compensate (to the detriment of their children) by providing less support for their children than for others.

Coaching your own children is a no-win situation. Communication has been cited as the major downfall. As we have mentioned throughout this book, it is important for coaches to communicate equitably with all athletes. If this communication with your own children is unsuccessful, you will fail in coaching and will probably disrupt your family life as well. Even if you do manage to be fair and equitable, others will probably perceive you as either biased towards your children or unfairly harsh with your children. There are more negative than positive experiences in stories we hear about parents coaching their own children. This book advocates that parents should not coach their own children for the sake of everyone on the team or squad, as well as for their own sons/daughters, their family life, and their own peace of mind.

POINT TO PONDER

Have you ever seen coaches give their own children extra playing time or attention even though others were better athletes or offered more team support? Alternatively, have you witnessed children being treated harshly because their parents as coaches were afraid of being seen to play favourites with their own children? How do you think these situations affect the children of the coaches? What about the other children?

SELF-REFLECTION

If you are considering coaching your own child or children, please reflect on the following questions to help you make an informed decision:

- What are the most important problems you can foresee in coaching your own child?
- What are the most likely conflicts?
- What can you do to avoid or solve these potential conflicts?
- What boundary or dual-role issues can you foresee (e.g., your child approaches you as a parent when you are in the role of coach)?

- Can you communicate with your child honestly? Sport may improve the quality of your relationship with your child, or it may destroy it.
- Does your child really want to participate? If so, do you want to coach your child because you feel you can best help your child accomplish his or her own dreams, or are you coaching your child to accomplish your own dreams?
- If you coach your own child, will your child come first?

Think carefully. You must be willing to accept your child as he or she is, no matter what the ability level or reasons for participating.

The points mentioned above also can be rephrased to apply to situations where you may be tempted to coach a sibling or partner. We only ask that you carefully consider if that course of action is the best for everyone involved (both on and off the field/court/track).

SUMMARY

1 Parents influence the decisions about their children's participation in sport.
2 A coach–parents meeting is a useful way to communicate the team's expectations to parents. The meeting should be carefully planned.
3 Coaches can have an influence on parents' behaviours on the sidelines.
4 Keeping the channels of communication open between coach and parents enhances the working relationship.
5 Some parents pressure their children through guilt when children do not meet their parents' expectations.
6 Some parents tend to increase pressure on their children through constant reminders of their sacrifices, both financial and time.
7 Some parents believe that pressure is good for their children and force their children to work beyond their capabilities or desires.
8 Some parents create pressure when they expect their children to follow in the footsteps of other family members who were great sport achievers.
9 Most parents are encouraging and supportive of their children's participation in sport.
10 Parents should not coach their own children.

CHAPTER 10

THE BALANCING ACT

Even with the multiple jobs that can become part of the coaching role (particularly when travelling), if the only responsibility we had in our lives was coaching we would probably all cope fairly easily. Similarly, coaching would be less stressful if we always had access to the specific facilities and equipment we needed when we wanted them. In this chapter we recognise that most, if not all, coaches have many demands placed on them at once and that venues and equipment are often shared with other teams, sports, or activities. Because coaches have a limited amount of time, they have to learn to balance the demands of family, schools, clubs, jobs, professional organisations, and friends.

EXTRA JOBS WHEN TRAVELLING WITH A TEAM

Coaches are often required to perform administrative or managerial functions when travelling with a team or being involved with a team during a weekend-long competition, because few coaches have managers to look after these tasks. These duties may include organising travel, equipment, alternative activities, food, and assorted other requirements.

Travel arrangements

Making individual athletes responsible for their own personal travel arrangements not only decreases opportunities for developing team cohesion that can be achieved when travelling or staying together as a unit, it can also result in athletes arriving at the wrong place or at the wrong time. Coaches may want to be involved in arrangements such as determining the condition of the vehicle used for travel (petrol, spare tyre, oil); knowing exactly where the competition venue is; verifying reservations for accommodation, cars, shuttles, or planes; providing maps; confirming departure and arrival times; and checking any required documentation such as registration forms, passports, or visas.

Equipment

It is important to check all equipment early enough to fix anything that might not be right. If travelling long distances it also can be worthwhile to find out in advance the location of relevant stores or repair shops at the intended destination, particularly if the sport involves equipment that can be damaged easily in transit. Assigning specific individuals to be responsible for different items such as drink bottles, uniforms, balls, first-aid supplies, or sunscreen can give athletes a sense of responsibility as well as help share the workload. Providing athletes with a checklist of equipment and personal gear they should bring increases the chances that nothing vital will be left behind. In some instances transporting equipment requires lots of advanced planning (e.g., pole vaulters can't take their equipment on all planes).

Filling time

Groups of excited young athletes can result in major headaches for the coach if careful consideration has not been given to what the athletes will do when they are not actually competing. Requiring participants to bring books, cards, or computer games is a useful first step. If large blocks of time need to be filled, it can be beneficial to establish in advance team activities that are fun but do not sap the athletes' energy. Check the venue and ask organisers to provide information about local attractions.

226

Older athletes also can benefit from guidelines regarding free time. There have been instances where experienced international competitors have made unwise decisions when filling time. For example, the seemingly relaxing activity of going to the beach can prove to be quite draining because of sun exposure.

Food

Prior to departing for longer-term competitions, the coach needs to establish what the meal arrangements will be. Age, experience, cooking facilities, and financial considerations will determine whether individual athletes will be responsible for supplying their own food, everyone will chip in to buy food and then take turns cooking, the team will eat out, a parent or manager will be full-time cook, or whether a combination of these methods will be used. When planning meals and snacks, remember to include water and other liquids as a form of rehydration. In addition, be sure you are aware of any food allergies or other dietary requirements of the team members. If you are planning to shop for food, it is useful to plan menus so that shopping can be made easier on the pocket as well as the shopper.

Being 10 people at once

Travelling with teams often requires coaches to fill a variety of roles at the same time. Only experience and practice can tell you which hat(s) to wear when, but you can be sure that multiple credentials will be required. These roles include (but are not limited to): mother, physiologist, nurse, technician, chauffeur, physiotherapist, psychologist, father, and friend. Be prepared for minimal sleep.

Given all of the demands that can be placed on coaches, time management is a prerequisite for survival, particularly when roles such as parent, partner, and employee are added to the mix.

Figure 10.1 So much to do and so little time

TIME MANAGEMENT

- Have you ever put off something important until later?
- Do you have trouble saying 'no' when people ask you to do things for them?
- Do you work best under pressure?
- Do you ever start new projects before finishing current ones?
- Do you find that you rarely have time to do the things you want to do?

If you answered 'yes' to one or more of these questions, you may have some trouble managing your time. The perception (whether actually true or not) that you do not have enough time to do everything you should is one of the most common sources of stress. When we do not accomplish everything we think we should, we often feel compromised, frustrated, and stressed.

A useful way to start evaluating your management of time is to discover first how you currently spend your time (Etzel & Monda, 2010). There are 168 hours in every week. Few people are able to make the most of all of this time on a regular basis.

ACTIVITY

Consider how you spend your time during an average week. In Weekly Timetable 1 (Figure 10.2), fill in your committed time. Be sure to include some sleep time as committed time. To be completely accurate with this task, actually record how you spend your time during one week, recording your activities as they happen. Be sure to pick a week that is fairly representative of your typical lifestyle.

Hours	Mon	Tues	Wed	Thurs	Fri	Sat	Sun
4–5 am							
5–6 am							
6–7 am							
7–8 am							
8–9 am							
9–10 am							
10–11 am							
11–12 am							
12–1 pm							
1–2 pm							
2–3 pm							
3–4 pm							
4–5 pm							
5–6 pm							
6–7 pm							
7–8 pm							
8–9 pm							
9–10 pm							
10–11 pm							
11–12 pm							
12–1 am							
1–2 am							
2–3 am							
3–4 am							

Figure 10.2 Weekly Timetable 1

When you have finished the first timetable, calculate how many hours of flexible or free time you have. Do you have time for relaxation? Is your life balanced? Circle the activities that cause you the most stress.

Now that you have some idea how you use your 168 hours each week, begin with a blank timetable (Weekly Timetable 2 in Figure 10.3) and block in the activities that you feel absolutely must be done every week. Once again, be sure to include time for sleeping. Once the committed time has

230

been scheduled, then allocate time for recreational activities and relaxation (Lakein, 1997b). If possible, try to have some relaxation time either before or after the activities that cause you the most stress. To some extent we are all restricted in the structure of timetables by work, family, training times, and the like. The idea is to create a timetable that allows for a balanced lifestyle. Try to adhere to this new schedule and determine if it is realistic.

Hours	Mon	Tues	Wed	Thurs	Fri	Sat	Sun
4–5 am							
5–6 am							
6–7 am							
7–8 am							
8–9 am							
9–10 am							
10–11 am							
11–12 am							
12–1 pm							
1–2 pm							
2–3 pm							
3–4 pm							
4–5 pm							
5–6 pm							
6–7 pm							
7–8 pm							
8–9 pm							
9–10 pm							
10–11 pm							
11–12 pm							
12–1 am							
1–2 am							
2–3 am							
3–4 am							

Figure 10.3 Weekly Timetable 2

After trialling your new schedule for a week, answer the following questions:

- How easy or difficult was it to stick to your new schedule?
- How well were you able to cope with stressful activities during the week?
- Is there anything you accidentally left out of your schedule that should be included?
- Was your relaxation time well placed?
- What changes do you think you should make to your schedule?
- Do you need to negotiate with others to make your schedule more balanced?
- Do you think you wasted much time during the week?

Time-wasting

All of us are capable of wasting time. We might waste time by watching TV, listening to music, talking on the phone, raiding the refrigerator, reading novels and magazines, taking naps, shopping, or having long baths or showers. These activities are not bad in themselves, but when coaches are feeling stressed because they have not accomplished everything they wanted and at the same time have spent hours doing some of the above, they should consider how they might be wasting time. Scheduling relaxation time is not wasting time; however, participating in relaxing activities when we should be doing other things could be considered wasting time.

Time-wasting also is an issue for athletes. Coaches with early morning training sessions (e.g., rowing, swimming) are probably familiar with lacklustre performances, bleary-eyed athletes and absenteeism that often result from athletes not going to bed early enough. Many athletes we have worked with blame their inability to turn off the television as a frequent source of late nights. So, using TV-watching as an example of time-wasting activities, let's consider some possible remedies. A drastic plan would be to sell or give away the television. More palatable alternatives include pre-selecting a limited number of hours of TV-watching by choosing programmes in the weekly TV guide, turning on music instead of the TV when walking in the front door, or just starting by having one TV-free night each week. This list of strategies is by no means exhaustive, but it does show how individuals should consider a number of different strategies when trying to overcome time-wasting.

232

List the two most common ways you waste time (meetings at work cannot be included in this list!). Do not include activities that are commitments you have with your job or your family. For each activity establish at least three alternative strategies you could use to help you curb that behaviour.

Time waster 1	Time waster 2
1	1
2	2
3	3

Procrastination

Procrastination is another way we manage to waste time. Procrastinating and putting things off, however, are not exactly the same thing. What distinguishes the two is the level of discomfort created. Procrastinating has a negative effect. If Carol procrastinates about watering her plants, they die (a definite negative effect). Similarly, if Kent procrastinates about cleaning the house, although no permanent negative consequences may result, there is still the negative effect of feeling guilty. The same activity (or rather non-activity) could be just putting something off for one person and procrastinating for another. Take, for example, the task of cleaning your windows at home. If you do not mind having dirty windows and the people you live with do not mind having dirty windows, failing to clean the windows is not an act of procrastination. If, however, you feel guilty when you have dirty windows or someone else criticises you for not cleaning the windows, then failing to clean them is an act of procrastination. Similarly, whether waiting to repair or replace specific sporting equipment is an act of procrastination is dependent on the potential negative effects of waiting. If there are feelings of guilt or harassment, or someone gets injured using the old equipment, then it is procrastination. People who procrastinate a lot are more likely to experience anxiety, distress, under-achievement, and illness than those who rarely procrastinate (Klassen et al., 2008).

One way to counteract procrastination is to set goals (Etzel & Monda, 2010). We discussed a goal-setting process in Chapter 5. This process can be used to help manage time, prevent distress, and complete those tasks that seem to hang over your head.

ACTIVITY

Think of an activity about which you procrastinate. Think of something that really bothers you because you have not done it. Some examples are completing a home project, getting your car serviced, making a dental appointment, getting a haircut, writing letters, paying, or getting insurance, taking a holiday, playing with the kids, having coffee with friends, cleaning the bathroom, or mowing the lawn.

Now, set a short-term, realistic, positive, controllable, and specific goal (see Chapter 5) regarding something you will do in the next week about the activity about which you procrastinate. Specify exactly when you will do it. If necessary, determine a number of strategies that could be used to help you achieve the goal. For added motivation to tackle this source of procrastination, tell a friend or a colleague your goal for this week. Ask them to check up on you to see that you have achieved it by the end of the week. Do it right now! If you are alone, email, text, or phone someone.

Source of procrastination:

Short-term goal:
When this will be achieved:
Strategies:

Mythical time

A common time management issue is the reliance on mythical time: the belief that as soon as the season is over, the house guests leave, the term finishes or a current project is completed, you will have all the time in the world to accomplish anything and everything you have been meaning to do. This mythical time never arrives. There is always another project, an unexpected development, or a competing activity that rushes in to fill the time. Few busy people ever experience a sustained period of inactivity. The lesson is to learn not to rely on this mythical time.

Making lists

Because we are unable to add hours to the day or days to the week, another useful technique to enhance time management is to create a 'To do' list. Some people feel they have so many things to do that they do not know where to start. Instead of sitting around feeling overwhelmed, it can be beneficial to create a 'To do' list and then establish priorities (Lakein, 1997a). Be careful with this technique, however, because some people take it to the extreme and end up wasting time by writing and rewriting lists. Used properly, this technique allows you to become decisive about time, overcome procrastination, and determine priorities.

ACTIVITY

1 Write a personal 'To do' list. Write for two or three minutes without censoring what you are writing.
2 Establish priorities for your list using As, Bs, and Cs (A = absolutely, positively must do; B = really should do; C = would be nice to do).
3 Prioritise the As using A1, A2, A3... (you can only have one A1).
4 On a fresh piece of paper write the A1 activity at the top, then write down all the activities you should do to achieve your A1 activity.
5 Go through the new list and prioritise them with As, Bs, and Cs.
6 Prioritise your new As using A1, A2...
7 *Do whatever your new A1 activity is.*

You may have noticed that little mention has been made of coaching so far in this section. Learning to manage your time better, however, can make you a less stressed coach. You will be less prone to stress-related illnesses, more relaxed and probably a lot happier overall if you are not stressed about how you are going to get everything done. You will probably also be a more patient and understanding coach.

Keep in mind that the time-management approaches mentioned in this chapter may also be useful for athletes. Few athletes only train for their sport. Most also have commitments with school, university, friends, family, and/or jobs. After completing the activities in this section, you should be able to help the athletes with the same process.

FACILITY AND EQUIPMENT MANAGEMENT

Because there are limited hours in a day but multiple demands to fill them, coaches need to manage or balance their time. Similarly, venues (and equipment) are in demand by many groups and activities and therefore need to be managed in a manner that allows balanced access (Fried, 2010). There is nothing worse than arriving to a sporting event and finding out that the secretary of the club has no key to the sporting shed and there is no way of getting the equipment out for the Saturday morning competition. So, what do you do? Panic? Send all the athletes and parents home? Or improvise? How many times have you been forced to improvise? What could you have done to prevent this from happening? Has it happened recently?

This section is about facility and equipment organisation and safety. Most coaches have an association with a sporting organisation, and need to function within its structure. It is important at the beginning of the season to organise training times and facilities. Approach your sport's organisation for equipment and facility bookings before the season starts. Some coaches meet their teams for the first time in the season and do not have enough equipment for everyone. Coaches often have a difficult time ensuring that athletes are on-task at training without the required equipment (see Chapter 4).

ACTIVITY

You are meeting your team/squad for the first time. List all the equipment you will need to coach for the year. Remember to include minor equipment such as witches' hats/cones, bibs, stopwatches, and anything else you need to organise activities or ensure your athletes are safe. An example is provided in Figure 10.4. A blank form is provided for you in Figure 10.5.

236

Equipment/facilities to be booked	Who do I need to contact/phone number	
Football field @ 4 pm, Tuesdays	R.U. Watching, Maintenance	555 1234
Football goals	Secretary, Joan Mackie	555 1111
Footballs (11)	Secretary, Joan Mackie	555 1111
Bibs	Local primary school	555 1212
Witches' hats/cones (12)	Local primary school	555 1212
Uniforms	Secretary, Joan Mackie	555 1111
Goalie gloves	Secretary, Joan Mackie	555 1111
Mouthguards, shin pads, football boots	Athletes are to arrange to get these	

Figure 10.4 A sample of equipment needs

Equipment/facilities to be booked	Who do I need to contact	Contact number or email

Figure 10.5 Your list of equipment needs

Sometimes the sporting organisation with which you are associated is not as well organised as you are. You will have to be proactive and take the first step to contact the people who can help you provide a safe and effective learning environment. It would be useful to attend your sport's administrative meetings and learn the way the organisation is managed and run. Promote your sporting organisation. There are too many coaches and parents who complain and are reactive to initiatives put forward by others, but never suggest or do anything constructive themselves. For the betterment of your team, be proactive and participate in club decisions. By being proactive, you will be able to find the best ways of providing effective training sessions for the athletes.

Safety first

People have become concerned about liability and negligence in coaching. Coaches are responsible for providing reasonable care and protection of the athletes against predictable risks inherent in the sport (Hackett & Hackett, 2004). If coaches fail to provide such care, they are considered to be negligent. If coaches have been negligent in their duties, then they are liable to anyone who is injured. It is important for coaches to consider the implications of their responsibilities or duties of care for the athletes. As part of those duties, they should ensure the equipment and facilities are safe for use.

ACTIVITY

For each of the following cases, indicate how you could have decreased the chances of the incident occurring.

CASE STUDY 1

You are coaching softball with a group of 12-year-olds for a local club. You would like to work on batting, so you have brought out all the bats to begin practising. You have asked the children to leave the bats where they are and you turn to go and get the rest of the equipment. When your back is turned, one of your players picks up a bat and begins swinging it. When swinging, a piece of the bat goes flying and hits another child in the head. The other child is rushed to the hospital with a suspected skull fracture. What are the possible implications for you as a coach?

CASE STUDY 2

You are coaching a senior team (A Grade) during a football match. It has been raining for three days and the ground is quite wet. You arrive at the game and notice huge mud puddles and a hole in the centre of the field. When the referee arrives, you ask her to have a good look at the field because you have noticed a big hole in the middle. The referee surveys the field and declares the field safe. Just before half time, one of the players from the other team steps in the hole and breaks her leg and is rushed to the hospital. What are the possible implications of this accident for you as a coach?

238

You are coaching a group of children in yachting. When you are out in the middle of the bay, one of the P Class boats breaks in half and sinks quickly to the bottom. As Matthew abandons the yacht, he hits his arm on the mast. His arm is broken and as you pick him out of the water you notice the injury. This is the first time that you did not check the boats before putting them in the water, but the club president indicated that he had checked all the boats. You assumed that he checked all the boats thoroughly and had no reason to question his judgement. What are the possible implications for you as a coach?

It is the coach's responsibility to provide athletes with as safe a facility as possible, with well-maintained equipment in proper condition for use (Olsen, 1996). Coaches are responsible for eliminating unsafe equipment and avoiding unsafe facilities. It is also their responsibility to inform the club or the facility manager when facilities and equipment are in need of repair or are inadequate. Coaches cannot guarantee safety (although they must take every step to do so), but they must provide and maintain facilities relatively free from injury-producing conditions. Most of the responsibility for keeping the area in which the athletes are participating safe belongs to the coach. The sport area should be inspected regularly and warnings given to athletes of potential hazards. Coaches should recommend to the sporting organisation changes required to potentially unsafe areas. If nothing has been done about a hazard that has been reported, coaches are responsible for protecting the area or piece of equipment. They can do so by not allowing athletes to use the facility or equipment, or by insisting on the use of protective gear to ensure safety.

Facilities

Facilities that are poorly maintained, improperly designed, contain defective equipment, or are eroded by weather pose risk to athletes. Some common injury causes are holes in the field, broken bottles on the grounds (not uncommon for facilities that have clubhouses attached), sharp objects that stick out into a participation area, or equipment that is not a permanent fixture. Some facilities are improperly designed. In some gyms the walls are too close to the participation area, or bars and other hanging equipment are in the way. Where defects are noticed, the sporting organisation should be advised and the equipment removed or protective devices put up to reduce the risk of injury (Fried, 2010). A coach has a partial responsibility to request upgrading or new facilities. Coaches should be aware of various funding schemes for which their clubs/schools or teams may be eligible to upgrade facilities and enhance safety.

Defective equipment in facilities is a common cause of injury. Basketball hoops can be improperly designed for dunking or football goals may not be permanent fixtures and can collapse. Defective equipment should be recorded and reported to the proper authorities. If the equipment is defective, do not allow athletes to use it.

Sometimes the weather can play havoc on facilities. Rain may create deep mud and holes in fields or slippery gym floors through wet shoes or leaky roofs. Athletes should not be allowed to use faulty facilities. Coaches should do as much as possible to reduce the risk, although it is impossible to entirely eliminate safety hazards.

There is a tendency to think that either improving facilities is too big a task or that you are only one of many to use the facilities, so surely someone else will look after them. Unfortunately, everyone else is probably thinking the same thing. To help ensure the facility is safe, follow the guidelines below:

- Make sure that proper standards are applied. Ensure athletes do not use a facility that has been declared unsafe and warn athletes about using such an unsafe facility.
- Conduct regular inspections to make certain the facility is safe and properly maintained for the sport.
- Develop facility rules and enforce them. Educate athletes about emergency procedures.
- Ensure there are preventive maintenance strategies for the facility. To follow up on an inspection, confirm that unsafe conditions are fixed and then maintained.
- Share the responsibility amongst members from the sporting organisation, including other athletes, coaches, parents, and administrators.

240

Figure 10.6 Take responsibility for the maintenance of facilities and equipment

Equipment

Equipment supplied by sporting organisations needs to be thoroughly checked to ensure safety. Some sporting organisations provide protective gear. Because body size can vary, some gear may not fit athletes properly. Coaches should be certain that the athletes receive gear that fits and will protect them. An example of questionable equipment is the use of bicycle helmets. There has been much research into how the helmets should be worn and how helmets should fit various sizes of heads. Yet there have been quite a few instances of bicycle accidents where, if the helmet had fitted well and had been worn properly, head injuries could have been prevented (Lee, 2009).

Much of what applies to ensuring facility safety can be said about equipment. Some considerations are the proper use of equipment, appropriate equipment selection, the provisions of warnings to players about hazards, and knowledge about current equipment safety issues (Walker & Seidler, 1993). Athletes are notorious for trying out unusual ways to use sports equipment. Coaches must monitor athletes' use of equipment. When coaches are selecting equipment to buy, current standards of safety should be met for each piece. Coaches are also responsible for warning athletes of the proper use of equipment. Many pieces of equipment carry warning messages. Athletes should be aware of such warnings. It is also important for coaches to set standards for the use of equipment. For example, if there is a mini-tramp in the gym you use, warn against its use without supervision or permission, or better still lock it away in a supplies cupboard. Protective equipment is essential to many of our sports, and it is the coach's responsibility to ensure the proper protective equipment is worn. For example, if participation in the sport involves body contact, then athletes should wear mouthguards and possibly headgear.

Some general guidelines for coaches to think about in ensuring a safe environment include:

■ Take reasonable safeguards to notice and fix any risk. Make sure that general conditions of a sporting activity involve no unnecessary risks (such as playing with broken equipment).
■ Appropriately limit the number of participants using equipment and a facility at any one time.
■ Give instructions and warnings about existing or potential risks.
■ Be sure to have efficient and thorough monitoring to protect all athletes.
■ Use reasonable care in selecting and fitting equipment, including protective gear.
■ Remove obstacles from the participation area.
■ Conduct regular safety inspections of equipment and facilities.
■ Record and report any unsafe equipment or facilities.

Coaches have a responsibility to organise the use of facilities and equipment as well as ensure the safe use and maintenance of facilities and equipment for athletes. It is impossible to design a completely safe facility and probably impossible to develop completely safe equipment. Nevertheless, it is up to coaches to take every possible precaution to provide a safe environment for athletes.

List all the sporting equipment and facilities you need to conduct your sport. Be sure to include protective gear and the types of facilities you need to run an effective training session. In the last column, list some common maintenance problems and possible concerns about the facilities. An example is provided in Figure 10.7. A blank form is provided for you in Figure 10.8.

Rock climbing and abseiling	Common concerns, risks	Safety precautions, how to care for equipment to ensure safety
Equipment		
Rope	Fraying, pressure	Supervise knots, keep a usage log, check ropes before use, include karabiners for connections
Harnesses	Rips, fit on participant	Keep a usage log, ensure the harness fits the climber, tie-in separate from abseil harness
Belay devices	Broken	Supervise tie-ins and belays, test before using
Descendeurs	Broken	Test before using
Anchors	Broken	Establish back-ups, separate anchors for protection
Protective gear		
Mats	Mats not in place, not thick enough, holes or worn areas	Ensure mats are in place and that they are fully maintained, with no holes or wearing
Helmets	Cracks, don't fit well	Examine helmets for use, ensure warning signs are placed in a helmet and adhered to by participants
Shoes	Worn rubber, don't fit well	Ensure shoes can grip, not too worn
Facilities		
Rock wall	Loose footsteps, mats not in place, climber alone	Ensure no loose rocks and that footsteps are secure, put mats in place to protect from fall, no solo climbing
Cliff face spectator area	Spectators get hit by falling rocks	Clearly designated area for spectators with no hazard of being in the line of falling rocks

Figure 10.7 An example of a list of safety concerns for rock climbing and abseiling

Your sport	Common concerns, risks	Safety precautions, how to care for equipment to ensure safety
Equipment		
Protective gear		
Facilities		

Figure 10.8 Your own list of safety concerns

SUMMARY

1 Coaches are often required to perform administrative or managerial functions when travelling with a team.
2 There are 168 hours in every week and time management enables coaches (and athletes) to make the most of this time.
3 Coaches need to learn to balance the demands of family, schools, clubs, jobs, professional organisations, and friends.
4 Allocate time in your busy schedule for recreational activities and relaxation. Relaxation before or immediately after stressful activities is beneficial.
5 All of us are capable of wasting time.
6 Procrastination is counterproductive and contributes to stress. One way to counteract procrastination is to set goals.
7 Avoid relying on mythical time.
8 Making 'To do' lists and establishing priorities can enhance time management.
9 Communicate with the local sporting organisation early in the season to book facilities and equipment.
10 As a coach, it is your responsibility to provide reasonable care and protection of athletes against predictable risks inherent in the sport.
11 Negligence is failure to provide reasonable care.
12 Common facility risks include poor maintenance, improper design, defective equipment, and weather erosion.

244

13 Common risks relating to equipment include lack of protective equipment, improperly fitted equipment, poorly maintained equipment, lack of appropriate coach supervision, and failure to adhere to warnings about equipment use.

CHAPTER 11

WHAT NOW?

In the discussion of the coaching process thus far, we have seen that successful coaching involves a complex web of decisions and strategies to help athletes perform. We have defined a successful coach as one who focuses on individual development and enables athletes to learn. This last chapter reviews the concept of self-reflective analysis and introduces coaches to a self-directed training approach to continue to develop their coaching and, ultimately, their athletes.

A self-directed training approach is a process involving the application of information that has been gained and practised, including self-reflective analysis. The aims of the approach include:

■ To develop an understanding of coaching strategies used in various sporting environments;
■ To develop the ability to self-reflect, so that you can facilitate the evaluation of your coaching strategies (behaviours);
■ To develop a self-directed learning package to facilitate desired changes in your coaching strategies;
■ To develop the ability to provide players/athletes with quality learning experiences.

246

SELF-REFLECTIVE ANALYSIS

In any sport, if athletes cannot gain basic physical, cognitive and psychosocial skills and understand the fundamentals of the sport, it is difficult for them to be able to achieve a high standard of performance. This concept applies to the coaching process. If coaches do not have the basic skills or understand the fundamentals of coaching, it is difficult for them to achieve a high standard of coaching performance. As part of your coach development, it is your responsibility to practise coaching strategies. A successful, effective coach should understand and apply the theoretical elements of sport to enhance athlete development. This book has provided you with some guidelines for coaching and psychological strategies in coaching. We have given you opportunities to apply practically some strategies through a coaching process labelled self-reflection. Self-reflection is a tool that empowers coaches to continue analysing their coaching (Cassidy et al., 2009).

Modifying one's own skills requires competence in applying the results of one's observations and analyses. Coaches can learn to modify their skills by applying learning and psychological theory (some of which is in this book) to their coaching process. You have participated in this modification process already, but can continue the process to develop further as a coach. Examples of questions that lead to further development include, 'What is it about the behaviour that I need to change?', or 'How will I go about making the change?'

The next step – re-evaluating yourself – requires the same competence and understanding of learning and psychological theory and involves asking questions such as 'How did the change go?', 'Was the change effective for me and the athletes?', or 'What more (if anything) could I do to improve?'

In summary, the coaching process involves five steps:

1 Observing and collecting information about your coaching;
2 Analysing your collected information based on your and others' knowledge;
3 Using the information to create a plan to change coaching behaviours;
4 Executing the plan of action;
5 Evaluating the plan of action. (Fairs, 1987)

247

As part of your ongoing development using this book, you have employed video as a tool of self-reflection. By continuing to view videos of your coaching, you can perform a subjective, self-reflective analysis using your knowledge and even intuition about your coaching. To supplement self-reflective analysis, we provide a list (not comprehensive) of coaching behaviours for you to consider. Understanding these behaviours will help you analyse how such behaviours may affect your coaching.

A summary of coaching behaviours

Included in this section is a list of coaching behaviours that coaches may notice when observing and analysing their own or colleagues' work. They are behaviours that relate to the coaching strategies of organising, managing, instructing, and communicating. Definitions and examples of the behaviours are given. The coaching behaviour label is provided in italics, followed by the main coaching action in bold type. Use the definitions as a resource to help you when engaging in a self-directed training approach (discussed later). The behaviours are not always worthwhile or beneficial for athletes. Their usefulness depends on how they are exhibited and whether it is a coachable moment when athletes are ready to learn. Use this list to identify coaching behaviours with which you are satisfied and want to keep, as well as those behaviours for which you would like to design a plan of action to improve, or any you wish to eliminate. Although this list is not complete, it gives an indication of some behaviours that you may want to consider.

High-order Questioning (see Chapter 7) – **The coach asks a question for feedback or understanding related to the subject matter that elicits a multitude of answers.** The subject matter is the focus of the session or moment. Examples are: 'Why do you want to get away from your defence?' and 'What is the best way to get to a free space?'

Low-order Questioning (see Chapter 7) – **The coach asks a question for feedback or understanding related to the subject matter. There is only one correct answer.** Examples are: 'What side do you throw from?' and 'In netball, what is the distance you need to be away from your opponent?'

Listening (see Chapter 5) – **The coach displays signs of trying to understand what an athlete is saying.** Some signs include eye contact with the athlete(s), silence, or nodding of the head.

248

ROLLing (see Chapter 5) – **This communication behaviour focuses on the use of non-verbal language. ROLLing is used when a coach is talking one on one with an athlete.** The coach remains relatively *Relaxed* with the athlete during the interaction, faces the athlete, and adopts an *Open* posture, *Leans* towards the athlete at times, and *Looks* at the athlete when communicating with him or her.

Body Language (see Chapter 5) – **This non-verbal communication behaviour provides a message through the use of a body signal.** The signal can be positive or negative and often sends the real intention of your message even though your words say something different (e.g., having your hands on your hips when you speak, smiling, or clapping your hands).

Informative Feedback (see Chapter 6) – **The coach provides specific information about what athletes did correctly or what they can do to make a satisfactory performance even better.** The information indicates one of two things: (a) the performance was satisfactory and should be repeated in the same manner; or (b) the performance was satisfactory but could be improved even further by incorporating additional features. Informative feedback can concern both skill and general behaviours and stipulates what to do on the next occurrence of behaviour. Examples are: 'The entry into the water was fine, but if you point your toes, it will be smoother' and 'The release of the bowl was adequate; if you bring your arm back a bit further, you will get more power.' Informative feedback is more than evaluative statements such as, 'Well done.'

Positive Feedback (see Chapters 5 and 6) – **The coach openly demonstrates pleasure with the behaviour of an athlete, group, or team.** The feedback is given in a rewarding way and can be verbal or non-verbal. This behaviour is different from informative feedback in that it is purely directed at a past performance and carries no instruction for future athlete behaviour. Examples are putting your thumbs up to show approval or statements such as, 'Great to see that Brooke is first in line' or 'It was superb that you held your position for five seconds.'

Correcting Feedback (see Chapter 6) – **The coach provides information that conveys to athletes that their performances were not satisfactory, and how they can be altered to improve.** The content should include the performance characteristics that need to be introduced to produce at least a satisfactory performance. This type of feedback contrasts with informative feedback in that (a) the athlete has not yet achieved an adequate performance, and (b) the coach stipulates what to do on the next occurrence of the behaviour. Examples are: 'You should be doing left-hand lay-ups on the left side' and 'The racquet is too high in your back swing, lower it.'

Cues (see Chapter 6) – **The coach provides verbal or non-verbal cues to remind the athletes of previous information about performance.** Cues are different from informative and positive feedback in that the skill has not already been performed and the coach wants the athletes to recall specific information already given, for the next performance. Examples are: 'Fingers spread' and 'Remember to put your right foot first.'

Hustle – **The coach makes verbal comments intended to motivate athletes to intensify their performances** such as 'hurry', 'faster', or 'come on'.

'Don't' Feedback (see Chapters 3 and 6) – **The coach openly displays displeasure with the skill as it is performed by athletes.** 'Don't' feedback conveys negative feelings about, or unacceptability of, the skill or skills performed. It can be verbal or non-verbal. 'Don't' feedback is different from correcting in that the informational content does not indicate what to do on the next occurrence. Examples are: 'Don't drop the ball!' and 'Don't serve into the net.'

Witticism (see Chapter 2) – **The coach makes a verbal remark often involving sarcasm, irony, or ridicule.** The remark has a perceived element of jest. Examples are: 'You throw like a girl' and 'You are such a wimp.'

Demonstrating (see Chapter 7) – **The coach provides a physical or visual demonstration of a skill or principle of a skill to the team.** The demonstration can be given by the coach, an athlete, or by video.

Directing (see Chapter 4) – **The coach directs an athlete, group, or team to do something.** The content does not refer to previous behaviour. Examples are: 'Come in, everyone' and 'Get into groups of three.'

Explaining (see Chapter 7) – **The coach clarifies, elaborates or summarises material.** The content must be related to the subject matter. This behaviour commonly occurs when new information is being presented. An example is when the coach is providing the information about how to do the next learning activity.

250

Justifying (see Chapter 7) – **The coach rationalises through explanatory remarks, direction, or additional information.** An example is after the coach has provided information about the paddle stroke and follows up with, 'We use this stroke to get more momentum to go forward.'

Organising (see Chapter 4) – **The coach engages in behaviours that lead up to, but are not directly related to, a learning situation or the subject matter.** An example is when a coach passes out bibs or organises the starting line-up for the next competition.

Transition (see Chapter 4) – **A transition is the time it takes to move from one learning activity to another, or the coach changes the focus, the team changes courts, or similar situations occur that involve changing from one task to another or from one variation of a task to another.** An example in athletics is when the athletes have finished high leg lifts and are moving on to sprint work.

Observing (see Chapter 6) – **The coach is observing athletes and their execution of skills.** Examples are where there is a break from coach talk and the coach appears to be analysing the skill of an athlete or observing the way in which a team is executing game strategies.

Socialising – **The coach is communicating to athletes on a topic not related to the purpose of the session.** An example is when the coach is interacting with an athlete regarding his or her friend, or about what the athlete did at the weekend.

Using these definitions of behaviours, coaches can analyse their own experiences. The process of self-reflection involves the skills of observation, analysis, modification, and re-evaluation of coaching behaviours that you have been developing while working through this book.

ACTIVITY

Look at a video of any coaching session for 15 minutes. Using the list of coaching behaviours from above, identify two behaviours that you think the coach should change. By doing this activity, you will be able to develop your observation and analysis skills and be able to help other coaches in their self-reflections.

Reflective questions

Self-reflective analysis in coach development is based on regular evaluation and modification. Reflective questions should be included as part of ongoing self-analysis. Reflective questions provide structured guidelines and information about coaching behaviours. Some reflective questions are provided in this book, but coaches should seek sport-specific personnel or other respected individuals and ask them to help develop reflective questions about a particular strategy that they would like to analyse or change. This expert or respected individual would also be a good source for advice about your coaching. Refer to Self-reflection activities in previous chapters to help formulate these questions.

Feedback from respected sport-specific experts or other coach educators is useful for coaches in the self-reflective analysis process. The function of the person who provides this feedback is to assist in enhancing and maintaining coaching behaviours. You can obtain feedback by supplying someone with a copy of your video. This 'critical friend' should be a person you respect, someone in your sport, a colleague, or another coach. The feedback provided will serve to further identify the behaviours for development and those that are effective. You should also be your own critic and source of feedback, but remember to look for positive coaching behaviours as well. As you improve, pat yourself on the back.

ACTIVITY

Write reflective questions for two coaching behaviours you identified in the last activity. You can use this book, other references that have been cited in this book, your own intuition based on the behaviour, or ideas from other colleagues. You may have to do some research, but once you formulate such questions, you will have them to share with other coaches and for your own future use.

CONTINUING TO DEVELOP AS A COACH

Now that you have worked through this book, continue to strive for best practice on your own. An advantage of using self-reflective analysis in coach development is the ease of application. Once coaches are trained in self-reflection, they can participate in a self-directed training

252

approach when it is suitable to their own needs and time. A self-directed training approach provides coaches with a means to change coaching behaviours at their own learning pace. A self-directed training approach also encourages coaches to share with other coaches and respected individuals so that they can help analyse videos and provide useful feedback.

Modify the approach to suit your needs. There are also other ways to determine if you are effective in applying sport science principles to coaching. For example, if you wanted to determine how you applied the biomechanical principles of force to your sport, you could video your coaching to observe and analyse how you interpreted and applied the principles, then design a plan to modify the application of these principles.

An example of a self-directed training approach

The following is an outline of a successful self-directed training approach (based on Fairs' (1987) work), a process to help analyse, change, or maintain coaching behaviours.

Step 1   Video at least two training sessions and perform a self-reflective analysis of your coaching behaviours. Identify one or two coaching behaviours that need attention.

Step 2   After identifying coaching behaviours that need attention, develop a plan of action for changing the identified behaviours. Ask yourself, 'How can I design a method to improve this behaviour?' Reflective questions about the targeted behaviours can be obtained from a critical friend, another respected individual or from written resources (such as this book or others that we have referenced).

Step 3   You will need several training sessions to attempt to improve each of the identified coaching behaviours. The first few training sessions will be used to practise the identified coaching behaviour requiring attention. Video a training session when you are ready to do a self-reflective analysis of that identified coaching behaviour. Ensure you have prepared some reflective questions to help in the self-reflective analysis.

253

Step 4 You will then self-reflectively analyse the videoed session, give the video to a critical friend and gather feedback about your application of the coaching strategy (behaviour) identified.

Step 5 Upon receipt of the feedback from the respected individual, repeat the above process for the second coaching strategy (behaviour).

Step 6 After completion of the self-directed training package, video one more session to self-reflectively analyse the changed or unchanged coaching strategies (behaviours).

POINT TO REMEMBER

You should only focus on changing one coaching behaviour at a time. When you are happy with the change, begin to target another. Just as athletes should focus on one skill at a time, coaches should learn and apply one aspect of coaching at a time.

This self-directed training approach is one method that will help you to continue developing as a coach. Use information gathered from this book and create your own self-directed approach. Remember that there are a multitude of coaching behaviours, so analyse your coaching and decide which behaviours you wish to change, decrease, or increase.

Self-evaluation (revisited)

An effective method of identifying the behaviours that coaches want to improve is self-evaluation. In the first chapter of this book you were asked to complete a simple self-evaluation form that had you rate strategies you use as a coach and characteristics about yourself on a five-point scale. The strategies and characteristics included listening, being prepared, being positive, giving effective feedback, being enthusiastic, keeping your cool, treating athletes equally, providing good learning experiences, varying your tone of voice, ensuring athletes enjoy the session, and enabling athletes to make decisions.

Chapter 8 provided an example of a self-evaluation form for an experienced volleyball team. The challenge now is to create a self-evaluation form for yourself, as a coach. Your self-evaluation form may

254

be in a format similar to the one presented in Chapter 8, or you can create an original format. Whatever format you select, be sure to include a place to record at least one thing you did really well during the session and at least one specific aspect of the coaching performance that you would like to improve. The content should include a combination of the behaviours listed near the beginning of this chapter, the strategies and characteristics used in the simple form in Chapter 1, and other points from this book that are significant to you. Once you have created your self-evaluation form, make multiple photocopies of it and place them in an easy-access folder or binder.

Coaching journals

To help the self-reflective analysis process and continue to develop as a coach, there are many useful resources (books, journals, magazines, websites) available. There are a multitude of books on coaching available, from an applied, practical perspective (such as this one) to a more theoretical aspect (such as *Understanding Sports Coaching*, by Cassidy et al., 2009), and many others that focus on specific aspects of coaching (e.g., sport sciences, psychology, sociology, pedagogy; see the References section at the end of the book for ideas). There has been an onslaught of research about coaching in the past few decades. Several journals are dedicated to research and other, more practical journals highlight coaching issues. Research journals tend to present new, investigative findings and are peer-reviewed. Because coaching is a vibrant area for research, new material continues to be developed. Such research informs sport sciences, pedagogy, psychology, sociology, and other disciplines in sports coaching. A list (not extensive) of some useful research journals in the area of pedagogy (art and science of coaching and learning) and psychology (to stay with the theme of this book) follows:

> *International Journal of Sports Science and Coaching*
> *Journal of Applied Sport Psychology*
> *Journal of Sport, Education and Society*
> *Journal of Sport and Exercise Psychology*
> *Journal of Teaching in Physical Education*
> *The Sport Psychologist*
> *Sociology of Sport Journal*
> *Journal of Physical Education and Sport Pedagogy.*

There are also many practical journals that are useful. Practical journals tend to inform, persuade, and express stories or personal opinions of people who have been involved in coaching. These sources are useful to gather 'how to' ideas. Some of these practical journals include:

Sports Coach (Australian Sports Commission)
Coaches Report (Coaches Association of Canada)
Journal of Physical Education, Recreation and Dance (USA)
Coach and Athletic Director (USA)
Coaching Edge Magazine (UK)
Journal of Sport Psychology in Action (USA).

Another useful source of research and information comes from business coaching and leadership areas. There are also a multitude of practical journals that are sport specific (e.g., *Soccer Journal, International Rugby Coaching, International Gymnast Magazine*). Online searches using Google Scholar or university-based search engines such as SPORTDiscus are helpful tools for finding articles about coaching.

Coaching websites

In our opinion, one of the best websites for sharing coaching information is Sport and Recreation New Zealand's website. On this website, anyone can download (free of charge) a full range of coaching resources (http://www.sparc.org.nz/en-nz/Information-For/Coaches/). Most countries also have sports-based websites with coaching information available (e.g., SportsCoach UK, Australian Sports Commission, Coaching Association of Canada). There are also many opinion-based websites that provide useful information to help coaches coach. The advice we give is to make sure that the opinions are not just those of people who are spouting off personal viewpoints, but that they are reliable in providing up-to-date, research-based information.

ACTIVITY

Perform a search of the internet and list two coaching websites that will help you develop as a coach. Share these websites with two critical friends and ask them to do the same exercise. When a list has been formulated, share some information that has been useful to your coaching with one of your critical friends.

256

SHARING IDEAS

One of the most important ways for coaches to continue developing is to share ideas with others. Coaches are notorious for keeping coaching secrets to themselves (Mallett & Rynne, 2009). The best way to learn about great coaching is to talk with other people, including coaches, parents, administrators, athletes, and educators. Coaches have insight into what they have experienced, what has worked, what has not worked. You may have a specific problem creating a learning activity to meet an objective, so go to another coach and ask for his or her advice. You are not admitting defeat, but are demonstrating a desire to search for knowledge or new methods. It cannot hurt to ask. The worst that can happen is that someone says 'no'.

Parents have had experience raising and dealing with children, and are therefore good resources if you are experiencing a particular problem with an athlete. Ask for some possible solutions or where to go for further advice, but be sure to keep the identity of the athlete confidential. Parents are often sources of community information. Some will have contacts or friends who may help.

Administrators have answers too. Many sport administrators have coached. They have seen a variety of coaches pass through their organisations. Most have opinions about good and bad ways to do things. You do not have to agree, but they may spark an idea.

Athletes may have experienced several different coaches. They may have been exposed to learning activities or methods that they enjoyed and others they hated. Many athletes would be honoured to be asked about what they know or experiences they have had that they can share. As we have advocated in this book, athletes' opinions and desires influence team culture. Putting their ideas into action develops feelings of competence and self-determination, thereby enhancing athletes' performances. As coaches we are there for the athletes, so we need to let them have a say about what to do at training or what strategies to apply during competitions.

Please do not forget the educators (teachers, university lecturers, coach educators). Although there are coaches who may see educators as being in another world, there are many who are available to help. Historically, there has been a gap between educators and coaches (Cassidy et al., 2009), but many coach educators are willing and eager to close this gap. Coaches should be empowered to enhance their effectiveness, thus the focus in the book on self-reflection. Most educators would like to share, to learn from coaches, and for coaches to learn from them. It would be useful to the coaching profession for educators and coaches to work together for the benefit of the athletes. The athletes are the most important consideration and we are all responsible for providing high-quality learning experiences. Coaches can make a difference by making the step to approach educators for advice. Educators will not have all the answers, but can sprout some ideas and ways of thinking. It has been our intention in this book to bridge this gap by empowering coaches to gain and apply knowledge at their own pace and in their own way.

ACTIVITY

Talk to another coach about a particular skill or tactical strategy that you have been trying to teach your athletes to understand and master. Ask the coach if he or she has a suggestion as to what learning activity or game could best be used to practise this skill or tactical strategy. After you have discussed the new game or learning activity, give the coach a learning activity or game that has been successful for you. You do not have to be in the same sport, but it would help if your sports were similar in nature, such as team ball sports or individual fitness work.

Because you have participated in the various activities of self-reflection, you should also be able to offer valuable information to other coaches. Ensure that you serve as a critical friend, one who can provide sound advice and at the same time identify the positive aspects of others' coaching.

One last caution. When seeking advice, ensure you get several opinions before taking action. Reflect on the ideas that you receive and relate them to your situation. Using the skills of self-reflection, adapt the ideas to meet your own and your athletes' needs. There is rarely only one way to improve the coaching process.

Coach development programmes

There are a number of countries where coach education programmes are available. Most are accredited, where coaches attend courses as part of a qualification framework (e.g., Australia's National Coaching Accreditation Scheme), programmes (e.g., Canada's National Coaching Certification

Program), certificates (e.g., United Kingdom Coaching Certificate) and national coaching strategies (e.g., The New Zealand Coaching Strategy and Coaching Strategy for Ireland; Cassidy and Kidman, 2010). Several international organisations, for example the International Council for Coach Education (ICCE – see http://www.icce.ws/), are focused on trying to standardise coach education.

Arguably, the intention of these various organisations is to enhance coaching performance so that athletes benefit. Nevertheless, we recommend caution because some of these coach accreditation schemes focus on formal coach education (e.g., knowledge-based classes with little application of coaching practice in realistic sporting environments). Research suggests that informal coach education is preferable for coaches' learning and development (Mallett et al., 2009) and many of the schemes do not offer informal learning opportunities. We contend that a move from an accredited and certified, standardised programme, to an ongoing professional development process informed by an applied athlete-centred philosophy, will help coaches to learn and develop (see box for a Recent Research sample on coach development). At the very least, existing standardised programmes should be embedded in practice with ongoing self-reflection. The New Zealand policy document for coaching (*Coach Development Framework*; SPARC, 2006) emphasises coach learning and developing (formally and informally) rather than focusing on coaches gaining qualifications. Many coaches learn most about their trade 'on the job' through self-reflective analysis, researching the needs of their specific group, and sharing with other coaches. (See box for Recent Research about coach development.)

CONTINUING COACH DEVELOPMENT USING COLLABORATIVE ACTION RESEARCH

For this research project, the first author took on the role of sports pedagogue, where he collaborated with a coach (practitioner in the field) who wanted to implement a player-centred approach, known as Game Sense in Australia. The coach participated in an eight-week intervention whereby, in collaboration with the sports pedagogue, he reflected on his ability to learn about and implement Game Sense. The intervention involved introducing training that represented relevant match conditions, involving the players in more decision making than he had in the past, and collaborating with the sports pedagogue in self-reflection. The elite rugby coach and five players served as the participants for this investigation.

Collaborative Action Research (CAR) is a method that uses 'reflection in process', produces new knowledge and increases understanding of coaching practice. Throughout the eight-week intervention, the sports pedagogue and coach collaboratively worked to develop the coach's practice. The CAR process (intervention) began with coach and sports pedagogue discussions, where the coach was initially provided with readings on constructivist learning theories and player-centred pedagogy. To gather data, the researcher used semi-structured interviews with five players and the coach (pre-, mid-, and post-intervention), observation notes of the sessions, informal dialogue between the coach and the researcher, completion of the Coaching Effectiveness Self Analysis Sheet, and players' completion of the Coach Behaviour Scale for Coaches (CBS-S). In gathering the data the focus was on players' perceptions of change, the coach's response to the intervention, and the coach's views on the process of CAR.

The players' perceptions of change results showed an increased motivation in training, an increased sense of player autonomy, and improvements in the relationship between the players and coach. The coach's perceptions showed that he was able to change his coaching practices by working with the sports pedagogue, developing training activities that better replicated game situations, developing his ability to give better explanations and justifications to the athletes during training, introducing individual and group feedback sessions, and using more player questioning. The coach also viewed the CAR process as valuable in the facilitation of his critical reflection upon his practice. The coach acknowledged the increased relevance of using Game Sense and highlighted the increase of player input to help to further their development. The coach also acknowledged that more time is needed in his development and that he would continue to use Games Sense in elite rugby. An implication for coaching was that the research method used (CAR) is a useful tool for coaches in self-directed coach development.

Source: Evans, J.R. & Light, R. L. (2008). Coach development through collaborative action research: A rugby coach's implementation of Games Sense pedagogy. *Asian Journal of Exercise and Sports Science*, 5(1), 31–37.

POSTSCRIPT

Congratulations, using this book demonstrates your interest in continuing to develop as a coach! We hope you have gained some useful ideas from our sharing.

REFERENCES

Anderson, L.W. & Krathwohl, D.R. (Eds.) (2001). *A taxonomy for learning, teaching and assessing: A revision of Bloom's taxonomy of educational objectives: Complete edition*. New York: Longman.

Andersson, C. (2000). *Will you still love me if I don't win?* Dallas, TX: Taylor.

Bandura, A. (1977). *Social learning theory*. Englewood Cliffs, CA: Prentice-Hall.

Baribeau, J.R. (2006). Adapting coaching methods to different learning styles. *Coach and Athletic Director*, 75(7), 51.

Barnett, N.P., Smoll, F.L., & Smith, R.E. (1992). Effects of enhancing coach–athlete relationships on youth sport attrition. *The Sport Psychologist*, 6, 111–127.

BBC News (2003, May 20). Parents banned from school sports day. Online. Retrieved May 14, 2010, from: http://news.bbc.co.uk/1/hi/education/3039553.stm

Bigelow, B., Maroney, T., & Hall, L. (2001). *Just let the kids play: How to stop other adults from ruining your child's fun and success in youth sports*. Deerfield Beach, FL: Health Communications.

Blom, L. & Drane, D. (n.d.). Parents' sideline comments: Exploring the reality of a growing issue. Online. Retrieved May 6, 2010, from: http://www.athleticinsight.com/Vol10Iss3/ParentsComments.htm, *Athletic Insight: The Online Journal of Sport Psychology*, 10(3).

Bray, S.R., Beauchamp, M.R., Eys, M.A., & Carron, A.V. (2005). Does the need for role clarity moderate the relationship between role ambiguity and athlete satisfaction? *Journal of Applied Sport Psychology*, 17, 306–318.

Buck, L.A. (1992). The myth of normality: Consequences for abnormality and health. *Social Behavior and Personality: An International Journal*, 20(4), 251–263.

Bunker, D. & Thorpe, R. (1982). A model for the teaching of games in secondary schools. *Bulletin of Physical Education*, 18(1), 5–8.

Burrows, L. (2004). Developing athletes. In T. Cassidy, R. Jones, & P. Potrac (Eds.), *Understanding sports coaching: The social, cultural and pedagogical foundations of coaching practice* (pp. 82–89). Abingdon: Routledge.

Butler, J. & Griffin, L. (Eds.) (2010). *More Teaching Games for Understanding: Moving globally*. Champaign, IL: Human Kinetics.

Carron, A.V., Colman, M.M., Wheeler, J., & Stevens, D. (2002). Cohesion and performance in sport: A meta-analysis. *Journal of Sport and Exercise Psychology*, 24, 168–188.

Carron, A.V., Hasenblas, H., & Eys, M. (2005). *Group dynamics in sport* (3rd ed.). Morgantown, WV: Fitness Information Technology.

Cassidy, T. & Kidman, L. (2010). Initiating a national coaching curriculum: A paradigmatic shift? *Physical Education & Sport Pedagogy*, 15(3), 307–322.

Cassidy, T. & Potrac, P. (2006). The coach as a 'more capable' other. In R. Jones (Ed.), *The sports coach as educator: Re-conceptualising sports coaching* (pp. 39–50). Abingdon: Routledge.

Cassidy, T., Jones, R., & Potrac, P. (2009). *Understanding sports coaching: The social, cultural and pedagogical foundations of coaching practice* (2nd ed.). Abingdon: Routledge.

Chow, J., Davids, K., Button, C., Renshaw, I., Shuttleworth, R., & Uehara, L. (2009). Nonlinear pedagogy: Implications for Teaching Games for Understanding (TGfU). In T. Hopper, J. Butler, & B. Storey (Eds.), *TGfU ... Simply good pedagogy: Understanding a complex challenge* (pp. 131–144). Ottawa: Ottawa Physical Health Education Association.

Clough, J.R., McCormack, C.E., & Traill, R. (1993). A mapping of participation rates in junior sport. *The ACHPER National Journal*, 40(2), 4–7.

Coaching Association of Canada (n.d.). Coaching code of ethics: Principles and ethical standards. Online. Retrieved January 30, 2010, from: http://www.coach.ca/eng/certification/documents/REP_CodeofEthics_01042006.pdf

Coakley, J. (2009). *Sports in society: Issues and controversies* (10th ed.). New York: McGraw-Hill Higher Education.

Cooper, P. (2010). Play and children. In L. Kidman & B.J. Lombardo (Eds.), *Athlete-centred coaching: Developing decision makers* (2nd ed., pp. 137–150). Worcester: IPC Resources.

Coté, J., Lidor, R., & Hackfort, D. (2009). ISSP position stand: To sample or to specialize? Seven postulates about youth sport activities that lead to continued participation and elite performance. *International Journal of Sport and Exercise Psychology*, 7, 7–17.

Crisfield, P., Cabral, P., & Carpenter, F. (Eds.) (2003). *The successful coach: Guidelines for successful coaching practice*. Leeds: The National Coaching Foundation.

Cross, N. & Lyle, J. (1999). *The coaching process: Principles and practices for sport*. London: Butterworth Heinemann.

Cushion, C. & Jones, R.L. (2006). Power, discourse and symbolic violence in professional youth soccer: The case of Albion F.C. *Sociology of Sport Journal*, 23(2), 142–161.

Davids, K., Button, C., & Bennett, S. (2008). *Dynamics of skill acquisition: A constraints-led approach*. Champaign, IL: Human Kinetics.

Davis, W.E. & Broadhead, G.D. (2007). *Ecological task analysis and movement*. Champaign, IL: Human Kinetics.

Dimmock, J.A. & Gucciardi, D.F. (2008). The utility of modern theories of intergroup bias for research on antecedents to team identification. *Psychology of Sport and Exercise*, 9, 284–300.

263

Duda, J.L., Chi, L., Newton, M.L., Walling, M.D., & Catley, D. (1995). Task and ego orientation and intrinsic motivation in sport. *International Journal of Sport Psychology*, 26, 40–63.

Edwards, C. (2010). Guy Evans: The challenge of change. In L. Kidman & B.J. Lombardo (Eds.), *Athlete-centred coaching: Developing decision makers* (2nd ed., pp. 173–200). Worcester: IPC Resources.

Electro-Mech (2009, July 6). Shortest players in NBA history. Online. Retrieved May 3, 2010, from: http://www.electro-mech.com/team-sports/basketball/shortest-players-in-nba-history/

Etzel, E. & Monda, S. (2010). Time management. In S.J. Hanrahan & M.B. Andersen (Eds.), *Routledge handbook of applied sport psychology: A comprehensive guide for students and practitioners* (pp. 528–536). Abingdon: Routledge.

Ewing, M.E. & Seefeldt, V. (2002). Patterns of participation in American agency-sponsored youth sports. In F.L. Smoll & R.E. Smith (Eds.), *Children and youth in sport: A biopsychosocial perspective* (pp. 39–60). Dubuque, IA: Kendall-Hunt.

Fairs, J. (1987). The coaching process: Essence of coaching. *Sports Coach*, 1(1), 9.

Farrey, T. (2008). *Game on: The all-American race to make champions of our children*. Holmes, PA: ESPN Books.

Fried, G. (2010). *Managing sports facilities* (2nd ed.). Champaign, IL: Human Kinetics.

Galipeau, J. & Trudel, P. (2006). Athlete learning in a community of practice. In R. Jones (Ed.), *The sports coach as educator: Re-conceptualising sports coaching* (pp. 97–112). Abingdon: Routledge.

Galwey, T.W. (2009). *The inner game of golf*. New York: Random House.

Gilbert, W. & Trudel, P. (2004). Analysis of coaching science research published from 1970–2001. *Research Quarterly for Exercise and Sport*, 75, 388–402.

Ginott, H. (n.d.) Dr Haim Ginnot quotes. Online. Retrieved August 6, 2010, from: http://thinkexist.com/quotation/i-ve-come-to-the-frightening-conclusioin-that-i/347295.html

Graham, G. (2008). *Teaching children physical education: Becoming a master teacher* (3rd ed.). Champaign, IL: Human Kinetics.

Griffin, L. & Butler, J. (2005). *Teaching games for understanding: Theory, research and practice*. Champaign, IL: Human Kinetics.

Hackett, P. & Hackett, S. (2004). *Creating a safe coach environment*. London: Coachwise.

Hadfield, D.C. (1994). The query theory: A sports coaching model for the 90s. *The New Zealand Coach*, 3(4), 16–20.

Halden-Brown, S. (2003). *Mistakes worth making: How to turn sports errors into athletic excellence*. Champaign, IL: Human Kinetics.

Hall, C.R., Stevens, D., & Paivio, A. (2005). *The sport imagery questionnaire: Test manual*. Morgantown, WV: Fitness Information Technology.

Hanlon, T. (2009). *The sports rule book* (3rd ed.). Champaign, IL: Human Kinetics.

264

Hanrahan, S.J. (2010). Culturally competent practitioners. In S.J. Hanrahan & M.B. Andersen (Eds.), *Routledge handbook of applied sport psychology: A comprehensive guide for students and practitioners* (pp. 460–468). Abingdon: Routledge.

Hanrahan, S.J. & Andersen, M.B. (Eds.) (2010). *Routledge handbook of applied sport psychology: A comprehensive guide for students and practitioners.* Abingdon: Routledge.

Hanrahan, S.J. & Carlson, T.B. (2000). *GameSkills: A fun approach to learning sport skills.* Champaign, IL: Human Kinetics.

Hanrahan, S.J. & Cerin, E. (2009). Gender, level of participation, and type of sport: Differences in achievement goal orientation and attributional style. *Journal of Science and Medicine in Sport*, 12, 508–512.

Horn, T.S. & Harris, A. (2002). Perceived competence in young athletes: Research findings and recommendations for coaches and parents. In F.L. Smoll & R.E. Smith (Eds.), *Children and youth in sport: A biopsychosocial perspective* (pp. 435–464). Dubuque, IA: Kendall-Hunt.

Hughes, M. (2008). Notational analysis for coaches. In R.L. Jones, M. Hughes & K. Kingston (Eds.), *An introduction to sports coaching: From science and theory to practice* (pp. 101–113). Abingdon: Routledge.

Jones, R. (Ed.) (2006). *The sports coach as educator: Re-conceptualising sports coaching.* Abingdon: Routledge.

Jones, R. & Standage, M. (2006). First among equals: Shared leadership in the coaching context. In R. Jones (Ed.), *The sports coach as educator: Re-conceptualising sports coaching* (pp. 65–76). Abingdon: Routledge.

Jones, R., Armour, K., & Potrac, P. (2004). *Sport coaching cultures: From practice to theory.* Abingdon: Routledge.

Kidman, L. (2001). *Developing decision makers: An empowerment approach to coaching.* Christchurch, NZ: Innovative Print Communications.

Kidman, L. (2005). *Athlete-centred coaching: Developing inspired and inspiring people.* Christchurch, NZ: Innovative Print Communications.

Kidman, L. & Carlson, T.B. (1998). An action research process to change coaching behaviours. *Avante*, 4(3), 100–117.

Kidman, L. & Lombardo, B.J. (Eds.) (2010a). *Athlete-centred coaching: Developing decision makers* (2nd ed.). Worcester: IPC Resources.

Kidman, L. & Lombardo, B.J. (2010b). Teaching games for understanding and humanistic coaching. In J. Butler & L. Griffin (Eds.), *More teaching games for understanding: Moving globally* (pp. 171–186). Champaign, IL: Human Kinetics.

Kidman, L. & McKenzie, A. (1998). *Your kids, their game: A children's guide for parents and caregivers in sport.* Canberra: Australian Sports Commission, Active Australia.

Kidman, L., McKenzie, A., & McKenzie, B. (1999). The nature and target of parents' comments during youth sport competitions. *Journal of Sport Behavior*, 22, 54–68.

Klassen, R., Krawchuk, L., & Rajani, S. (2008). Academic procrastination of undergraduates: Low self-efficacy to regulate predicts higher levels of procrastination. *Contemporary Educational Psychology*, 33, 915–931.

Kretchmar, R.S. (2005). Teaching Games for Understanding: The delights of human activity. In L.L. Griffin & J. Butler (Eds.), *Teaching Games for Understanding: Theory, research and practice* (pp. 199–212). Champaign, IL: Human Kinetics.

Lakein, A. (1997a). *Give me a moment and I'll change your life.* Kansas City, MO: Andrews McMeel.

Lakein, A. (1997b). *How to get control of your time and your life.* New York: Penguin.

Launder, A. (2001). *Play Practice: The games approach to teaching and coaching sports.* Champaign, IL: Human Kinetics.

Lawrence, G. & Kingston, K. (2008). Skill acquisition for coaches. In R.L. Jones, M. Hughes & K. Kingston (Eds.), *An introduction to sports coaching: From science and theory to practice* (pp. 16–27). Abingdon: Routledge.

Lee, R.S. (2009). A systematic review of correct bicycle helmet use: How varying definitions and study quality influence the results. *Injury Prevention*, 15(2), 125–132.

Leidl, D. (2009). Motivation in sport: Bridging historical and contemporary theory through a qualitative approach. *International Journal of Sports Science and Coaching*, 4(2), 155–172.

Lidor, R. (2010). Pre-performance routines. In S.J. Hanrahan & M.B. Andersen (Eds.), *Routledge handbook of applied sport psychology: A comprehensive guide for students and practitioners* (pp. 537–546). Abingdon: Routledge.

Lombardo, B.J. (1987). *Humanistic coaching.* Springfield, IL: Charles C. Thomas.

Lyle, J. (2002). *Sports coaching concepts: A framework for coaches' behaviour.* Abingdon: Routledge.

Mageau, G.A. & Vallerand, R.J. (2003). The coach–athlete relationship: A motivational model. *Journal of Sports Sciences*, 21, 883–904.

Malina, R., Bouchard, C., & Bar-Or, O. (2004). *Growth, maturation, and physical activity* (2nd ed.). Champaign, IL: Human Kinetics.

Mallett, C.J. (2005). Self-determination theory: A case study of evidence-based coaching. *The Sport Psychologist*, 19, 417–429.

Mallett, C. & Hanrahan, S.J. (1997). Race modelling: An effective cognitive strategy for the 100m sprinter? *The Sport Psychologist*, 11, 72–85.

Mallett, C.J. & Rynne, S. (2009). Agency and affordances in high performance coaches' learning. In *Petro-Canada Sport Leadership Sportif and ICCE Global Coach Conference*, Vancouver, Canada.

Mallett, C.J., Trudel, P., Lyle, J., & Rynne, S.B. (2009). Formal vs. informal coach education. *Journal of Sports Science and Coaching*, 4, 325–364.

Martens, R. (2004). *Successful coaching* (3rd ed.). Champaign, IL: Human Kinetics.

McCullagh, P., Matzkanin, K.T., Shaw, S.D., & Maldonado, M. (1993). Motivation for participation in physical activity: A comparison of parent–child perceived competence and participation motives. *Pediatric Exercise Science*, 5, 224–233.

McMorris, T. & Hale, T. (2006). *Coaching science: Theory to practice.* Hoboken, NJ: John Wiley & Sons.

McNamee, M.J. (2010). *The ethics of sport: A reader.* London: Taylor & Francis.

Metzler, M. (2005). *Instructional models for physical education* (2nd ed.). Boston, MA: Holcomb Hathaway.

Mitchell, S.A., Oslin, J.L., & Griffin, L. (2006). *Teaching sport concepts and skills: A tactical games approach* (2nd ed.). Champaign, IL: Human Kinetics.

Moran, A. (2010). Concentration/attention. In S.J. Hanrahan & M.B. Andersen (Eds.), *Routledge handbook of applied sport psychology: A comprehensive guide for students and practitioners* (pp. 500–509). Abingdon: Routledge.

Morgan, J.K. (2008). Pedagogy for coaches. In R.L. Jones, M. Hughes & K. Kingston (Eds.), *An introduction to sports coaching: From science and theory to practice* (pp. 3–15). Abingdon: Routledge.

Morris, T. (2010). Imagery. In S.J. Hanrahan & M.B. Andersen (Eds.), *Routledge handbook of applied sport psychology: A comprehensive guide for students and practitioners* (pp. 481–489). Abingdon: Routledge.

Murphy, S. (1999). *The cheers and the tears: A healthy alternative to the dark side of youth sports today.* San Francisco, CA: Jossey-Bass.

Nakamura, R. (1996). *The power of positive coaching.* Sudbury, MA: Jones & Bartlett.

Newell, K.M. (1986). Constraints on the development of co-ordination. In M.G. Wade & H.T.A. Whiting (Eds.), *Motor development in children: Aspects of co-ordination and control* (pp. 341–360). Dordrecht, the Netherlands: Martinus Nijhoff.

Olsen, J.R. (1996). *Facility and equipment management for sport directors.* Champaign, IL: Human Kinetics.

Parvis, L. (2003). Diversity and effective leadership in multicultural workplaces. *Journal of Environmental Health*, 65(7), 37.

Penney, D. (2006). Coaching as teaching: New acknowledgements in practice. In R. Jones (Ed.), *The sports coach as educator: Re-conceptualising sports coaching* (pp. 25–36). Abingdon: Routledge.

Purdy, L. & Jones, R.L. (in press). Choppy waters: Elite rowers' perceptions of coaching. *Physical Education and Sport Pedagogy*.

Rees, T. & Hardy, L. (2004). Matching social support with stressors: Effects on factors underlying performance in tennis. *Psychology of Sport and Exercise*, 5, 319–337.

Reeve, J. (2009). *Understand motivation and emotion* (5th ed.). Hoboken, NJ: John Wiley & Sons.

Reeves, J.L. (1989). TV world of sports: Presenting and playing the game. In G. Burns (Ed.), *Television studies: Textual analysis* (pp. 205–219). New York: Praeger.

Renshaw, I. (2010). A constraints-led approach to talent development in cricket. In L. Kidman & B.J. Lombardo (Eds.), *Athlete-centred coaching: Developing decision makers* (2nd ed., pp. 151–172). Worcester: IPC Resources.

Renshaw, I. (n.d.). Constraints-led approach. Online. Retrieved June 1, 2010, from: http://www.sparc.org.nz/en-nz/communities-and-clubs/Coaching/Coach-Development--Education/Framework-programme-materials/Coach-Development-Modules---Learning-Resources-and-Materials/

Roberts, G.C. (Ed.) (2001). *Advances in motivation in sport and exercise.* Champaign, IL: Human Kinetics.

267

RugbyFootballHistory.com (n.d.). History of the laws of rugby union. Online. Retrieved February 12, 2010, from: http://www.rugbyfootballhistory.com/laws.htm

Ryan, R.M. & Deci, E.L. (2000). Self-determination theory and the facilitation of intrinsic motivation, social development, and well-being. *American Psychologist*, 55, 68–78.

Sadker, M. & Sadker, D. (1986). *Classroom teaching skills*. New York: D. Heath & Co.

Scanlan, T.K. & Lewthwaite, R. (1988). From stress to enjoyment: Parental and coach influences on young participants. In E.W. Brown & C.F. Banta (Eds.), *Competitive sports for children and youth* (pp. 63–73). Champaign, IL: Human Kinetics.

Schmidt, R. & Wrisberg, C. (2004). *Motor learning and performance: A problem based learning approach* (4th ed.). Champaign, IL: Human Kinetics.

Shumway-Cook, A. & Woolacott, M.H. (2007). *Motor control: Translating research into clinical practice* (3rd ed.). Philadelphia, PA: Lippincott, Williams & Wilkins.

Siedentop, D. & Tannehill, D. (2000). *Developing teaching skills in physical education* (4th ed.). Mountain View, CA: Mayfield.

Smith, G. (Ed.) (1997). *Celebrating success: Inspiring personal letters on the meaning of success*. Dearfield Beach, FL: Health Communication Inc.

Smith, R.E., Smoll, F.L., & Cumming, S.P. (2007). Effects of a motivational climate intervention for coaches on young athletes' sport performance anxiety. *Journal of Sport & Exercise Psychology*, 29, 39–59.

Smith, W. (n.d.). Athlete learning and decision-making resource. Online. Retrieved April 27, 2010, from: http://www.sparc.org.nz/en-nz/communities-and-clubs/Coaching/Coach-Development--Education/Framework-programme-materials/Coach-Development-Modules---Learning-Resources-and-Materials/

Smoll, F.L. & Smith, R.E. (Eds.) (2002). *Children and youth in sport: A biopsychosocial perspective*. Dubuque, IW: Kendall/Hunt.

Sousa, C., Smith, R.E., & Cruz, J. (2008). An individualized behavioral goal-setting program for coaches. *Journal of Clinical Sport Psychology*, 2, 258–277.

Southard, D. (2007). Manipulating a control parameter in overhand throwing. In W.E. Davis & G.D. Broadhead (Eds.), *Ecological task analysis and movement* (pp. 97–114). Champaign, IL: Human Kinetics.

SPARC (2006). *The coach development framework*. Wellington, NZ: Astra Print.

Sportstec (n.d.). Welcome to Sportstec. Online. Retrieved May 5, 2010, from: http://www.sportstec.com/Default.htm

Statler, T.A. (2010). Developing a shared identity/vision: Benefits and pitfalls. In S.J. Hanrahan & M.B. Andersen (Eds.), *Routledge handbook of applied sport psychology: A comprehensive guide for students and practitioners* (pp. 325–334). Abingdon: Routledge.

Staurowski, E.J. (1998). Critiquing the language of the gender equity debate. *Journal of Sport & Social Issues*, 22(1), 7–26.

Thorpe, R. (2005). Teaching Games for Understanding. In L. Kidman, *Athlete-centred coaching: Developing inspired and inspiring people* (pp. 229–244). Christchurch, NZ: Innovative Print Communications.

Turner, M.M. (2007). Using emotion in risk communication: The anger activism model. *Public Relations Review*, 33, 114–119.

Van Raalte, J. (2010). Self-talk. In S.J. Hanrahan & M.B. Andersen (Eds.), *Routledge handbook of applied sport psychology: A comprehensive guide for students and practitioners* (pp. 510–517). Abingdon: Routledge.

Vealey, R.S. & Greenleaf, C.A. (2010). Seeing is believing: Understanding and using imagery in sport. In J.M. Williams (Ed.), *Applied sport psychology: Personal growth to peak performance* (6th ed., pp. 267–299). Boston, MA: McGraw-Hill.

Vealey, R.S. & Vernau, D. (2010). Confidence. In S.J. Hanrahan & M.B. Andersen (Eds.), *Routledge handbook of applied sport psychology: A comprehensive guide for students and practitioners* (pp. 518–527). Abingdon: Routledge.

Walker, M.L. & Seidler, T.L. (1993). *Sports equipment management*. Boston, MA: Jones & Bartlett.

Walsh, J.A. & Sattes, B.D. (2005). *Quality questioning: Research-based practice to engage every learner*. Thousand Oaks, CA: Sage.

Walsh, J.A. & Sattes, B.D. (2010). *Leading through quality questioning: Creating capacity, commitment and community*. Thousand Oaks, CA: Corwin.

Weinberg, R.S. (2010). Activation/arousal control. In S.J. Hanrahan & M.B. Andersen (Eds.), *Routledge handbook of applied sport psychology: A comprehensive guide for students and practitioners* (pp. 471–480). Abingdon: Routledge.

Weinberg, R.S. & Gould, D. (2007). *Foundations of sport and exercise psychology* (4th ed.). Champaign, IL: Human Kinetics.

Whitmore, J. (2002). *Coaching for performance: GROWing people, performance and purpose*. London: Nicholas Brealey.

Williams, J.M. (2010). Relaxation and energizing techniques for regulation of arousal. In J.M. Williams (Ed.), *Applied sport psychology: Personal growth to peak performance* (6th ed., pp. 247–266). Boston, MA: McGraw-Hill.

Williams, J.M., Nideffer, R.M., Wilson, V.E., Sagal, M., & Peper, E. (2010). Concentration and strategies for controlling it. In J.M. Williams (Ed.), *Applied sport psychology: Personal growth to peak performance* (6th ed., pp. 336–358). Boston, MA: McGraw-Hill.

Woodman, W.F. & Grant, M.R. (1977). The persistence and salience of small group structures within a successful athletic team: A case study over time. *International Review for the Sociology of Sport*, 12(2), 73–87.

INDEX

abdominal breathing 192–3, 204
ability levels: planning for different 73–4, 89
achievement motivation theory 48, 51, 52
activation: control of 120, 191–3, 204; decreasing 192–3; increasing 191–2; optimal 178–80, 203
administrators, sport 257
affective objectives 68, 70, 89
affiliation incentive 50–1
affirmations 32, 194–5, 201
analysing strategies 133–6, 144; and video 134–6
anxiety 48–9; and self-confidence 184–5
appropriate behaviours: defining 80–1; reinforcing 78, 79, 90
athlete-centred approach 9, 12, 16, 28
athletes: backgrounds and experiences 49–50, 65; developing a team from a collection of individuals 54–61; expectations of coach 14–15; and learning 72–3; managing of see managing athletes; participation motives 50–3, 65; personality attributes 46–9, 65; physical characteristics 40–2, 65; and rights 28; and senses 42–6, 65
attention 178, 196–7; internal/ external 47; narrow/broad 47; style 46–7
attention-seekers 80
attitudes, athlete 46
Australian Coaching Council 27

backgrounds, athlete 49–50, 65
balance 45
ball sports 44
Bandura, A. 30
basketball 65, 134, 147
behaviours: ignoring negative 79, 80, 82, 90; praising expected 81; reinforcing appropriate 78, 79, 90; stopping inappropriate 82
biases, personal 28, 29–30
bicycle helmets 241
body build 40
body language 100–1, 249
breathing 192–3, 204
Bryant, Kobe 147
buddy system 65
Bunker, D. 125, 128
burnout 106
'butterflies in the stomach' 179

Campbell, J. 71–2
Cassidy, T. 14
Chambers, K.L. 161–2
Chappell, Greg 111
cheating 23
children: parents' expectations of and pressures put on 220–2; reasons for playing sport and dropping out 215
choking 178
cliques 65
coach-centred coaching 8, 12
coach development programmes 258–9
coach–parents meeting 211–17, 218, 224; agenda 214–16; benefits of 212–13; conducting of 213–14
coaches: athletes' expectations of 14–15; coaching own children issue 222–3; continuing development of see continuing coach development; expectations of 31–3, 35, 94–5; influence of

270

performance: relationship between self-confidence and 184
performance objectives 68, 70, 89
persistence: and motivation 106–7, 111
personality (of athletes) 46–9, 65
physical characteristics (of athletes) 40–2, 65
positive approach 93–8, 121; and feedback 95–6, 141, 249; 'good, better, how' analyses 95–6, 122, 141; and punishment 97–8; and realistic expectations of athletes 94–5; reasons for using 97; and rewards 93–4
positive environment 91–122; and communication 98–105, 122; facets of 91–3; and motivation 106–18, 122; self-control 118–21; *see also* positive approach
positive feedback 95–6, 141, 249
positive management 78–82, 88–9, 90; emphasising clear expectations and rules 81; ignoring negative behaviour 79, 80, 82, 90; praising expected behaviours 81; reinforcing appropriate behaviour 78, 79, 80; stopping inappropriate behaviour 82; ultimate goal in 82
positive reinforcement 63, 79, 86, 87, 91, 167–8
potential 95
praise 32, 79, 81, 82, 86, 94, 141, 168 *see also* positive reinforcement
pre-competition routines 199–201, 204
pre-start focus 200
probing 169–70
procrastination 233–4, 244
prompts/prompting 86, 168–9
protective equipment 241, 242
psychological factors *see* mental skills
psychological warm-up 199–200
punishment 81, 97–8
Purdy, L. 14

query theory 138–9, 144, 160, 163
questioning/questions 139, 146, 154–72, 173; effective 172; encouragement of athlete responses 156, 166–8; evaluating 156, 171; gaining athletes' attention 165–6; and guided discovery 170–1, 173; high-order 158, 159, 166, 173, 248; leading 166; low-order 158, 173, 248; and movement responses 163, 173; planning 156, 157–63; positive impact of in swimming study 161–2; presenting of 156, 165–6; and probing 169–70; processing athlete responses 156, 168–71; and prompting 168–9; reflective 7, 12, 252; rhetorical 166; solving problems through 155, 166; tactical 159–60; technique 159, 160; and wait time 166–7

'read the game' 47
reflective questions 7, 12, 252
relaxation methods 192–3
reminder demonstrations 151
rewards 81; extrinsic 8, 93; and positive approach 93–4
rhetorical questions 166
ridicule 91, 250
rights, athletes' 28
Riley, Pat 111
rock climbing/abseiling 243
role identities: and team cohesion 64
role models: coaches as 30–1
ROLLing 100, 101, 122, 249
Ross-Steward, L. 182–3
rotation 21–2, 64
routines: pre-competition 199–201, 204; training sessions 84–6
rowing 153
rugby 25, 134, 179
rules: emphasising of to athletes and parents 81; respecting of 25

safety 92, 238–43
screams, team 192
self-awareness 46, 137, 170, 186–90; and query theory 138–9, 144; and self-evaluation forms 186–9
self-confidence 194–5; and anxiety 184–5; and imagery 182–3
self-control 118–21
self-determination 9, 92, 107, 108, 109–10

276

Routledge Sport

The Ethics of Sports Coaching
Alun R Hardman & Carwyn Jones,
University of Wales Institute Cardiff, UK

Combining powerful theoretical positions with clear insights into
the everyday realities of sports coaching practice, this is an
agenda-setting book.
Paperback: 978-0-415-55775-7

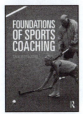

Foundations of Sports Coaching
Paul E. Robinson, University of Chichester, UK

This textbook provides the student of sports coaching with all the
skills, knowledge and scientific background they will need to
prepare athletes and sports people technically, tactically, physically
and mentally.
Paperback: 978-0-415-46972-2

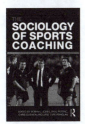

The Sociology of Sports Coaching
Robyn L. Jones, Paul Potrac, Chris Cushion, Lars Tore Ronglan

Establishing an alternative conceptual framework from which to
explore sports coaching, this textbook firstly introduces the work
of key social theorists, such as Foucault, Goffman and Bourdieu
among others, before highlighting the principal themes that link
the study of sociology and sports coaching, such as power,
interaction, and knowledge and learning.
Paperback: 978-0-415-56085-6

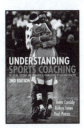

Understanding Sports Coaching
The Social, Cultural & Pedagogical Foundations of
Coaching Practice
Tania G. Cassidy, Otago University, New Zealand, Robyn L. Jones,
University of Wales Institute, Cardiff and Paul Potrac, Hull University

This book is essential reading for all students of sports coaching
and for any professional coach looking to develop their coaching
expertise.
Paperback: 978-0-415-44272-5

A selection of new and bestselling titles
- visit www.routledge.com/sport for more.